Where Is God When We SUFFER?

What The Bible Says About
SUBJECTS YOU CARE ABOUT

Power from On High: What the Bible Says about the Holy Spirit
Jack Cottrell

Where Is God When We Suffer? What the Bible Says about Suffering
Lynn Gardner

Other Topics in the Planning:
Headship & Submission (Cottrell); Preaching; Prayer

What The Bible Says About
SUFFERING

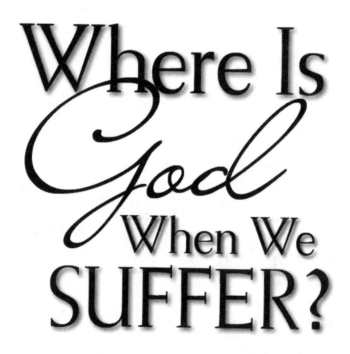

Where Is God When We SUFFER?

Lynn Gardner

COLLEGE PRESS PUBLISHING COMPANY· JOPLIN, MISSOURI

Library of Congress Cataloging-in-Publication Data

Gardner, Lynn.
    Where is God when we suffer?: what the Bible says about suffering /
by H. Lynn Gardner.
        p. cm.
    Includes bibliographical references and index.
    ISBN 978-0-89900-719-9 (hardback)
    1. Suffering—Biblical teaching. I. Title.

    BS680.S854G37 2007
    231'.8--dc22

2007023167

To

My wife and best friend,

Barbara

together with Christ,
in joy and in sorrow,
in sickness and health

Abbreviations Used in this Book and Others in the Series

AD......................*Anno Domini*
ASV ....American Standard Version
BC......................Before Christ
BEB...................*Baker Encyclopedia of the Bible.* Ed. by W.A. Elwell.
                      2 vols. Grand Rapids, 1988.
CSB ....Holman Christian Standard Bible
CEV...................Contemporary English Version
ESV...................English Standard Version
KJV....................King James Version
LB......................Living Bible
LXX ....*Septuagint*
MT ....Masoretic Text
NAB ....New American Bible
NASB ....New American Standard Bible
NEB...................New English Bible
NIV ....New International Version
NKJV.................New King James Version
NLT ....New Living Translation
NRSV ....New Revised Standard Version
NT......................New Testament
OT......................Old Testament
RSV ....Revised Standard Version
TEV ....Today's English Version
TNIV ....Today's New International Version

ABOUT THE SERIES

W hat does the Bible say about that?" This is a question that should concern every Bible-believing Christian, whatever the particular subject being discussed. Granted, we know there are situations and activities that are not directly addressed by the Bible, because of changes in society, culture, and technology. However, if we truly believe that the Bible is to be our guide for living and especially for developing our relationship with God, then we need to look to it for information that will impact our everyday decisions. Even what may seem like abstract doctrinal matters will affect our religious practices, and if the Bible is indeterminate on a particular issue, then we need to know that too, so that we don't waste time on the kinds of controversies Paul warns about in 1 Timothy 1:4.

College Press Publishing Company is fully committed to equipping our customers as Bible students. In addition to commentary series and small study books on individual books of the Bible, this is not the first time we have done a series of books specifically dedicated to this question: "What DOES the Bible say?" Part of this stems from the background of CPPC as a publishing house of what has generally been known as the "Restoration Movement,"[1] a movement that gave rise to Churches of Christ and Christian Churches. The "restoration" of the movement's name refers to the desire to restore biblical teaching and emphases to our religious beliefs and activities.

---

[1] In order to be more specific and recognize that these churches are not necessarily unique in the plea to restore the church of the apostles, it is also known as the "Stone-Campbell Movement," after the names of some of the 19th-century leaders of the movement.

It is important to understand what this series can and cannot do. Every author in the series will be filtering the exact words of the biblical text through a filter of his or her own best understanding of the implications of those words. Nor will the Bible be the only source to be quoted. Various human authors will inevitably be referenced either in support of the conclusions reached or to contradict their teachings. Keeping this in mind, you should use them as tools to direct your own study of the Bible, and use the "Berean principle" of studying carefully every part of the Bible to see "whether these things [are] so" (Acts 17:11, ASV). We would not be true to our own purpose if we encouraged you to take any book that we publish as the "last word" on any subject. Our plea, our desire, is to make "every Christian a Bible Student."

A WORD ABOUT FORMAT

In order to emphasize the theme of "What the Bible Says," we have chosen to place Scripture quotations and Scripture references in distinct typestyles to make them stand out. Use of these typestyles within quotations of other works should not be taken as an indication that the original author similarly emphasized the highlighted text.

FOREWORD

When it comes to the topic of suffering, Lynn Gardner has earned the right to be heard. First, he has demonstrated a firm grasp of Bible truth. His years as professor and dean of Ozark Christian College along with his many books and articles establish him as a careful scholar.

In addition, his life experiences give him a unique perspective on the subject. In recent years, he has gone through suffering and tragedy at a level not known by many. He has been confronted with the death of an adult child, the diagnosis of his own terminal illness, and his wife's cancer. Out of the context of these experiences he offers empathy to his fellow-sufferers, their families and friends, and all who want to help them.

This book is solid both theologically and practically. It corrects many mistaken views about suffering, while providing helpful insights for those who *are* suffering and the people who want to help them.

All of us suffer, but some people seem to have more than their share.

That's Lynn Gardner.

Some people seem to handle suffering better than others.

That's Lynn Gardner too.

This book provides a valuable overview of the biblical teaching on suffering, but it does much more. It is filled with practical counsel, drawn both from the teaching of Scripture and a lifetime of ministry.

Where Is God When We Suffer? addresses the topic from various perspectives. It begins with a study of both Old and New Testament examples of people who suffered. Why did they? How did they deal with it? What can we learn from their experiences? The book also includes a philosophical discussion of evil and suffering for those who want an analysis of this difficult topic from a biblical perspective. How can an all-powerful, all-loving God permit such pain and tragedy in the world He created?

The book lists scriptural principles that offer help and hope for those going through hard times and for the family and friends trying to help them. The bibliography suggests the latest and best books in this field, without overlooking the classics.

Several of these chapters first appeared in an earlier form as essays in *Christian Standard*. They were warmly received. Their inclusion in this volume ensures that Dr. Gardner's helpful observations will be available to an expanded audience for years to come.

Although he gives only succinct reports of his own firsthand experience with suffering, these serve to validate his counsel about how to help others. As we look into his heart, we don't get the feeling that he is just venting. Neither does he pontificate solutions for everyone else based on what has happened to him. Instead Lynn frames biblical principles in real-life situations that we all face.

Sharing his own observations as well as the testimony of many others, he explains what *does* help and what *doesn't* help as we try to minister to those who are suffering. The book includes helpful quotations from a wealth of sources, all designed to help the reader answer some of life's most difficult questions. Preachers and teachers will find a wealth of helpful illustrative material.

Always the author points us back to what the Bible itself says about suffering. And in the end, that's the best place anyone can go.

Sam E. Stone

ACKNOWLEDGMENTS

I am greatly indebted to three men who read the entire manuscript as it was being written and gave valuable suggestions: Sam Stone, Willard Black, and Dr. Wayne Bigelow. Several others read parts of the manuscript and made good suggestions: Peter Buckland, Larry Pechawer, Gary Reed, Jeff Robertson, Darold and Shirley Nelson, Jim and Marje Taylor.

My family—Bryce and Nancy, Kara and Bob, Cean and, most of all, my wife, Barbara—have been a great support. They were especially helpful to me in the writing of Chapter 1. Barbara read the manuscript and gave excellent suggestions. Kara read several chapters and made helpful comments.

Four of the chapters (10, 11, 16, and 18) and a portion of chapter 2 appeared in an earlier form in *Christian Standard*.

Some of the material in this book I taught in my Apologetics courses in my forty years of teaching in Bible college (6 years at Central Christian College of the Bible, Moberly, Missouri, and 34 years at Ozark Christian College, Joplin, Missouri). My students helped sharpen my ideas.

I am honored to have Sam Stone write the foreword for this book. I watched him for years ministering to the needs of his wife Gwen (my sister) when she was recovering from a serious auto accident and, along with Gwen, he gave tireless and unselfish care for his handicapped brother-in-law (my brother).

I am grateful to College Press Publishing Company for bringing this work to the light of day.

IN THIS BOOK

13

Part 2 — Facing Suffering with Faith, Joy, and Hope

Part 3 — The Problem of Evil and Suffering

In This Book

Part 4 — Helping the Hurting

INTRODUCTION

The psalmist faced taunts from his adversaries who constantly questioned, *"Where is your God?"* (**Ps 42:10**). Malachi told the people that they had wearied the Lord by asking, *"Where is the God of justice?"* (**Mal 2:17**). When forced to watch the hanging of a child, an Auschwitz prisoner cried out, "Where is God? Where is He?" Grieving the death of his wife from cancer and frustrated by heaven's silence, C.S. Lewis, asked "Where is God?" Soon after September 11, 2001, a reporter asked a believer, "Where was God when the towers fell?"

"Where is God?" may be an unbeliever's taunt of believers or a justification for one's unbelief. For the believer it may be an anguished cry for understanding and help. This question, whether it is an attack from without or anxiety within, presents a serious challenge to the Christian's trust in a loving, all-powerful God. The question, "Where is God when we suffer?" demands our best response.

> **"Where is God?" presents a serious challenge to the Christian's trust in a loving, all-powerful God.**

Serious questions need to be addressed. "We prayed for their safety, why didn't God answer our prayers when our loved ones were killed in a car accident?" "Why do I have to suffer when I have served Christ all my life?" "If God created the world and is good and sovereign, is He responsible for the evil in the world?" "Why does the Bible say we are to rejoice in trials?" "What do I say to those who reject God because of the evil and suffering in the world?"

The problem of suffering and evil is a very old and complex one. *Where Is God When We Suffer?* seeks to teach biblical truth concerning suffering. It does not claim to be a definitive solution to this complex problem. Oversimplified, pat answers do not help. No attempt is made to give a comprehensive discussion of the many issues related to suffering and evil. The main message is trusting God and seeing that His role in human suffering enables believers to cope with suffering. This book is written for Christians. Other interested parties are invited to join in the study.

The church needs to help Christians think biblically about the issues related to suffering. This book seeks to help believers prepare to understand and approach suffering in their own lives with a perspective that will enable them to persevere through and benefit from suffering. A second purpose is to provide guidelines and insights equipping Christians for ministering to the hurting. This resource will assist church leaders (ministers, elders, deacons, teachers, and counselors) in preaching, teaching, and ministering to those suffering.

D.A. Carson observes:

> One of the major causes of devastating grief and confusion among Christians is that our expectations are false. We do not give the subject of evil and suffering the thought it deserves until we ourselves are confronted with tragedy. If by that point our beliefs—not well thought out but deeply ingrained—are largely out of step with the God who has disclosed himself in the Bible and supremely in Jesus, then the pain from the personal tragedy may be multiplied many times over as we begin to question the very foundations of our faith. (*How Long?* 11)

In times of intense grief, unbearable pain, and suffering most people do not want to read a book about suffering. When broadsided by tragedy, we may not be able to think logically or concentrate or read.

When broadsided by tragedy, we may not be able to think logically or concentrate or read.

Believers should think through these issues *before* the storm clouds of pain and suffering assail. Churches need to include biblical teaching and instruction on issues related to suffering. I pray that this book will help prepare Christians to cope with suffering in their own or loved ones' lives, as well as preparing them to be effective caregivers and sympathetic helpers to the hurting.

I hope that the biblical principles and insights will give the reader strength to face the ups and downs of life. Various explanations of the problem of suffering will be discussed. The reader will not find a neat set of answers for believers to use to defeat unbelievers. The problem of suffering is so deep and complex that it would be foolish to think that one can state a complete and final solution. I desire to treat with respect and compassion those who find suffering to be unsettling to their faith and life. We must listen to those who have real, honest questions. I cannot give a total answer to every question. I will share clues I've learned from God's Word to help the reader formulate his or her own way of dealing with suffering.

I write not as an expert on this subject but as a fellow struggler. I do not approach this subject as an academic analyst or outside observer but as a participant. Many have suffered far more than I have. However, my life has been touched with grief and suffering. I write out of this experience and out of a lifetime of Bible study and teaching.

While every effort has been made to provide a work of competent research, it is my desire to communicate clearly with the thinking person without being too technical. Illustrations, charts, and questions enhance the discussion. Selected quotations from competent authorities give depth and credibility.

In the first chapter, "Suffering, Up Close and Personal," I tell the story of the suffering and grief my wife and I have faced. We have found strength from trusting God and His Word, as well as support from His people.

Each of the four parts of the book stands on its own. They do not build on one another. The reader may start with any of the four parts of the book if he or she has a personal interest in that section. As the issue of suffering is multifaceted, so the book approaches the subject from several different angles. Part 1 is biblical theology. Part 2 contains exegetical studies. Part 3 is apologetic and philosophical. Part 4 is practical ministry. The following overview summarizes each part.

Part 1, "A Biblical Approach to Suffering," sets forth biblical teaching on suffering. Chapter 2 shows how God fits into the big picture in regard to suffering in the world. This chapter functions

God's creation was marred by human rebellion bringing about disease, disruption, and death.

as an overture highlighting the key points of this section. God's good creation was marred by human sinful rebellion against God bringing about the consequences of disease, disruption, and death. A Christian view of suffering must include Jesus as God in the flesh dying on the cross and rising from the dead. Through the sacrifice on the cross, God's justice was preserved, and at the same time He freely offered salvation to those who believe. Since sin is the ultimate cause of suffering, salvation through Christ is the ultimate answer to suffering.

Rather than following a systematic theology model (organizing the material under topics) in this section, I have used an inductive method following a biblical theology approach (treating the material as it unfolds in the biblical text).

Chapters 3, 4, and 5 consider Old Testament sufferers and their response to suffering. Job, the psalmists, and Jeremiah and Habakkuk represent OT perspectives on suffering. Chapter 6 on the sufferings of Christ covers the OT predictions and Christ's predictions, Christ's teaching about His suffering, His actual sufferings, the meaning of the cross, and its relevance to our suffering today. Chapter 7 discusses the sufferings of the Twelve, Stephen, and then Paul. Chapter 8 summarizes the NT teaching about sufferings faced by Christians—from the Gospels, Acts, the letters, and Revelation. Chapter 9 discusses some of the benefits of pain and suffering. This section closes with a summary of the Bible's teaching on suffering, answering specific questions with biblical texts.

Part 2 is "Facing Suffering with Faith, Joy, and Hope." Sufferers must cope with discouragement, helplessness, alienation, hopelessness, and even despair. Sufferers sometimes struggle with prayer requests not granted. They find it difficult to rejoice in trials. Some sufferers feel God is silent and unresponsive to their plight. Facing death raises questions about meaning in life and hope beyond the grave. Chapters 11–15 present exegetical studies which give Christian teaching which can help one cope with these troublesome attitudes and issues when confronted with suffering.

Some sufferers feel God is silent and unresponsive to their plight.

Part 3 addresses the problem of evil and suffering. Chapter 16 discusses the various responses people make to God when suffering.

Chapter 17 seeks to understand and respond to the problem of suffering. The age-old problem of evil and suffering presents itself as an intellectual puzzle—*How can we reconcile a good, all-powerful God with the reality of evil in the world?* For some this is more of an emotional struggle. "How can an all-powerful, loving God allow evil things to happen in His world?" Chapter 18 identifies several wrong solutions to this problem. Human philosophy does not have the answer. While many questions go unanswered, still the most satisfying solution is the biblical approach summarized in Chapter 1.

| **Human philosophy does not have the answer.**

Part 4, "Helping the Hurting," discusses ministering to those who are suffering and grieving. Chapter 19 addresses several facets of the grieving process. Chapter 20 identifies things said and done that do not help the hurting. Chapter 21 gives suggestions as to what genuinely helps those who are hurting.

The book concludes with brief definitions of terms used in the book, a select annotated list of books on suffering, a list of sources cited and/or consulted, and indexes on persons, biblical references, and subjects mentioned in the book.

I write as a lifetime Bible student and teacher and as a fellow struggler in the experience of suffering. It is my hope and prayer that this book will assist you in developing a Christian approach to suffering and help you avoid some wrong turns. The fact of suffering does not defeat belief in the God of the Bible. Trust in the God of the Bible can give us the strength to overcome whatever suffering we face in this world. The ultimate solution and the best response to suffering is to trust in God our Father and in the Lord Jesus Christ.

> I walked a mile with Pleasure.
>> She chattered all the way,
> But left me none the wiser
>> For all she had to say.
> I walked a mile with Sorrow.
>> And ne'er a word said she,
> But, oh, the things I learned from her
>> When Sorrow walked with me![1]

H. Lynn Gardner, May, 2007

Introduction

CHAPTER ONE

SUFFERING, UP CLOSE AND PERSONAL

Even though I walk through the valley of the shadow of death,
I will fear no evil.
For you are with me;
Your rod and your staff,
They comfort me.
Psalm 23:4

October 11, 1999, started as an ordinary day. I went to my study at Ozark Christian College, where I taught. My wife, Barbara, went to her job in the reference department at the Joplin Public Library. The day soon became unlike any day we have experienced.

OUR SON'S DEATH

I received a phone call from a lady at a local hospital. She wanted to reach Dr. Arnce, our son-in-law, because his brother-in-law had been killed in a wreck. She did not know that his only two brothers-in-law were my two sons. Our 34-year-old son, Mark, had been killed in a truck accident on I-44, near Waynesville, Missouri, about 8:00 A.M. In shock I drove to the library and found my wife, Barbara. "Mark has been killed in a wreck," I blurted out. It was the darkest day of our lives.

We don't know the cause of the one-vehicle accident. For some reason his truck had gone between parallel guardrails and hit the concrete overpass post in the center of a divided highway. On the day of the accident, I talked with the highway patrolman. He said they did not know what

23

happened. He may have lost control because he went to sleep or because the sun was in his eyes. At that time of the year, the sun was just above the horizon at 8:00 in the morning. Those who later looked at the wrecked truck said the right tie-rod was broken. We don't know if mechanical failure could have figured in the accident. A few weeks after the accident, I had a dream in which I was talking with God about the wreck. He was about to tell me what happened. To my dismay, I woke up without hearing the answer! It has been difficult, but we have had to accept that we will never know the cause of the accident.

As we came out of the library, our daughter, Kara, and her husband, Bob, drove up. Not knowing that we had heard, they had come to tell us. We drove the few miles to Mark's house. Several friends awaited us. It was hard to think coherently and to talk. We were in shock. A vast emptiness opened up within and crowded everything out. We remember little of what people said, but we will long remember their presence and support.

> **We remember little of what people said, but we will long remember their presence and support.**

Words cannot describe the loss we felt and still feel and the gaping hole this has left in our family. My wife's anguished words, "I have never hurt so much," were the first words I said to my sister and brother-in-law when they came the next day. Our trust in God and the comfort of family and friends helped all of us move through the initial impact of grief. It helps to know you aren't alone when you hurt so deeply. Those who helped the most did not try to explain why Mark was killed. I found strength from those who said they didn't know what to say but wanted us to know they cared.

We did not agree with people who told us that because it was God's time for Mark to die, He took him to heaven. We felt Cean, his wife, and family needed him. She is a Type 1 diabetic and was pregnant at the time. Their son, Dane, who was almost three, needed him.

Three months later their daughter, Hope, was born with serious physical problems. A few hours after birth, she had to be air-flighted three hundred miles to St. Louis Children's Hospital for her special medical needs. She underwent four surgeries in the first year and a half of her life.

Mark gave a strong witness for Christ in the church and community. Many people relied on him for practical help in many ways. Many men told us how he had influenced their lives. We were strengthened by the many expressions of love and appreciation for him. I can't express how much we miss him. Mark's campus minister, Bob, wrote in a note to Cean,

> His life was an incredible example of integrity and honesty, and I can only tell you that if he were my son, I would have been very proud. He was no shallow 'Sunday' Christian relying on his family's good name. He quietly split wood or raked leaves for a widow; he chimed in during a Bible study and then challenged the group to live it. He knew high-minded theological ideas and yet lived the simple truth of loving God which means loving people, which means taking care of them, which means getting a little dirty.

In the College Heights Christian Church, where Mark and his family attended, he led a Home Time Ministry which provided household repairs for elderly widows and singles. They repaired toilets, floors, roofs; made rooms handicap-accessible; and did whatever needed to be done.

Christians often look for some purpose God has in a tragedy like this. A few days after Mark's death our family was discussing such comments. Our older son, Bryce, said, "Don't they realize that accidents just happen?" While we didn't know what caused the accident, we didn't think God caused it, and we didn't blame God for it.

Just as with other tragedies, parents who lose a child experience indescribable pain and hurt. Each person must deal with grief and suffering in his or her own way. We are grateful for the biblical teaching we have received. As we faced this devastating loss, our confidence in the Word of God gave us a solid rock as a place to stand.

Each person must deal with grief and suffering in his or her own way.

Barbara found help in the Genesis account of creation. The world God created He declared good. The account of man's fall into sin explains how suffering came into the world. In this fallen world everything that happens is not what God wants to happen. Man's sin has brought about a world in which there are accidents, disease, and death. Perfection is gone.

Later Barbara wrote some of her thoughts,

> When Mark died, I realized this is indeed a fallen world that has been marred by sin. Bad things happen to people who love God. God was not punishing us through Mark's death. Jesus himself pointed out that the people who died when a tower fell did not die because they were worse sinners. Life in this world is not perfect. It has had sorrow since the day sin entered into this world through the choice of man.

There is no reason to be angry with God. We should be angry with sin and death.

We did not believe that God directly caused Mark's death. Bad things happen in a fallen world. People die in this world ultimately as a consequence of the introduction of sin. There is no reason to be angry with God. We should be angry with sin and death.

Our caring family members and friends helped us begin the adjustment from loving Mark in his presence to loving him in his absence. Our trust in God has seen us through the jolt of losing our son. The thirty-four years of having him here with us were wonderful. Our thankfulness for the hope of the resurrection grows as life continues.

Every day we miss his presence. Often when we face a problem with our car, house, computer, or other things, we want to call Mark and ask him to stop by and help us. We miss being able to hear his opinions about issues in life. Even seven and one-half years later we still hurt for Cean in the loss of her husband and Dane and Hope who miss having a father. We also hurt for our son, Bryce, and daughter, Kara, and their families when we see the continuing gaping hole left in their lives. His absence is loudly present in family gatherings, especially at holidays and birthdays.

We all grieve in our own way. Personally, for two or three years I didn't want to read books on grief and suffering. I didn't want to talk about my inmost feelings. In fact the feelings were so deep I wasn't sure if I knew how I felt. In the last few years I have read extensively on the subject of suffering. To be honest, I did not want to write this chapter, but so many have told me that I should tell my story because they felt it could be a help to others. I can only hope that this will be true.

MY TERMINAL LUNG DISEASE

A week before Mark's death, we learned that I had a serious health problem but no diagnosis had been made. A nonproductive cough had punctuated my life since about 1992. My pulmonologist ruled out several things—asthma, sleep apnea, pulmonary hypertension. A local radiologist read my chest x-ray as COPD (Chronic Obstructive Pulmonary Disease). My pulmonologist was sure that diagnosis was wrong because I had never smoked. He wanted me to get a high-resolution CT scan at St. Louis or Denver. We went to St. Louis for this test on February 14, 2000.

The radiologist at Barnes Jewish Hospital said I had idiopathic pulmonary fibrosis (IPF), which my local pulmonologist had suspected. IPF is characterized by progressive scarring and deterioration of the lungs. Currently there is no known cause or cure. IPF is usually a fatal disease. For a few months he debated what steps to take in treatment. I grew impatient of waiting so I made an appointment to go to National Jewish Research Center in Denver.

During June and July 2000, I made two trips to Denver for testing and a lung biopsy. After the biopsy, the surgeon said to Barbara, "Have you considered a lung transplant?" That prospect had never entered our minds. "You do not have cancer but you have a disease just as serious," the doctor informed me. He said the life expectancy, after diagnosis, was an average of three years. Since medical science knows no cure for IPF my only hope was a lung transplant. In the meantime, he started me on the usual medicine for this disease.

"You do not have cancer but you have a disease just as serious."

We had a lot to think about. I started pulmonary rehabilitation at a local hospital in August 2000. I knew very little about a lung transplant and I initially resisted the idea. However, I decided to research my disease. While at rehab I visited with a man who had received a lung transplant a year earlier. After this visit and consulting with my wife, I decided to accept my doctor's advice to go to Barnes Jewish Hospital in St. Louis to be tested to see if I could qualify to be on the waiting list for lung transplantation. In December 2000, after a week of tests, my doctor gave us the news that I would be put on the waiting list.

Realizing that I may not have long to live before a lung was available, we made several decisions. Because I had great difficulty navigating stairs, we needed to move from our tri-level house to a single level. We purchased another home nearby and moved in February 2001. I wanted to make preparations for my passing so it would be as smooth as possible for my wife. We purchased a new car. We paid off the new mortgage as quickly as possible.

In early 2001, I began using supplemental oxygen. I resisted the idea, but one doctor told me, "It will prolong your life longer than any medicine we can give you." By the summer it was obvious that the usual medical treatment of IPF was not slowing the progress of my disease.

My doctor at National Jewish in Denver started me on interferon gamma, an experimental drug for IPF. Thanks to my insurance company's covering most of the cost, I was able to take this medicine. I gave myself shots three times a week. The health of my lungs deteriorated at a slower rate.

We returned to Denver every six months for checkups as my doctor at National Jewish guided my clinical treatment. I began regular trips to St. Louis to Barnes Jewish Hospital because that was where I would have the transplant. My disease stabilized and in March 2003, I went on the inactive lung transplant list.

My disease stabilized and I went on the inactive transplant list.

During the school years, 2002–3 and 2003–4, I only taught two classes at the college and the school provided another teacher to assist me in these classes. The college also scheduled my classes in the building with my office and made sure I had access to the elevator. They also provided a chair so I could lecture seated because I did not have sufficient strength and energy to stand for 50 minutes. My lectures were regularly interrupted with my coughing, but my students ignored that and were understanding about my limitations.

Since my condition had seemingly stabilized, I began to think maybe I could live like this—with limited function on medicine and oxygen. During my visit to Barnes in the summer of 2003, my doctor said he would not recommend a transplant at that point because he could not promise that after the transplant I would be better than I was at that point.

However in the fall of 2003 my pulmonary function numbers started to decline. In my November visit to St. Louis, the doctor said, "You need to get on the active list and prepare for transplantation."

I told him that I was not ready to do so at that time. I had been receiving a checkup every four months. I bargained, "Maybe these numbers are just unusual. Could I come back in two months? If my numbers are continuing to worsen, I'll agree to go back on the active list." I had difficulty reorienting my thinking again to accept the fact that I really needed the transplant.

A DOUBLE LUNG TRANSPLANT

Tests in January 2004 made clear that I would not survive without a transplant. I agreed to go back on the active list. Before I could be on the active list, I had to have a transportation plan to travel three hundred miles from our home to St Louis in two- to two-and-one-half hours. The other option was to move to St. Louis. After investigating several medical transportation options, we decided to move to an apartment near the hospital in St. Louis.

Barbara and I had to fulfill another prerequisite for the transplant: pretransplant and posttransplant education. We traveled to St. Louis two weeks in a row in March to receive this teaching. The teaching helped the patient and caregiver see the reality of what was involved in the transplant. They explained the steps in the preparation for the surgery and actual transplant surgery itself.

We learned all the things that could go wrong and understood the warnings that the result may not be successful. Our instructor pointed out the limitations and potential problems posttransplant patients can face: rejection, infection, renal failure, etc. Also being immune suppressed would leave me more vulnerable to diseases for the rest of my life. They explained that the average life expectancy after transplant is five years.

We learned all the things that could go wrong.

This time was a particularly difficult time. We had to weigh the evidence on both sides of the issue. I had to decide how important it was for me to live. I faced a clear-cut, either-or matter. I could choose to seek the transplant or prepare to die soon. In spite of the potential risks, I decided I wanted to live, if possible, so we continued to make preparations for having the transplant.

With six weeks left in the spring semester, I told our president and dean that I had better not wait until the end of the semester to move to St. Louis. With conflicting emotions I suggested that I would like to teach three more weeks and then let my coteachers finish the classes. My president and dean supported this suggestion. We moved to St. Louis to an apartment about four miles from the hospital on April 17, 2004. In a couple of days I was put on the active list for transplantation and started pulmonary rehabilitation at the hospital.

With my energy level lessening, going to pulmonary rehab was my primary activity. Barbara and I had planned to have one outing a week, visiting the many interesting places and things to do in St. Louis. As it turned out, I did not feel like getting out much besides going to church on Sunday and rehab every weekday.

Moving up to St. Louis when we did was a blessing in many ways. Barbara got used to driving in St. Louis. We became familiar with the hospital. We became established with a local church, pharmacy, the library, and the post office. We found a grocery store and other stores.

Our daughter, Kara, asked me what I wanted for Father's Day, and I told her "new lungs." Monday evening after Father's Day, June 14, 2004, being unusually tired, I went to bed about 8:00 P.M.

About 12:30 A.M. we received a call from Barnes Jewish Hospital telling me, "We have lungs available and offer them to you. Will you accept them?" I gladly said, "Yes." They asked me to be at the hospital in one hour.

Barbara called our children and I sent a quick email to our family and friends, "If all goes well, I will have the transplant in a few hours." We drove to the hospital and I was admitted at about 1:30 A.M.

We had repeatedly been warned that even after being readied for surgery, it still could be a dry run, if, for some reason, the offered lungs proved not to be suitable. After being admitted, they took my vital signs and a doctor explained what would happen. I waited in the bed several hours. The surgical team harvesting the lungs called back and reported that the lungs were good.

About 5:30 A.M. nurses took me to the floor where the surgery would be performed. In the preparation room I received further instruction from the anesthesiologist and others about what to expect.

They inserted an IV and began some sedatives. I remember talking briefly to Barbara at this point, but drowsiness began to overtake me. The last thing I remember was being taken from this room toward the surgery unit at about 6:30 A.M. The new lungs arrived at the hospital at 9:30 A.M. The surgeons completed their work about 1:30 P.M. My transplant was the 840th lung transplant done at Barnes Hospital.

> **My transplant was the 840th lung transplant done at Barnes Hospital.**

A new friend stayed with Barbara at the hospital until some family arrived. We had incredible prayer support. My college family assembled at 9:00 A.M. during the surgery for prayer. They prayed that I would have fifteen more years like God gave Hezekiah.

I woke up after 8:00 A.M. Wednesday morning greeted with the words that I had new lungs. They had taken out my breathing tube and said my numbers were good. Experiencing a lot of pain made breathing difficult. They had a difficult time finding effective pain control, trying various methods including an epidural and a morphine pump.

I also developed drug-induced sleep apnea. I would fall asleep and stop breathing when I took a bite of food. Barbara would tell me to wake up and to breathe. So they withdrew the morphine pump and used pain pills which were less effective in controlling the pain.

A few days after my transplant I was improving and had one chest tube removed. On Sunday, a tech walked me without properly adjusting the pressure on my oxygen supply. I started puffing up with air under my skin. My family noticed it and asked the nurse about it. She said I had subcutaneous emphysema (air under the skin). The next morning the respiratory therapist said I must walk. I told her of my problem. She didn't believe me and forced me to walk which only increased my problem.

I puffed up so much my eyes almost swelled shut. I was put in a special observation unit. I had an MRI which appeared to indicate a hole in my lung. However, when the surgeon did a bronchoscopy, he found I had only a small leak in the lung and surgery wasn't necessary. An additional chest tube was inserted to help with removing the air from under the skin. This episode was one of the most difficult times of my hospitalization.

I had great support from my family. My wife was with me every day. Our children and their spouses and the grandchildren were there. My sister and husband, my brothers, a nephew, some coworkers from my college, and other friends visited. I can't even estimate the number of people who prayed for me.

> **I can't even estimate the number of people who prayed for me.**

While recovering in the hospital I thought of the things I had lost due to the disease that I had now recovered. The most obvious was I could breathe on my own. Nine days after surgery I no longer needed any supplemental oxygen. For several years I had not been able to sing in church because, when I did, I began coughing. The thought came to me that I would be able to sing again. When Barbara came into my room one morning, I surprised her by singing, "Let Me Call You Sweetheart."

The hospital released me 15 days after my transplant. The transplant medical team of doctors closely monitored my progress for the next three months. So we stayed in our apartment in St. Louis during this time. I had regular and frequent blood tests, x-rays, pulmonary function tests, and bronchoscopies. I went to pulmonary rehabilitation Monday through Friday.

At first I was so weak that I needed help with everything, even putting on my socks and taking a shower. The main thing I did outside of rehab was sit in my recliner and watch Cardinal baseball games. I didn't even care about reading at first. I have generally been a decisive person, but I had trouble making decisions. I don't think I am usually a pessimistic person, but I must have given my wife and daughter plenty of reasons to keep encouraging me to be positive.

I didn't want company. We requested that visitors not come for a time. Barbara was extremely lonely being in a new town. She needed company, but she respected my weakness on this issue. In our marriage we have worked together on things. Now I could not contribute in any way to the work that needed to be done. Barbara did everything—carried everything, drove the car, ran all the errands, and took care of my every need.

In mid August we made our first weekend trip home. We attended the Convocation service at the beginning of the fall semester at my college. What a great blessing and boost to our spirits! Again, we came back to Carl Junction in September anticipating moving permanently back home soon. While home, I had trouble with breathing, and my oxygen saturation in the blood had dropped. I also had a fever. I waited until near morning before I called my coordinator at Barnes Hospital in St. Louis. She told me to go to the emergency room at the local hospital. My son-in-law, an ER physician, said I probably had a collapsed lung and took me to his ER. After a surgeon inserted a chest tube I was admitted to the hospital. I was in the hospital for five days recovering. This setback slowed my recovery. It was a few weeks before I was as strong as before.

After our return to St. Louis and another hospital stay, I made sufficient progress that I was allowed to move back to our home in Carl Junction. We moved home the first of October 2004. During October I was very weak and did not go to rehab. I started back to rehab in early November and have been faithful to this three-days-a-week responsibility ever since. Doctors

> **Regular exercise is something we can do for ourselves to be as healthy as we can be.**

and medicine can only do so much. Regular exercise is something we can do for ourselves to be as healthy as we can be. A man at rehab commented to me that I was serious about my exercise. I told him, "You have to be when your life depends on it." I know it has been a key ingredient in my being able to function as well as I can.

Tests and a bronchoscopy in December revealed that I had mild rejection to my new lungs. Three sessions of intravenous steroids took care of the problem. My next bronchoscopy in February showed no rejection. However, during the fall of 2004, I had noticed a lump in the soft tissue on the right side of my chest. It hurt all the time. Several doctors had differing opinions about it but no measures were taken to determine the nature of the lump.

While in St. Louis on February 15, 2005, for a bronchoscopy, a CT scan revealed the lump. I returned a week later for an ultrasound biopsy which indicated an infection. Barbara had a serious surgery on February 28. (I'll tell about her health problems later in this chapter.) My longtime friend, Gordon, went with me to St. Louis. On March 2, I met with the surgeon, and had my pre-op testing. I had surgery on March 10 to clear out the abscess. I made five trips to St. Louis in six weeks. After this surgery I began feeling better and did not have the constant pain from the swelling on my chest.

A transplant is not a perfect solution and many things can go wrong. I have experienced some "bumps in the road." However, I tell people, "It sure beats the alternative!"

When I went back to St. Louis in June 2005 for my one-year check-up, I was feeling pretty well. I hoped that they would say, "You're doing fine. Come back in one year." However, again, my bronchoscopy showed mild rejection. The doctors changed one of my immunosuppressant drugs and told me to return in August for an evaluation. When I returned, my bronchoscopy showed no rejection. In June 2006, I went back to the Lung Center at Barnes Jewish Hospital for my two-year checkup. My tests were all good. This time the doctor did tell me, "You're doing well. Come back in a year."

During the 2004–2005 school year I offered readings classes and worked on research for the college. This research resulted in a book entitled *Choosing a Commentary* (College Press, 2006). I taught one class in the fall and spring semesters and offered readings courses in the 2005–2006 school year. Teaching in the classroom at least one more year after having my transplant brought great satisfaction and fulfillment.

In June 2006, I retired from a rewarding 40 years of teaching and administration in Bible college. I am grateful to God to be able to spend more time with my family and teach my grandchildren and do some writing.

BARBARA'S HEALTH CHALLENGES

My wife Barbara has also dealt with some health challenges. I won't go into detail, but with her permission I will share briefly about these situations. Between 1984 and 1994 she was under treatment for a disease which we understood had no cure. Either this condition is now in remission or God has healed her.

In 2003, an x-ray revealed a large cyst attached to the lining of her heart. Because of the unusual size of the cyst our primary care doctor scheduled her to see the head thoracic surgeon at Barnes Hospital in St. Louis. He performed the surgery and removed a pericardial cyst the size of a grapefruit.

My illness and all that was involved in the transplant put a great deal of responsibility and stress on my wife. She unselfishly put aside her own interests and instead served my needs. This took a toll on her both physically and emotionally.

In February 2005, she had another surgery which did not accomplish its goal and resulted in complications. Her recovery was frustratingly slow, taking at least four months.

In October of 2005, we learned she had breast cancer. In the following four months she had four surgeries. One of the surgeries was to implant a port for receiving chemo treatment. In the process the surgeon punctured her lung causing a painful pneumathorax (collapsed lung) and a hospital stay. After her third chemo treatment the port became defective, so she had another surgery to remove that port and implant a new one. She completed her last chemo treatment in April 2006.

I have observed that even in her suffering she has been able to have a thankful spirit. When diagnosed with cancer, she was thankful that the doctors found the cancer so it could be treated. When the cancer center discovered that her port had a crack in it and they could not give the chemo, she was thankful that they found the defective port before they gave her the chemo infusion.

> **I have observed that even in her suffering Barbara has been able to have a thankful spirit.**

During this time several people provided meals and helped in various ways. Her friend, Marje stayed with Barbara a few times when I needed to be away. Our daughter helped in too many ways to list.

Very helpful was her longtime friend, Linda, who said she would bring a meal every time we returned home from her chemo treatment at Tulsa. We usually arrived home on Friday afternoons. Each time Linda and Newt brought a large, warm meal. This practical and helpful service was a great encouragement.

Through all of this Barbara has continued as reference librarian at Ozark Christian College. Usually she was not able to work much the week after the chemo treatment. It has not been an easy time, but she has endured each difficulty with grace and faith. We decided that she did not need the stress of working fulltime. She retired from her job as reference librarian at the end of December 2006. She saw how much fun I was having teaching our grandchildren. We both hope to have more time for family and especially our grandchildren.

PERSONAL REFLECTIONS

When I was a teenager, my brother Greg was born. He had cerebral palsy from birth and could not care for himself. I know firsthand the suffering his condition caused him and my family through the years. He could not walk. Talking was extremely difficult, and it often would take fifteen to thirty minutes just to understand one word he was saying. In spite of these physical limitations, he knew the Lord and had a strong Christian witness. He had a keen mind and good heart. Being imprisoned in a body that did not work properly did not keep him from having the values that really matter.

In 2003, Greg died at the age of fifty. I saw suffering up close and personal in Greg's life. I also watched my parents suffer, especially my mother who provided around-the-clock care for him. My sister, Gwen, and brother-in-law, Sam, oversaw his care after our mother died in 1984. I observed the time-consuming attention they unselfishly gave to meeting his special needs and the stress that came with that care. Perhaps this schooling in suffering helped my wife and me deal with suffering when it abruptly intruded directly into our lives.

Experiencing suffering makes you rethink many things. I will express some of my personal reflections. When you are told you have a terminal disease and have about three years to live, *you take a hard look at your life and basic convictions.* I asked myself, "Am I ready to die? Do I really believe the promises of God which I have been teaching for over forty years?"

Experiencing suffering makes you rethink many things.

I decided I was ready to die and did in fact believe with all my heart in the Christian message which I have taught and lived. At that point I thought I would likely die soon and was making peace with that fact. Facing life-threatening diseases and losing our adult son has caused us to focus more on the real purpose and meaning of life. The really important things in life have to do with loving God and loving others.

When my health was deteriorating and I was recovering from the transplant, *I sensed the power and presence of God in a deeper way.* I was so weak I would just ask God to help me do whatever I was trying to do. "Lord, help me eat this food, even though I don't want to eat anything." After several hours trying to get to sleep, "Lord, help me get to sleep." Sometimes I would ask, "Help me take a shower." I had an ongoing conversation with the Lord and sensed He was with me all the way. The statement from *Psalm 16:3*—*"In your presence there is fullness of joy"*—came to mean more to me. This joy is not back-slapping gladness but rather a deep joy and peace because all is well in my relationship with God.

> **This joy is not back-slapping gladness but deep joy and peace that all is well in my relationship with God.**

More than ever before, I learned how much I am dependent on others. I am the kind of person who likes to do things myself. The experience of suffering helped me realize more than ever my dependence upon God and other people. I don't know how I would have ever endured without the help, most of all, of my wife and my family, my friends, and the medical staff. I hope through this experience I am more sensitive to the needs of others and ready and willing to help where I can. My experience has helped me be a better caregiver to my wife while she has faced health problems and undergone cancer treatment.

The prayers of Christian brothers and sisters have sustained us. It would be impossible to count all the people who prayed for healing for me and for my wife. Many prayed every day and for years. Bethlehem Bible College in India has regularly sent me cards with about 95 signatures affirming they regularly pray for me. I keep these cards on my desk. They have also prayed for our granddaughter and my wife in their health needs. My colleagues and the students at Ozark Christian College and other Bible colleges prayed for me. My local church and many others kept my wife and me on their prayer list.

A minister friend of ours told of reading to his congregation Barbara's emails reporting on my progress with the transplant. They were upholding us in their prayers. He said when he read the email about my singing to Barbara, the congregation applauded. It warms your heart and sustains your spirit when you sense this kind of support.

Now I am thankful for every day of life. I have been given a new lease on life. Every day is holy. Each day is a special gift of God. I have added motivation to make the most of every day by using what I have left to seek to serve the Lord. In the light of Barbara's health challenges, I feel a heightened sense of privilege for the extended time we are having together.

This concentrated study of the Bible gave us an understanding of life and the world that provided us with a foundation and framework for dealing with suffering. We both believe that knowing and trusting God and His Word are keys to enduring suffering. Our faith and understanding of His Word have helped us to survive the collapse of our private world when our son, Mark, died.

> **Knowing and trusting God and His Word are keys to enduring suffering.**

We are both graduates of Ozark Bible College, now Ozark Christian College. Our Bible college training gave us grounding in the faith and a biblical basis for life. I have taught Bible and Bible-related courses in Bible college for forty years. No other source can provide the wisdom and strength that comes from knowing, believing, and obeying the Word of God.

It is my prayer that this book will help you learn a Christian approach to suffering informed by the Word of God. It is also my prayer that churches will provide biblical teaching about suffering to help people withstand the vicious trials experienced in suffering and to be more effective helpers to hurting people.

Part 1

A Biblical Approach to Suffering

CHAPTER TWO

WHERE IS GOD IN SUFFERING?

If, because of one man's trespass, death reigned through that one man,
much more will those who receive the abundance of grace
and the free gift of righteousness reign in life through the one man Jesus Christ.
Romans 5:17

What is God's role in human suffering? If God is loving and all powerful, why does He not stop suffering? Why does He let good people suffer? These serious questions deserve careful thought. The fact of suffering presents the most common objection to belief in a loving God. A national survey revealed that the question people would most like God to answer was "Why is there pain and suffering in the world?"

Deep grief and intense suffering force us to think about our relationship with God. We ask, "Who is responsible for the bad things in the world?" If God made the world, isn't He ultimately responsible? Should the blame be placed on the devil? Are human beings to blame for evil and suffering? In spite of devastation, disease, and death in the world, do we have a basis for trusting in a loving, all-powerful God? Since an absolutely good God would not create evil, what is the origin of evil? To answer our own questions and to be effective helpers of the hurting, we must have a sound biblical view of God's role in suffering.

This chapter looks at the big picture of God's role in human history. The sovereign, holy God created a good world and good human beings. This creation was marred by

> **The big picture is crucial to answering the question, "Where is God when we suffer?"**

the introduction of sin, which resulted in evil and suffering. Throughout history God has carried out His plan to reclaim and redeem fallen sinners and the fallen world. This big picture is crucial to answering the question, "Where is God when we suffer?"

THE INTRODUCTION OF EVIL AND SUFFERING INTO THE WORLD

THE CATHEDRAL AND THE ARCHITECTS

Before World War II, A.E. Wilder-Smith frequently visited the impressive Gothic cathedral in Cologne on the Rhine River in Western Germany. He admired the impressive structure with its flying buttresses, high-domed roof, two towers, and stained-glass windows. He also admired the architects and masons, who over the centuries had planned and built the cathedral. Its sturdy endurance and beauty gave testimony to the excellence of their craftsmanship.

During World War II Cologne suffered extensive damage from the bombing. When Dr. Wilder-Smith returned to Germany in 1946 after the end of the war, he was amazed at the sight of the cathedral. Most nearby buildings were destroyed but the cathedral stood. Gaping holes in the towers revealed the massive masonry that kept the building from collapsing. Though badly damaged, it was not destroyed.

While he observed the chaos and remembered the former beauty, he said he never once connected that chaos with any defect on the part of the architects and masons. They did not make it for this ruin. Observing the damaged building, he did not doubt the existence of the architects or the masons. Even as it stood in ruins, it bore testimony to the intelligent design and masterful workmanship of its builders.

No one would accuse the builders of producing the ruins. The mixture of chaos and order did not lead one to assume it had no architects nor that its creators were responsible for both its construction and destruction. Something had happened between its creation centuries before and its condition in 1946 (**Wilder-Smith, *Paradox*, 46-50**).

In our world today we see evidence of a grand Designer, but we also see much disorder. We see beauty and ugliness, hope and despair, health and sickness, life and death. It is bad logic to conclude that because bad things happen in this world that God does not exist or that He caused the bad things to happen.

CREATION

When God created the heavens and the earth, He said it was good. When He created man and woman, He declared that was good (**Gen 1:1,27,31**). It was a world without sin or suffering. God made human beings in His image with the ability to understand, the ability to choose, and the ability to love. Without free will the concepts of morality and love lose their meaning. God did not create amoral programmed robots but persons made in His image. In giving human beings free will, God risked rejection. However He offered a choice so that love for Him would be genuine and not coerced.

> **Without free will the concepts of morality and love lose their meaning.**

Adam and Eve were in fellowship with God, capable of reasoning, choosing between obedience and disobedience. They were genuinely free. They had the freedom to respect God's role as the supreme authority in the universe and to enjoy loving community with Him. They also possessed free will to commit the supreme evil of rebelling against God with all the horrible consequences that would bring. They chose to obey themselves rather than God.

God did not create evil. Rather, He is responsible for creating the possibility of evil, not the actual practice of evil. Adam and Eve had the option of obeying God and enjoying perfection or rejecting God and experiencing a world of evil and suffering. When they chose to rebel against God, we see the beginning of suffering, pain, and death (**Genesis 3**).

Jack Cottrell states,

> But he [God] did create free-will beings for whom moral evil was a possibility. Why did God do this? The Bible does not give an explicit answer to this question; but we infer from other teaching in Scripture that God's chief purpose and desire were to have creatures who would love, serve, and glorify him of their free choice and not by coercion or manipulation. (**220**)

God's love enters the issue. God created man out of love. Real love is impossible without free choice to accept or reject it. When a man expresses his love to a woman and asks her to marry him, he must consider the real possibility of rejection. God made human beings with the possibility of loving Him or rejecting Him. Genuine love requires this free acceptance.

Evil came into the world when His creatures rejected God's love. God permitted evil to occur in the world, but He did not directly cause it.

> **To be morally responsible, one must be able to choose the right in preference to the wrong.**

The risky gift of free will helps explain the existence of evil. The best moral system must have free will. To be morally responsible, one must be able to choose the right in preference to the wrong. God invested man with a free will.

C.S. Lewis states that

> badness is only spoiled goodness. And there must be something good first before it can be spoiled. . . . evil is a parasite, not an original thing. . . . If a thing is free to be good it is also free to be bad. And free will is what has made evil possible. Why, then, did God give them free will? Because free will, though it makes evil possible, is also the only thing that makes possible any love or goodness or joy worth having. (**Problem**, 35, 37)

Lewis also comments,

> We can, perhaps, conceive of a world in which God corrected the results of this abuse of free-will by His creatures at every moment: so that a wooden beam became soft as grass when it was used as a weapon, and the air refused to obey me if I attempted to set up in it the sound waves that carry lies or insults. But such a world would be one in which wrong actions were impossible, and in which, therefore, freedom of the will would be void. (**ibid.**, 24)

Much suffering is due to the exercise of free will in a world of natural law. When a sledgehammer hits a glass, the glass breaks. When the sledgehammer hits your finger, your finger feels pain. Much pain is caused by the exercise of free will to do that which can cause pain. Much suffering occurs because people choose to be in situations where accidents happen or germs are contacted.

To those who complain that God did a bad job in creating the world, we could ask, "Would you want a world without free will? Would you want a totally capricious world without the regularity described by natural law?" We exercise the gift of freedom in a world of uniform natural laws. When you choose to run on the ice, your free choice may result in a fall causing a collision with the sidewalk. A painful broken bone may result. Gravity seems uncomfortable at the time. God did not direct this fall to happen, but He set up a world in which we can choose to exercise our free will, and He set in motion uniform ways nature behaves. The fall was in the permissive will of God, but not the directive will of God. Even though gravity may be involved in a fall on the ice resulting in a broken bone, would we want a world without gravity? Do you want your possessions as well as your body floating in space? If the world did not have individuals with free will and an order described by natural laws, then human life, as we know it, would be excluded. I prefer a world with gravity instead of a world without gravity. But sometimes pain will result when my free will collides with the uniform behavior of nature. Much pain is caused by the exercise of free will to choose destructive behaviors.

Hugh Silvester said you can't claim your dog is well-trained until the leash is off. God created humans with the leash off, with real freedom (**60**). Genuine freedom to love and obey God leaves open the possibility of disobeying God. "Man is responsible for his actions, otherwise judgment would be a farce. And we are only 'responsible' when we could have acted otherwise; that is, we are free to choose and we choose wrongly" (**ibid., 62**).

> **God created humans with the leash off.**

Alvin Plantinga stated the Free Will Defense:

> A world containing creatures who are significantly free (and freely perform more good than evil actions) is more valuable, all else being equal, than a world containing no free creatures at all. Now God can create free creatures, but He can't *cause* or *determine* them to do only what is right. For if He does so, then they aren't significantly free after all; they do not do what is right *freely*. To create creatures capable of *moral good*, therefore, He must create creatures capable of moral evil; and He can't give these creatures the freedom to perform evil and at the same time prevent them from doing so. As it turned out, sadly enough, some of the free creatures God created went

wrong in the exercise of their freedom; this is the source of moral evil. The fact that free creatures sometimes go wrong, however, counts neither against God's omnipotence nor against His goodness; for He could have forestalled the occurrence of moral evil only by removing the possibility of moral good. (*Freedom*, 30)

If God made us so that we would be internally compelled to do His will, we would not be free.

THE FALL

Adam and Eve's free-will decision to sin brought devastation, pain, disease, and death to a good creation. It resulted in childbirth pain, the ground cursed, and painful toil necessary to survival (*Gen 3:16-17*). Death was brought into the world (*Rom 5:12-14*). Sin changed everything from the original creation. Sin not only introduced moral evil, but also brought physical evil into the universe. Our physical world has suffered disruption because of the fall and groans in this current condition (*Rom 8:18-22*).

D.A. Carson says, "Between the beginning and the end of the Bible, there is evil and there is suffering. But the point to be observed is that from the perspective of the Bible's large-scale story line, the two are profoundly related: evil is the primal cause of suffering, rebellion is the root of pain, sin is the source of death" (*How Long?* 40). We live in a fallen world, not a perfect universe. Suffering, even for the Christian, must be expected and accepted as a part of life in a fallen world.

> **"Evil is the primal cause of suffering, rebellion is the root of pain, sin is the source of death."**

R. C. Sproul says,

> Death is unnatural. It may be natural to fallen man, but it was not natural to man as he was created. Man was not created to die. He was created with the possibility of death but not with the necessity of death. Death was introduced as a consequence of sin. If there is no sin, there is no death. But when sin entered, the curse of the Fall was added. All death and suffering flow out of the complex of sin. (**47-48**)

Lewis observes that

> when you have a self, there is the possibility of wanting to be

the center, in fact, wanting to be God. Satan put this temptation into the minds of our first ancestors that they could "be like gods"—could set up on their own as if they had created themselves—be their own masters—invent some sort of happiness for themselves outside God, apart from God. And out of that hopeless attempt has come nearly all that we call human history—money, poverty, ambition, war, prostitution, classes, empires, slavery—the long terrible story of man trying to find something other than God which will make him happy. (*Christianity*, 39)

Man has rebelled against God and practiced inhumanity to his fellow man. True happiness apart from God does not exist.

The blame for evil in the world rests with human beings, not with God. The original sin was a declaration of moral independence from God. Sin is rebellion against God. That is what makes sin an evil thing. As Lewis says, we are not imperfect people who need to be improved; we are rebels who need to unconditionally surrender (**ibid.,** 44). We still bear the image of God, but what God created as good has gone bad. As sinners we are abnormal in contrast to what God originally created. God did not make the world as it now is. The chaos in our world has resulted from man's rebellion against God.

> **The original sin was a declaration of moral independence from God.**

Yancey asks, "Is God somehow responsible for the suffering in this world?" He answers that in an indirect way He is. "But giving a child a pair of ice skates, knowing that he may fall, is a very different matter from knocking him down on the ice" (***Where***, 65-66). Yancey observes,

> Any discussion of the unfairness of suffering must begin with the fact that God is not pleased with the condition of the planet either. . . . To judge God solely by the present would be a tragic mistake. . . . The Bible communicates no message with more certainty than God's *displeasure* with the state of creation and the state of humanity. (**ibid.,** 67)

Some physical evil and suffering comes from one's free choices that are not morally wrong. Choosing to build houses in areas subject to frequent floods, hurricanes, tornadoes, or earthquakes may result in suffering. Choosing occupations or activities that involve the risk of injury often result in suffering. Many find the thrill of bull riding or even riding motorcycles worth the risk.

Some suffering is a result of sinful choices. A doctor remarked that the first room he entered in his residency had three men who were dying: one from lung cancer from smoking, the second of cirrhosis of the liver from drinking alcohol, and the third from syphilis contracted through sexual immorality. Overeating, worry, hate, jealousy, and illicit anger can cause physical suffering. Hate, jealousy, greed, and uncontrolled anger all reap painful consequences. Ungodly people suffer *"wrong for their wrongdoing"* (*2Pet 2:13*). Such suffering does not absolve one of the responsibility and the guilt of one's sin. However, sometimes the consequences of sinful behavior are so harsh that the sinner wakes up and repents, turning to God.

Much suffering is caused by the direct free choices made by others. Child and spousal abuse, rape, murder, and war are examples. If a man chooses to drink alcohol and drive, his judgment is impaired. He may lose control of his vehicle, hitting and killing a man who chose to be walking on the sidewalk at that time. The tragedy here is the direct result of the driver's actions, not the pedestrian's. Children of dysfunctional and divorced families suffer greatly as a result of the choices of others. Disease, death, and destruction follow in the wake of the AIDS epidemic, wars of aggression, civil wars, and genocide. Various forms of slavery, such as sex trafficking, cause indescribable suffering to their victims.

Geisler summarizes the Christian understanding of the origin of evil and suffering,

> God is good, and he created good creatures with a good power called free will. Unfortunately, they used this good power to bring evil into the universe by rebelling against their Creator. So evil did arise from good, not directly but indirectly, by the abuse of a good power called freedom. Freedom in itself is not evil. It is good to be free. But with freedom comes the possibility of evil. So God is responsible for making evil possible, but free creatures are responsible for making it actual.
>
> God gave the power of choice. However, God is not responsible for the exercise of that free choice to do evil. God does not *perform* the free action for us. . . . God produces the *fact* of free choice, but each human performs the act of free choice. God then is responsible for the *possibility* of evil, but we must bear the responsibility for the *actuality* of it. (***Encyclopedia***, **219**)

GOD'S RESPONSE TO EVIL AND SUFFERING

THE BALCONY AND THE ROAD

Alister McGrath uses an analogy to describe perspective and suffering. Picture a Spanish home with a balcony on the second floor overlooking the roadway below. The balcony represents the perspective of the *observer* who watches people on the road below struggling with their suffering. Those on the road have the experience of the *participant*. They struggle with difficulties that at times seem insurmountable. To stand on the balcony is to learn from the wisdom of those who have gone before. You are on the road when pain, suffering, and death enter your life and your family. You are forced to wrestle with the deep issues of life and your relationship with God (*Suffering*, 11-16).

God gives us much information in the Bible to help us see the big picture—the creation, the fall, and His plan and program of redemption. This is the view from the Balcony.

When the Israelites suffered captivity in Egypt, God heard their groaning and rescued them (*Ex 2:25*). God knew exactly what was going on and He cared. The prophets indicated that God sees the evil done on the earth and hears the cries of the distressed and He cares. The book of Hosea teaches that when people sin, God suffers, and His compassion seeks their return to Him (*Hos 11:5-9*). Hugh Silvester states,

> So the Old Testament is the story of God who sees, hears, suffers and acts. God *does* something. He brings His people out of Egypt; He protects them in the wilderness; He leads them to their land; He sends them leaders, priests, prophets, kings; He judges them in exile and brings them back home. He makes promises and fulfils them. He does not always act as expected, but He hears the cry of the oppressed and is the deliverer of those who suffer. (99-100)

Where is God when we suffer? He came down from heaven and joined us on the Road. Jesus was God in human form facing the temptations and sufferings that are common to human beings on this planet. He faced the frustrations and difficulties of every-

To those who ask, "Why doesn't God do something about suffering?" we must answer, "He did."

day life. He was despised, betrayed, rejected, tortured, and killed. He was "a man of sorrows and acquainted with grief" (*Isa 53:3*). To those who ask, "Why doesn't God do something about suffering?" we must answer, "He did. He became a man and suffered and died to save us from our sins."

GOD SUFFERS WITH US

Alister McGrath remarks, "The God in whom the nineteenth and twentieth centuries came to disbelieve had been invented only in the seventeenth century." He continues, "The god of philosophical theology is a human invention, a product of human reason. Yet the God to whom Christian faith and theology respond is a living and loving being, who makes himself known to us through Christ, Scripture, and personal experience—including, as we shall see, suffering." The God and Father of the Lord Jesus Christ "is creator of the world, who chose to enter into the pain, sorrow, and sadness of the fallen world in order to restore it to its wholeness" (*Suffering*, 44).

Our Heavenly Father is not an unfeeling stoic. He is compassionate. Paul writes,

> *Blessed be the God and Father of our Lord Jesus Christ, the Father of mercies and God of all comfort, who comforts us in all our affliction, so that we may be able to comfort those who are in any affliction, with the comfort with which we ourselves are comforted by God. For as we share abundantly in Christ's sufferings, so through Christ we share abundantly in comfort too.* (*2Cor 1:3-5*)

Isaiah predicted of the coming Messiah,

> *He was despised and rejected by men;*
> *a man of sorrows, and acquainted with grief;*
> *and as one from whom men hide their faces*
> *he was despised, and we esteemed him not.*
> *Surely he has borne our griefs and carried our sorrows;*
> *yet we esteemed him stricken,*
> *smitten by God, and afflicted.*
> *But he was wounded for our transgressions;*
> *he was crushed for our iniquities;*
> *upon him was the chastisement that brought us peace,*
> *and with his stripes we are healed.* (*Isa 53:3-5*)

"Through the mystery of God's compassion and care, the servant is prepared to suffer in order that others might be thought of as being righteous (*Isa 53:11*). He was content to be treated as if he were a sinner, bearing their sin, and suffering beside them (*Isa 53:12*)" (**McGrath, Suffering, 64**). Christ understands our sufferings. He was made *"perfect through suffering"* (**Heb 2:10**). He took on the same nature as flesh and blood so he could defeat death and the devil. He was *"made like his brothers in every respect, so that he might become a merciful and faithful high priest in the service of God, to make propitiation for the sins of the people. For because he himself has suffered when tempted, he is able to help those who are being tempted"* (**Heb 2:16-18**).

John Stott acknowledged that suffering is "the single greatest challenge to the Christian faith." He said, "I could never myself believe in God, if it were not for the cross." In contrast with the image of Buddha sitting cross-legged, indifferent to the agonies of the world, stands Christ on the cross.

> **Suffering is "the single greatest challenge to the Christian faith."**

> . . . that lonely, twisted, tortured figure on the cross, nails through hands and feet, back lacerated, limbs wrenched, brow bleeding from thorn-pricks, mouth dry and intolerably thirsty, plunged in God-forsaken darkness. That is the God for me! He laid aside his immunity to pain. He entered our world of flesh and blood, tears and death. He suffered for us. Our sufferings become more manageable in the light of his. There is still a question mark against human suffering, but over it we boldly stamp another mark, the cross which symbolizes divine suffering. (**Cross, 311, 335-336**)

Charles Wesley sang:

> Amazing love! how can it be
> That thou, my God, shouldst die for me? (**270**)

The divine Son of God suffered on the Cross to give us the victory over suffering and evil.

McGrath states:

> Christ's death and resurrection draw the sting out of suffering. They declare that suffering is not meaningless. God worked out the salvation of the world through the suffering of Christ. Suffering does not always result from sin or lead to separation from God; the suffering of the sinless Christ and his resurrection to glory make this point more powerfully than we could

ever have hoped. Through faith we are bonded to Christ in a "fellowship of sharing in his sufferings" (**Phil. 3:10**). And suffering does not mean that this world lies beyond the power or love of God. The Almighty God stooped down in humility to suffer for us, to show us the full extent of his love for us. (**Suffering, 68**)

Looking to the cross of Christ does not explain cancer. However, when we see what God did for us on the cross, we can know that God cares and shares our suffering and that He can be trusted. God does not explain why we have specific sufferings but He does share our sufferings with us as a loving Father.

God demonstrated His love for the world by becoming a man, suffering, and dying on the cross. *Christ's death and resurrection give us the ultimate answer to sin which is the ultimate cause of suffering and death.* In the cross and the resurrection we see the love and power of God as well as the reality of evil demonstrated in a vivid way. God did not give us only a balcony view. Jesus came not as a tourist observer but as a fellow struggler on the road. The sufferings of Christ will be studied in more detail in Chapter 6.

ULTIMATE VICTORY OVER EVIL IS ASSURED

In this life we will never have a total understanding of evil and suffering. God has not chosen to explain everything to us about evil and suffering. He has taught us of the introduction of evil into the world and of its ultimate answer in Christ. We know the reality of evil by experience. We know of its beginning and answer by revelation. We have convincing reasons to trust the power and goodness of God. For our understanding of evil—its origin, its nature, and its consequences—we must trust what God has revealed in His Word.

> **In this life we will never have a total understanding of evil and suffering.**

God has chosen not to destroy evil in the world at this time. He has promised that when this world and human history are concluded, evil will be defeated. Even during our lives He has assured us that evil can be overcome. *"For everyone who has been born of God overcomes the world. And this is the victory that has overcome the world—our faith"* (**1Jn**

5:4). We will have ultimate victory through the Lord Jesus Christ (*1Cor 15:54-57*). Paul says,

> For I consider that the sufferings of this present time are not worth comparing with the glory that is to be revealed to us. For the creation waits with eager longing for the revealing of the sons of God. For the creation was subjected to futility, not willingly, but because of him who subjected it, in hope that the creation itself will be set free from its bondage to decay and obtain the freedom of the glory of the children of God. (*Rom 3:18-21*)

The Lord revealed to John, the promise of a new heaven and a new earth where

> the dwelling place of God is with man. He will dwell with them, and they will be his people, and God himself will be with them as their God. He will wipe away every tear from their eyes, and death shall be no more, neither shall there be mourning nor crying nor pain anymore, for the former things have passed away. (*Rev 21:3-4*).

A young man struggling with the problem of suffering was told by a wise philosophy teacher he would not find the answer in philosophy. The Christian philosopher said he too had struggled with this issue but his advice was to "Hold on to the person of Jesus." God does not offer us a logical argument to deal with suffering. The problem of suffering is not *solved by reason*, but is ultimately *resolved by faith* in our crucified and risen Lord.

The problem of suffering is not *solved by reason*, but is ultimately *resolved by faith.*

The best answer is the person of Jesus. He can identify with us. Cling to the person of Jesus Christ. He deserves our absolute trust. He is the ultimate answer for those struggling with suffering.

(See next page for "Think about It" questions.)

Think about It

1. Why is the question "Why do good people suffer?" important?

2. How does the story of the cathedral and the architects relate to the question of God and suffering in the world?

3. How does free will relate to the introduction of evil and suffering into the world?

4. Give an example of how free will and natural law account for some of the suffering in the world.

5. Can you imagine a world without natural law and humans without free will? Would such a world be an improvement?

6. We live in a fallen world. Explain.

7. Identify some causes of suffering.

8. Explain the illustration of the balcony and the road.

9. What effect does understanding that God suffers with us have on the sufferer?

10. How does the cross of Christ relate to the problem of suffering?

11. What is the ultimate cause of suffering? What is the ultimate solution?

CHAPTER THREE

JOB, A CASE STUDY IN SUFFERING

> *Though he slay me, yet will I trust in him.*
> **Job 13:15 (KJV)**

While the Bible does not explain suffering systematically or philosophically, suffering is accepted as a fact of life in a fallen world. Living in this world includes enduring unpleasant painful experiences. When we face hard times and suffering, we want to know where God is in all of this. The Bible does not ignore suffering but wrestles honestly with the problem of evil and suffering in the world.

Especially troublesome is the question of "Why do God's people suffer when often the wicked seem to prosper?" Job says of God, *"He destroys both the blameless and the wicked. When disaster brings sudden death, he mocks at the calamity of the innocent. The earth is given into the hand of the wicked; he covers the faces of its judges—if it is not he, who then is it?"* (**Job 9:22-24**). *"Why do you hide your face and count me as your enemy?"* (**Job 13:24**). *"Why do the wicked live, reach old age, and grow mighty in power?"* (**Job 21:7**).

Other Bible writers struggle with this question, David cries out, *"How long, O God, is the foe to scoff? Is the enemy to revile your name forever?"* (**Ps 74:10**). Habakkuk asks, *"Why do you make me see iniquity, and why do you idly look at wrong?"* (**Hab 1:3**). Jeremiah complains, *"Why does the way of the wicked prosper? Why do all who are treacherous thrive?"* (**Jer 12:1**). How did these men resolve their frustration with God as they faced seemingly inequitable suffering? By looking at Old Testament books of poetry and prophecy we can glean insights into coping with suffering. This chapter will present insights we can gain from the sufferings of Job.

THE THEME OF
THE BOOK OF JOB

In the words of Peter Kreeft,

> It is universally recognized that Job is one of the greatest books ever written: a masterpiece, an all-time classic. . . . It is fascinating, haunting, teasingly mysterious, tender, and yet powerful as a sledge-hammer. . . . If Job is about the problem of evil, then Job's answer to that problem is that *we do not know* the answer. We do not know what philosophers from Plato to Rabbi Kushner so helpfully but hopelessly try to teach us: why "bad things happen to good people". Job does not understand this fact of life, and neither do we. We "identify" with Job not in his knowledge but in his ignorance. (*Philosophies*, 61)

Job is not meant to be a prototype of the typical suffering every believer is expected to suffer. Rather it is a case study of one individual's unique sufferings from which we can draw some insights and perspectives.

The book of Job is a story of a believer who struggles with questions, doubts, and despair. His trial and victory are instructive for all believers. Job wants to know why he is experiencing this unanticipated and seemingly undeserved suffering. It seems to him senseless and unwarranted. The book portrays the suffering of a godly person. The insensitivity of his friends increased Job's anguish. They wrongly assumed that suffering is *always* caused by one's sin. The Bible rejects this false view (e.g., *Lk 13:1-3; Jn 9:1-3*).

The book is a story of a believer who struggles with questions, doubts, and despair.

Gleason Archer states that the book of Job is "an accurate and authentic record of an experience that actually befell a godly believer in ancient times" who was "badly advised by three would-be comforters who were ill equipped to counsel" and then was "finally admonished, humbled, and corrected by the direct teaching of the Lord Yahweh Himself" (**11-12**). While the book is written as an epic drama, it is a true account of what happened. The New Testament recognizes Job as an actual historical person (*Jas 5:11*).

Archer summarizes the theme and purpose of the book of Job:

> What is the issue? Nothing less than the chief stumbling block to all men's faith in the goodness and power of God as the ruler and judge over all the world. How can it ever be that calamity may befall the godly? How can a sincere and earnest believer who has all his life followed the Lord with true devotion and furnished an exemplary pattern of conduct be stricken with deadly illness or assassination, or suffer the loss of his loved ones, just as if he were some wicked offender who is ripe for judgment? And conversely, how can it be that heartless, self-seeking materialists, who care nothing for God and despise their fellow man, go through life untouched by such disasters? If God is all-powerful and all-just, how can he allow the innocent to suffer and the guilty (in some cases, at least) to be exempt from tragedy and loss? The all-too-frequent disparity between merit and fortune, between wickedness and prosperity, furnishes one of the most serious obstacles to faith that can beset the mind of the observer. Is God not really concerned about justice? Or is He too limited in power to maintain and enforce righteousness upon earth? What useful purpose can be achieved by the painful afflictions of heart-breaking bereavements that occasionally overtake even the godliest and most sincere? (17)

The book of Job makes a profound and powerful statement to trusting God completely, even when we cannot understand why we are suffering. It realistically portrays the overwhelming misfortune Job faced and how his steadfastness led to victory over bitterness and frustration.

Archer finds in Job a threefold answer to the problem of undeserved suffering.

1) "God is worthy of our total love, adoration, and praise, even apart from all of His benefits to us."

2) "God permits suffering in the life of the believer in order to strengthen his faith and purify his soul."

> The more we are deprived of the temporal supports for our earthly happiness, the more we are driven to the Lord for our comfort and support. . . . Our greatest maturing takes place in times of affliction and deep privation, because it is at such times that we learn to appreciate more fully those immeasurable blessings that no adversity can ever take from us: the assurance of God's love, joy in the Holy Ghost, peace of conscience, increase in grace, and perseverance therein to the end.

3) "The surpassing wisdom of our infinite God." His ways are beyond our understanding. We have an earthbound perspective and He has the eternal perspective. "Our part must be simply to trust Him even when we cannot understand what He is doing—or permitting." God's thoughts and actions having eternity in view are deeper and more profound than our limited human point of view can comprehend (19-22).

Job's sufferings included:

1) Sudden loss of all his earthly possessions (*1:13-17*);
2) Deaths of all his ten children in one day (*1:18-19*);
3) Loss of his own good health (*2:7-8*);
4) Rebuke and bad advice from his wife (*2:9*);
5) Flesh caked with worms and dirt; he grew black and was feverish (*7:5; 30:30*).

D.A. Carson makes these observations based on the first three chapters:

1) "The Book of Job frankly insists that suffering falls within the sweep of God's sovereignty."
2) "The emphasis on Job's goodness is meant to highlight the fact that there is such a thing as innocent suffering."
3) "The degree to which we struggle with this question is likely to be related to the extent of our own sufferings."
4) "God does not blame us if in our suffering we frankly vent our despair and confess our loss of hope, our sense of futility, our lamentations about life itself."
5) "Already the theme of mystery has intruded. Neither at the beginning of the affliction nor at the end does God tell Job about Satan's challenge and his own response."
6) "That is why Job's initial lament, and his later question must be placed within the right framework. At no point does Job abandon faith in God. . ." (*How Long?* 139-141).

Job did not accept his affliction quietly. He questioned God. He cursed the day he was born. He argued with his friends. He rebuked his wife. He cursed himself. But he never cursed God. Yet he desperately wanted God to explain to him why he was suffering.

In his lament in *chapter 3*, Job asks why he was not stillborn and longs for death. In fact he asks "why" four more times in *3:12-23*. Life for him is "turmoil" and no "rest" (*3:26*).

Job desperately wanted God to explain to him why he was suffering.

Job is a righteous man, yet he suffers the fate that seemingly should be for the wicked. He believes that if he understood why he was suffering, it would help him understand. God remains silent.

DIALOGUE WITH HIS FRIENDS

Three friends visit Job. The best thing they did was to sit silently with him for seven days. However, they are merciless in their condemnation of Job when they do speak. The main part of the book is made up of two of the friends speaking to Job three times and Zophar speaking twice with Job answering each.

Thoughts for Sufferers from the Book of Job
By Wilbur Fields[1]

1. Both God and Satan are watching our responses to suffering (*1:8-10; 2:3-5*).
2. God has always allowed His people to be tested (*Jer 17:10; 1Th 2:4*).
3. Suffering does not imply wickedness, nor does prosperity imply righteousness (*1:3,5,8; 2:3; 21:22-26; Lk 13:1-3; Jn 9:2-3*).
4. Satan lies to God about people (*1:9-11; 2:5*), just like he lies to people about God (*Gen 3:5*).
5. It is Satan who wants to hurt us, not God (*1:11; 2:4-5,7; Lam 3:33; Eze 33:11*).
6. God sets limits on how far Satan can test us (*1:12; 2:6; 1Cor 10:13*).
7. Some things (like our sincerity) can only be proved to Satan and to Satan's people by the sufferings of God's people.
8. Huge troubles may come upon us, one on top of another, until they are far beyond our endurance (*1:13-19*). The suffer-

---

[1] Wilbur Fields, class handout, Ozark Christian College.

ings may go on for months (*7:3*) until we cry out, *"How long, O Lord?"* (*7:19; Rev 6:10*).

9. Those closest to us may not understand us or be supportive or stand with us (*2:9; 19:13,14,17,19*).
10. We may be misunderstood and accused wrongfully (*11:5-6; 18:5-21; 30:9-10*).
11. Suffering believers may wish they had never been born or would have already died (*3:3,11; 6:9; 10:18*) and wonder why they have to live in their misery (*3:20*).
12. We may never understand why we suffer (*3:11; 10:18; chs. 38–41*) and may wonder what sin we have committed to make God treat us so badly (*13:23*).
13. We may experience no rest (*3:26*).
14. Our friends may misjudge us and say unkind things about us (*4:7-8; 8:6; 11:6; 15:2,7-8; 22:5,23*). Our "friends" may claim special enlightenment to guide us (*4:12; 5:27*).
15. We may be accused wrongly of doing evil and suffering punishment for it (*4:7-8; 5:6; 8:6,20*).
16. We may get crabby with our friends (*6:14,21; 12:1-3; 13:4-5; 16:2-3; 21:3*) and may blurt out things we should not say (*7:11; 10:1*).
17. We may accuse God wrongly (*6:4; 7:20-21; 9:17,22; 10:16; 13:24; 16:11-12; 19:6,11,21; 27:2; 29:5; 30:21*). God forgave Job for this (*42:9-10*), but God does not like our grumbling (*38:2; 40:2,8; Php 2:14*).
18. We may try to figure out why all this has happened (*7:1,3; 10:2*).
19. We may try to bargain with God and argue with Him (*7:21; 10:2-3,9; 14:15*). We may even try to "go to court" with God (*9:32-33; 23:3-5*).
20. We must put our trust in God, even when we do not understand what He is doing (*13:15-16*).
21. We may give a great testimony in suffering, possibly even greater than at other times (*1:21; 2:10; 16:19; 17:9; 19:25-27; 23:10; 26:7-14; 28:12-28*).
22. Remember that our Redeemer is living and will come again for us (*19:25; 16:19*).
23. We may come out of sufferings as pure gold (*23:10*).
24. We may fall into self-pity (*29:2-3*) and feel our prayers are not answered (*30:20*).

25. We may feel righteous in our own eyes (*32:1*). We must realize that we are sinners, even when we are suffering. Job finally came to be aware of that (*42:3-6*). We may have blamed God in order to justify ourselves (*40:8*).
26. We are ignorant even about God's creations in nature. How then can we expect to understand the harder questions of God's moral government in the world? (*38:2-3*).
27. We must forgive and pray for those who have spoken wrongfully about us (*42:10*).
28. Those who are faithful to God shall certainly be rewarded at last (*42:12-16; Jas 5:11; Heb 11:6*).

The friends know why Job is suffering. Their logic is that all who suffer do so because of their sin. Eliphaz says, *"Remember: who that was innocent ever perished? Or where were the upright cut off? As I have seen, those who plow iniquity and sow trouble reap the same. By the breath of God they perish, and by the blast of his anger they are consumed"* (*Job 4:7-9*). The friends reason that it is unthinkable that God would be unjust, so Job must be suffering for his sin. The heart of their argument is "Job, you are suffering. All suffering is caused by one's sin. Therefore you are suffering because of your sin." The problem with this argument is that the second premise is false. They also commit the fallacy of false dilemma contending that only two options exist: Live godly and experience no suffering or live wickedly and experience suffering. They failed to understand that God may have good reasons why godly people suffer.

They commit the fallacy of false dilemma.

Job resents their insensitivity and responds to each attack insisting on his innocence (*Job 6:28-30; 16:17; 23:10-12; 27:2-6*). Earlier God verified his innocence (*Job 1:1,8; 2:3*). Job honestly believes his suffering is undeserved. D.A. Carson states, "Job's speeches are the anguish of a man who knows God, who wants to know him better, who never once doubts the existence of God, who remains convinced, at bottom, of the justice of God—but who cannot make sense of these entrenched beliefs in the light of his own experience" (*How Long?* 146).

Job complains bitterly to God (*Job 7:11; 10:1; 23:2*). He says, "I desire to argue my case with God" (*Job 13:2*). He calls on God to explain the justice in all this (*9:19,32; 14:3-4; 23:7; 31:35-37*). Responding to God's silence, Job says, *"I call for help, but there is no justice"* (**Job 19:7**; see also **27:2**). He cries out, *"Let the Almighty answer me!"* (**Job 31:35**).

In Job's long speech (*26:1–31:40*) he blames God for making him taste of bitterness and defends his integrity (*27:2-6*). He describes his lifestyle: honesty, generosity, discipline, helping the needy, comforting the mourning, hospitality to strangers, fearing God, not looking lustfully at women, not practicing idolatry, not mistreating slaves, not rejoicing over the misfortune of others, not trusting his wealth or following unfair business practices (*chs. 29–31*). Yet, neither Job nor his friends took into account the influence of Satan on people.

"So these three men ceased to answer Job, because he was righteous in his own eyes" (**Job 32:1**). Later, after God spoke to Job from the whirlwind, *"The Lord said to Eliphaz the Temanite: 'My anger burns against you and against your two friends, for you have not spoken of me what is right, as my servant Job has'"* (**Job 42:7**). God tells Job he *"darkens counsel by words without knowledge"* (**Job 38:2**), yet Job is right that he was not suffering for his sin. He is right in that he kept his trust in God.

Elihu, a young man who has listened to the debate, can't hold his tongue any longer (**Job 32–37**). He tells the three friends that *"they had found no answer, although they had declared Job to be in the wrong . . . there was none among you who refuted Job or who answered his words"* (**Job 32:3,12**). He also rebukes Job *"because he justified himself rather than God"* (**Job 32:2**) and for accusing God of injustice (**Job 33:8ff.**). He tells Job that God speaks to man in many ways, even through pain (**Job 33:14-22**). He suggests that Job has not prayed, confessing his sin, and submitting to God's discipline (**Job 33:26-30**). He emphasized God's justice and omnipotence. While Elihu is an improvement over the three friends, he, too, charges Job with wrongdoing (**Job 35**). He is arrogant, claiming he is perfect in knowledge (**Job 36:4**). His positive contribution was to inform Job that the proper response to suffering is faith not resentment (**Job 36–37**).

> **The proper response to suffering is faith not resentment.**

John Mark Hicks observes,

> Job struggled to believe despite his circumstances. He trusts even when there seems to be no reason to trust. Job's wife

thought the best resolution was to curse God and die (*2:9*). But this was the essence of the test. Will Job believe even when he has no reason to believe? Will he maintain his integrity where there is no gain or profit? Everything was taken from him materially, physically, and emotionally. Will Job maintain his integrity, his fear of God, even in this desperate circumstance? The answer throughout the book's dialogue is "Yes."

Throughout his vacillations between despair and anger, between doubt and terror, Job maintained an implicit trust in God. Job would not deny his integrity, but neither would he curse his God. (*Trust,* 165)

Even in his darkness Job kept his faith. Note these statements: *"Though he slay me, I will hope in him"* (**Job 13:15**). *"Even now, behold, my witness is in heaven, and he who testifies for me is on high"* (**Job 16:19**). *"I know that my Redeemer lives, and that in the end he will stand upon the earth. And after my skin has been destroyed, yet in my flesh I will see God; I myself will see him with my own eyes—I, and not another. How my heart yearns within me!"* (**Job 19:25-29, NIV**).[2] *"Behold, the fear of the Lord, that is wisdom, and to turn away from evil is understanding"* (**Job 28:28**). His trust and hope in God leads Job to believe he would be vindicated and restored to fellowship with God even if he dies in his present misery (*13:15-16; 14:7-14*). Job maintains a basic confidence in God in spite of the apparent contradictions in his present circumstances.

John Mark Hicks summarizes,

Job's faith endured. He did not curse God. He maintained his integrity. He retained his hope. However, his enduring faith was mixed with doubt, despair, disappointment, and sharp accusations. Yet it was still faith. It was a struggle of faith, but it was a victorious faith. . . . Genuine faith is a faith that ultimately trusts and hopes in God even though it struggles through doubt and despair. Job teaches us that genuine faith is not perfect faith. Rather, genuine faith is a faith that retains its integrity through the struggle.(*Trust,* 171)

GOD RESPONDS TO JOB

When Job is at the end of his resources, God answers, but not as Job expects. Job wants an audience with God. He wants God to

---

[2] See the New American Standard Bible on **Job 19:25-26**.

answer his questions. But God comes to him not as the Answerer but as the Questioner. God throws at him rhetorical question after question to drive home the point of what Job cannot know and do in contrast to the power and wisdom God possesses. God reveals to him the marvels of His infinite wisdom and power. Job flunks God's demanding scientific examination (*chs. 38–39*; note especially *38:4,12,22-23,31-32,39-41*). After the torrent of unanswerable questions, the Lord said to Job, *"Shall a faultfinder contend with the Almighty? He who argues with God, let him answer it"* (*Job 40:2*). Job confesses his unworthiness and inability to answer God (*Job 40:4-5*).

God presses Job with direct questions, *"Will you even put me in the wrong? Will you condemn me that you may be in the right?"* (*Job 40:8*).

> ## God doesn't explain everything neatly for us.

God doesn't say Job is suffering because of this sin. In fact God does not explain the reason for Job's suffering, but He does make clear that Job is not suffering as a punishment for his sin.

God doesn't explain everything neatly for us. Mystery surrounds the Creator and Lord of the universe. Some do not like the God revealed in Job, but as Peter Kreeft says, "our likes and dislikes do not change reality. If we cannot take the God of Job (and the rest of the Bible), that is skin off our noses but not off God's. We do not make the universe hold its breath by holding ours" (*Philosophies*, 61).

JOB RESPONDS TO GOD

Job realizes his ignorance and presumption in telling God how He must act. He has drawn conclusions based on appearance and human thinking rather than understanding what is in reality the case.

> Then Job answered the LORD and said:
> "I know that you can do all things,
>   and that no purpose of yours can be thwarted. . . .
> I have uttered what I did not understand,
>   things too wonderful for me, which I did not know. . . .
> I had heard of you by the hearing of the ear,
>   but now my eye sees you;
> therefore I despise myself,
>   and repent in dust and ashes." (*Job 42:1-3,5-6*)

Job admits his guilt of foolishly misjudging and criticizing God and telling Him how He should act. In humility and faith Job trusted God even though he could not understand.

God reveals Himself wise, powerful, and sovereign. *Rather than answering Job's questions, God answers Job's need.* Answers in words alone would not have met the burning quest of his heart. Knowing God Himself is the answer Job receives. A satisfied Job says, *"I had heard of you by the hearing of the ear, but now my eye sees you" (Job 42:5).*

Knowing God is the ultimate key to enduring suffering. The better we know Him, the more we know He is worthy of our trust. Acceptance and confidence in the supreme wisdom of God is not evasion, but is the best and most reasonable response to the experience of suffering.

> **Knowing God is the ultimate key to enduring suffering.**

We can't find fulfillment in life until we accept our role as persons created by God. Because of our ignorance as human beings we can't expect to understand the why behind everything that happens. We are not in a position to know fully why God allows specific things to happen.

God is active in human affairs. The complex interplay of factors in God's sovereignty and human freedom are beyond our understanding. God is faithful and consistent, but circumstances change. We are not God. We should not try to explain the reasons behind God's actions where we have no divine revelation.

Those who insist that God must explain everything to human beings miss the main point of the book of Job. We will not understand some things in this life because of our human limitations. Repentance, not understanding, was the proper response for Job. "He does not repent of sins that have allegedly brought on the suffering; he repents of his arrogance in impugning God's justice, he repents of the attitude whereby he simply demands an answer, as if such were owed him. He repents of not having known God better" (**Carson, *How Long?*** 153).

The book rejects the simplistic notion that the righteous always prosper and the wicked always suffer. The family and prosperity that God returned to Job were not payments for faithfully enduring suffering but are described as a free gift of God (*Job 42:10-17*).

C.S. Lewis, grieving the death of his wife, asked, "Where is God?" He was frustrated by God's silence in regard to his plight (*Grief,* 5). Faith that endures suffering must be more than an intellectual faith. A faith that is more reason than trust will fail. In our day the pendulum has

A faith that is either more reason or more experience than trust will fail. swung away from reason to experience. But a faith that is more experience than trust will fail.

The experience of suffering leads some to question God. Experiences are real, but they need to be interpreted. Job does not understand why he is suffering. He wrongly interprets God's silence as absence and indifference.

Job doesn't realize that God was testing his faith. We need to trust God not only when things are going well and faith comes easily. We need to trust God when our experience seems to contradict our faith. We must trust God even when a bitter experience challenges our faith. On the cross Jesus senses abandonment by God, but He commits His Spirit to the Father. We will have experiences when God seems distant and not attentive to our needs. We need to interpret those experiences in the light of our loving and faithful God. We must not interpret our God only in the light of our experiences. Truth explains experience. Experience does not establish truth. Knowing God is the key to being able to deal with our experience.

Kreeft says Job found God but his friends did not. "Why? Because Job asked God! Job prayed. His three friends only philosophized. Job talked *to* God, his three friends only talked *about* God" (**Sense,** **23**). When we face suffering, it is important that we keep the conversation going with God. We need to tell Him our feelings and ask for wisdom and understanding. We need to pray for His help and strength. Even when we do not understand, it is essential that we trust in God with our whole being.

Think about It

1. Give Old Testament expressions of the question "Why do God's people suffer when often the wicked seem to prosper?"

2. How would you summarize the theme and purpose of the book of Job?

3. Give Archer's threefold answer to the problem of undeserved suffering.

4. Discuss the extent and impact of Job's losses and sufferings.

5. Which two or three of the "Thoughts for Sufferers from the Book of Job" by Wilbur Fields are most interesting to you? And why?

6. What was the main point made by the three friends?

7. What did the Lord mean when He told Eliphaz *"You have not spoken of me what is right, as my servant Job has"*? (*Job 42:7*)

8. How does Elihu characterize Job's problem? What does he see as the key for Job to deal with his suffering?

9. Quote Job's statements showing Job's deep faith even in the midst of his suffering.

10. How does the Lord rebuke Job in *38:1–42:6*? What is Job's response?

11. For what specifically was Job repentant?

12. State in one sentence the most important lesson you see in the book of Job.

CHAPTER FOUR

THE SUFFERER'S SONGBOOK

Even though I walk through the valley of the shadow of death,
I will fear no evil, for you are with me;
your rod and your staff, they comfort me.
Psalm 23:4

T he psalmists relate their experiences with God. They express confidence, praise, worship, and thanksgiving to God. They also express despair, doubt, and questioning. "There is no attempt in Scripture to whitewash the anguish of God's people when they undergo suffering. They argue with God, they complain to God, they weep before God. Theirs is not a faith that leads to a dry-eyed stoicism, but a faith so robust it wrestles with God" (**Carson,** *How Long?* **67**). The Psalms have much to teach us as we deal with suffering. This chapter will focus attention on insights for enduring suffering gleaned from the Old Testament psalmists.

INSIGHTS FROM THE PSALMISTS

The psalmists speak the language of the soul—whether in triumph or defeat, joy or sorrow, praise or anger. Pat and David Alexander speak of the relevance of the psalms,

> The psalms express the whole range of human feeling and experience, from dark depression to exuberant joy. They are rooted in particular circumstances, yet they are

timeless, and so among the best-loved, most-read, parts of the Bible. In our modern age we are stirred by the same emotions, puzzled over the same fundamental problems of life, cry out in need, or worship, to the same God, as the psalmists of old. We find it easy to identify with them. And we find their sheer, dogged faith, the depth of their love for God, both a tonic and a rebuke. (359)

Psalms is a hymnbook for those who want to live their lives in a right relationship with God. In the face of suffering, persecution, and sickness, the psalmists express praise, thanks, and trust in God for His mighty power, His steadfast love, and His judgment of the wicked.

Reading the Psalms can bring comfort to the grieving and help for those struggling.

Many people find them valuable for counseling. The words of this book strike a sympathetic chord with many people because they see how the writers of Scripture went through the same struggles they are going through. No matter what the situation in which we find ourselves, probably at least one psalm speaks to the issue at hand. The psalms state God's truth in a beautiful style that speaks to both our minds and our hearts. (**Arnold & Beyer, 305**)

The Psalms are the most popular section of the Old Testament Scriptures. Samuel Schultz observes,

The popularity of the Psalms rests in the fact that they reflect the common experiences of the human race. Composed by numerous authors, the various Psalms express the emotions, personal feelings, attitudes, gratitude, and interests of the average individual. Universally people have identified their lot in life with that of the Psalmists. (**286**)

The people of God voice their appeal to God for help. Facing anxieties, dangers, afflictions, oppressions, dryness of soul, and depression, the psalmists turn to God for divine assistance.

Joni Eareckson Tada and Steven Estes write, "If emotions are the language of the soul, then the Book of Psalms gives us the grammar and syntax, teaching us how to wrestle, inviting us to question, and vent anger in such a way as to move up and out of despair. The Psalms wrap nouns and verbs around our pain better than any other book" (**157**).

Since it is difficult to know the historical setting of many of the psalms, it has been helpful to group them according to themes or types. Various types have been identified including, laments, hymns of praise, thanksgiving psalms, psalms of trust, wisdom psalms, Torah psalms, royal psalms, liturgical psalms, penitential psalms, messianic psalms, imprecatory psalms, and songs of Zion. Since these psalms grow out of varied experiences of life, it is not surprising that many do not fit neatly into any one category, often having elements of two or more groupings.

Types of Psalms

Imprecatory Psalms—prayers that God would exercise His wrath on His enemies (e.g., *35, 69, 109*).

Lament Psalms—usually state one's miserable condition, express trust in God, and conclude with praise to the Lord (e.g., *3, 4, and 6*).

Messianic Psalms—make predictions about the person or ministry of Christ (e.g., *2, 16, and 22*).

Penitential Psalms—express repentance, sorrow, and confession for sin and appeal for forgiveness (e.g., *38 and 51*).

Psalms of Trust—are dominated by deep confidence in God and His goodness (e.g., *23 and 27*).

Praise Hymns—extolling God's might and majesty, often including a call to praise and the reason for the praise (e.g., *8, 19, and 145–150*).

Royal Psalms—composed for an event in the life of the king (e.g., *2, 18, 45, and 110*).

Songs of Zion—celebrate Mt. Zion in Jerusalem as the earthly center of the Lord's presence (e.g., *46, 48, 84, and 122*).

Thanksgiving Psalms—identify a crisis, indicate it has passed, and then express thanksgiving for the deliverance (e.g., *116 and 118*).

Torah Psalms—descriptions of life lived according to the Torah (law) (e.g., *1, 19, and 119*).

Wisdom Psalms—reflections on the problems of life (e.g., *73 and 127*).

This chapter will focus on psalms of trust, psalms of lament, and psalms of thanksgiving, observing how they relate to suffering.

Reading the identified psalms in conjunction with reading this chapter will prove profitable.

PSALMS OF TRUST

C. Hassell Bullock lists these elements which are usually present in psalms of trust: a declaration of trust, an invitation to trust, the basis for trust, a petition, a vow to praise, and an interior lament (implied or expressed). (167) These psalms can be divided into individual psalms of trust and community psalms of trust. The depth of confidence grows out of intense suffering. Some psalms of trust would also be labeled as laments.

Psalms of Trust

Individual Psalms of Trust—
    4, 16, 23, 27, 62, and 73.
Community Psalms of Trust—
    90, 115, 123, 124, 125, and 126.
Other Psalms Listed by Some as Psalms of Trust—
    11, 28, 31, 46, 56, 61, 63, 116, 131, 138, and 139.

These psalms often begin with an affirmation of gratitude to and affection for God. Even though the crisis has not passed, "the psalmist can face it now because experience has taught him that Yahweh is good and answers when his children call. These psalms are expressions of faith, not cries of victory" (168). Attention will be given to a few of the psalms of trust.

PSALM 23

Drawing on his background as a shepherd, David pictures God as the Great Shepherd. Surrounded by enemies, he can face death because he entrusts himself to the loving care and powerful protection of the Heavenly Shepherd. The shepherd with his weapons guards the sheep. While they were with the shepherd, they needed to fear nothing. David voiced his confidence in the protection provided by the powerful Shepherd,

> *Even though I walk through the valley of the shadow of death,*
>   *I will fear no evil,*

> For you are with me;
>> your rod and your staff,
>>> they comfort me. (**Ps 23:4**)

Even in the darkest valley, whether death, disease, or tragedy, our security rests not on our circumstances, but in God. When He is with us, we fear and lack nothing.

No psalm is more loved than *Psalm 23*. Through the centuries it has been a source of comfort to millions of sufferers. Bullock states, "*Psalm 23* is the psalm of trust par excellence. The psalmist has rested his whole life in the loving care of the divine Shepherd" (**173**).

My wife and I both learned *Psalm 23* as children—yet in the last few years it has ministered in profound ways to our spirits. During some difficult times when we were awake

> ## In the last few years Psalm 23 has ministered in profound ways to our spirits.

during long nights, we would quote it together. Its depth of meaning brought comfort to our souls.

PSALM 27

David's confidence in the Lord permeates this psalm. His enemies are seeking to harm him. He looks to the Lord for guidance, deliverance, and refuge.

> The LORD is my light and my salvation;
>> whom shall I fear?
> The LORD is the stronghold of my life;
>> Of whom shall I be afraid?
> When evildoers assail me to eat up my flesh,
> My adversaries and foes,
>> it is they who stumble and fall.
> Though an army encamp against me,
>> my heart shall not fear,
> though war arise against me,
>> yet will I be confident. (**Ps 27:1-3**)

Beginning with **verse 8**, confidence changes to urgent request. He seeks God's face, wanting Him to receive him. He does not want God to forsake him but to guide him in His will. The psalm ends in triumph:

> I believe that I shall look upon
>> the goodness of the LORD
>>> in the land of the living! (**Ps 27:13**)

A Christian leader in Africa, when sick and in prison in 1885, wrote in his journal "Comforted by Psalm 27" (**Stott**, *Psalms*, **38**). David's confidence and hope can inspire and comfort us.

Though she was blind, Fanny Crosby found strength to endure her suffering from the Psalms. Here she found inspiration for many of her 6,000 hymns. Contemplating on *Psalm 27* led her to write the hymn, "He Hideth My Soul."

> He hideth my soul in the cleft of the rock
> That shadows a dry, thirst land;
> He hideth my life in the depths of His love,
> And covers me there with His hand
> And covers me there with His hand.[1]

PSALM 34

When the righteous cry for help,
the LORD hears
and delivers them out of all their troubles.
The LORD is near to the brokenhearted
and saves the crushed in spirit.
Many are the afflictions of the righteous,
but the LORD delivers him out of them all. (**Ps 34:17-19**)

PSALM 46

God is our refuge, and strength
a very present help in trouble. (**Ps 46:1**).

No matter what life-shattering experiences the psalmist faced, he put his confidence in God as his fortress. Instead of running from troubles we need to *"Be still, and know that I am God"* (**Ps 46:10**). Knowing God in a personal way takes time, experience, and attention. When the 17th-century Scottish Covenanters were hunted, jailed, exiled, and killed, they took comfort in the Psalms, especially this one. When Luther faced oppression from the pope, this psalm was an inspiration for writing "A Mighty Fortress Is Our God." God's presence gives us security and sustains us when encompassed with troubles. Our confidence is strengthened as we review what He has done through the centuries (**Ps 46:8**). Accept His peace to rule in your heart.

[1] Fanny Crosby, "He Hideth My Soul," public domain.

Psalm 73

The problem of explaining the sufferings of righteous people and the apparent prosperity of the wicked is dealt with in the psalms—notably in *Psalms 37, 49, and 73*—as well as in Job and the prophets. "The divine perspective, which a man may share in the sanctuary, and the preciousness of the fellowship which the godly enjoy with God, outweighing all other considerations, are the means by which the psalmist is lifted out of his depression in *Psalm 73*" (*BEB*, 2:1803).

Asaph declares *"Truly God is good to Israel, to those who are pure in heart"* (*Ps 73:1*). He confesses he almost stumbled because he envied the arrogant. He says,

> For they have no pangs until death;
>> their bodies are fat and sleek.
> They are not in trouble as others are;
>> they are not stricken like the rest of mankind.
> Behold, there are the wicked;
>> always at ease, they increase in riches. (*Ps 73:4-5,12*)

He begins to think that his purity of life has been in vain because God is so good to the wicked (*Ps 73:13-14*). However when he worships God, he sees the big picture. He realizes the wicked will perish (*Ps 73:18-19*). He admits he failed to realize this because of his bitterness and ignorance (*Ps 73:21-22*). Carson observes,

> But he has now not only learned a negative lesson—that God's justice catches up with the wicked—but two positive ones as well: it is better to be with God *now*, and this present relationship with God must also be assessed on the long term. (*How Long?* 126)

Asaph affirms,

> Nevertheless, I am continually with you;
>> you hold my right hand.
> You guide me with your counsel,
>> and afterward you will receive me to glory. (*Ps 73:23-24*)

When he focuses on God and senses His presence, he realizes his favored position whether in this life or the next.

> Whom have I in heaven but you?
>> and there is nothing on earth that I desire but you.
> My flesh and my heart may fail,
>> but God is the strength of my heart and my portion forever.
> For behold, those who are far from you shall perish;
>> You put an end to everyone who is unfaithful to you.

> But for me it is good to be near God;
> I have made the Lord GOD my refuge,
> that I may tell of all your works. (**Ps 73:25-28**)

Carson concludes,

> Thus, everything depends on where you start. If you begin by
> envying the prosperity of the wicked, the human mind can
> "interpret" the data so as to rule God out, to charge him with
> unfairness, to make piety and purity look silly. But if you
> begin with genuine delight in God, both in this world and in
> the world to come, you can put up with "flesh and heart fail-
> ing," and be absolutely confident that, far from being the vic-
> tim of injustice, you are in the best possible position: near to
> the good (**v. 1**) and sovereign (**v. 28**) God. (**ibid., 126-127**)

The rich expressions of faith in the Psalms can enrich and deepen our
faith and spiritual experience.

PSALMS OF LAMENT

More psalms fit into the category of lament than in any other type
of psalm. Lament psalms usually include most of the following: a cry
for help, description of trouble, expression of trust, request for help, and a word of praise that God has heard his plea and will intervene. Complaint is followed by petition and praise.

More psalms fit into the category of lament than in any other type of psalm.

In an individual lament, one person complains about some trouble, for example, being sick or hounded by enemies. In a community lament, the nation has a problem, such as famine, locust infesta-
tion, or enemy attack. In the laments, often a complaint is expressed
to God for not intervening or for delaying to help in time trouble. As
the psalm progresses, the psalmist expresses trust or thanksgiving for
anticipated deliverance.

James Limburg describes the expressive and colorful language in
the Psalms,

> The complaint section of the laments is rich in figurative lan-
> guage. The one suffering may use comparisons from animal
> life, calling himself a worm (**22:6**) or comparing his situation
> to a vulture of the wilderness, an owl of the waste places, or a
> lonely bird on the housetop (**102:6-7**). His longing for the

Lord's deliverance is more than the longing of a night watch-
man for the morning (*130:6*); it is like the thirst of a person
about to faint (*63:1*), or a deer yearning for flowing streams
(*42:1*), or a parched land needing water (*143:6*). The present
situation of the people is like that of a dry creek in the Negeb
(*126:4*). The psalmist describes his personal distress as being
poured out like water, having a heart like wax, with his
strength dried up like a potsherd (*22:14-15*). He is shriveled
up like a dried out wineskin (*119:83*), broken like a pot
(*31:12*), lonely as a person who is deaf and dumb (*38:13-14*).
His life is passing away like a shadow that disappears at sun-
down, or it will vanish as quickly as a grasshopper that is
shaken away (*109:23*). (*5:531*)

The psalmists frequently ask "How long?" *"My soul also is greatly
troubled. But you, O LORD—how long?"* (*Ps 6:3*; see also *Pss 35:16-17;
74:10-11; 79:5; 80:4; 89:46; 90:13; 94:3; 119:84*). They call on the sovereign Lord to end the suffering of His people. Being in a covenantal
relationship with God, the psalmists ask the question common to
sufferers, "Why?" *"Why, O LORD, do your stand afar off? Why do you hide
yourself in times of trouble?"* (*Ps 10:1*; see also *Pss 22:1; 42:9; 43:2; 44:23-
24; 74:1; 79:10; 80:12; 84:14*). (Hicks, *Trust*, 201-203) When suffering
encompasses us, we must express our deep questions to God who listens and cares.

Lament psalms request God's help. *"But you, O GOD my Lord, deal
on my behalf for your name's sake; because your steadfast love is good,
deliver me!"* (*Ps 109:21*; see also *Pss 7:1; 25:20; 31:2; 59:1; 70:1-2; 109:26;
143:9*). They want God to deliver them to bring honor to His name.
Their complaint and praise arise out of a confidence in God's love
and presence. *"This is my comfort in my affliction, that your promise
gives me life"* (*Ps 119:50*).

Psalms of Lament

Individual Psalms of Lament of the Sick and Anguished—
> *6, 13, 22, 30, 31, 32, 35, 38, 39, 41, 51, 69, 71, 88, 91, 102,
> 103, and 130.*

Individual Psalms of Lament of the Persecuted and Accused—
> *3, 4, 5, 7, 11, 17, 23, 27, 57, and 63.*

Other Individual Psalms of Lament—
> *9, 10, 16, 25, 26, 28, 36, 40, 42, 43, 52, 54, 55, 56, 59, 61,
> 62, 64, 70, 77, 86, 94, 109, 120, 140, 141, 142, and 143.*

PSALM 3

As David was fleeing from Absalom, his son, he cries out to God. *"O Lord, how many are my foes! Many are rising against me; many are saying of my soul, there is no salvation for him in God"* (**Ps 3:1-2**). David says God is *"a shield about me"* and *"the lifter of my head"* (**Ps 3:3**). David can sleep without fear because God has sustained him (**Ps 3:5**). He is moved to say, *"Salvation belongs to the LORD; your blessing be on your people!"* (**Ps 3:8**).

PSALM 6

In anguish of soul, David cries out to God, then acknowledges God's answer to his prayer.

> O LORD, rebuke me not in your anger,
>   nor discipline me in your wrath.
> Be gracious to me, O LORD, for I am languishing;
>   heal me, O LORD, for my bones are troubled.
> My soul also is greatly troubled.
> But you, O LORD—how long? (**Psalm 6:1-3**)
>
> Depart from me, all you workers of evil,
>   for the LORD has heard the sound of my weeping.
> The LORD has heard my pleas;
>   the LORD accepts my prayer.
> All my enemies shall be ashamed and greatly troubled;
>   they shall turn back and be put to shame in a moment.
>   (**Ps 6:8-10**)

PSALM 7

When David is mistreated by Saul and chased as an outlaw, he says,

> O LORD my God, in you do I take refuge;
>   save me from all my pursuers and deliver me. . . .
> I will give to the LORD the thanks due to his righteousness,
>   and I will sing praise to the name of the LORD, the Most
>   High. (**Ps 7:1,13**)

Psalm 13

Psalm 13 moves from complaint (*vv. 1-2*) to petition (*vv. 3-4*) and then to praise (*vv. 5-6*). David begins by asking the Lord how long He will let the wicked triumph and concludes rejoicing in his salvation.

> How long, O LORD? Will you forget me forever?
> How long will you hide your face from me?
> How long must I take counsel in my soul
>   and have sorrow in my heart all the day?
> How long shall my enemy be exalted over me? (*Ps 13:1-2*)
>
> But I have trusted in your steadfast love;
>   my heart shall rejoice in your salvation.
> I will sing to the LORD,
>   because he has dealt bountifully with me. (*Ps 13:5-6*)

Psalm 22

As a messianic psalm, *Psalm 22* foreshadows the sufferings of Christ, which is the subject discussed in chapter 6. It is also a psalm of lament moving from suffering to triumph. It has an invocation (*vv. 1-5*), a description of the sufferer's condition (*vv. 6-8; 14-18*), a petition to God for aid (*vv. 11, 19-21*), and an affirmation of certainty that God has heard his prayer, ending with praise (*vv. 22-31*).

> My God, my God, why have you forsaken me?
>   Why are you so far from saving me,
>   from the words of my groaning?
> O my God, I cry by day, but you do not answer,
>   and by night, but I find no rest.
>
> The afflicted shall eat and be satisfied;
>   those who seek him shall praise the LORD! (*Ps 22:1-2,26*)

Psalm 42

The psalmist is thirsting for God, but apparently something is keeping him from attending the festivals at Jerusalem, and he is being taunted by challenges, *"Where is your God?"* (*Ps 42:1-3*). "These, then, were the causes of his depression of soul: the absence of God to comfort him and presence of men who mocked him. Each stanza reverts to this double theme" (**Stott**, *Psalms*, **55**). He is writing from the north but longs to be in Jerusalem and worship.

He was disappointed and depressed, brooding and feeling sorry for himself; he asked, *"Why are you cast down, O my soul, and why are* you in turmoil within me?" (*Ps 42:5,11*). Admitting he was discouraged, he turned to the Lord and asked why He had forsaken him. He needed to remember that problems are inevitable in this fallen world. He decided to quit moaning in self-pity. He prays to God and exhorts himself to *"Hope in God; for I shall again praise him, my salvation and my God"* (*Ps 42:5,11*)

PSALM 63

David does not give in to fatalism or doubt but rather seeks God.

> *O God, you are my God; earnestly I seek you;*
> *my soul thirsts for you; my flesh faints for you,*
> *as in a dry and weary land where there is no water.*
> (*Ps 63:1*)

PSALM 74

A major disaster to Jerusalem stands in the background of this psalm. God seems to have abandoned His city and His people. The temple has been destroyed. The psalmist calls on God to destroy their enemies which are considered as God's enemies. No separation of religion and state existed because the covenant people were the nation of Israel. Imprecatory psalms use "rhetoric of outrage" (**Carson, How Long? 87**). igniting the people's opposition to those who oppose God.

> *How long, O God, is the foe to scoff?*
> *Is the enemy to revile your name forever?*
> *Why do you hold back your hand, your right hand?*
> *Take it from the fold of your garment and destroy them!*
> (*Ps 74:10*)

PSALM 142

> *With my voice I cry out to the LORD;*
> *with my voice I plead for mercy to the LORD.*
> *I pour out my complaint before him;*
> *I tell my trouble before him.*
> *When my spirit faints within me,*
> *you know my way!*
> *In the path where I walk*
> *they have hidden a trap for me.*
> *Look to the right and see:*
> *there is none who takes notice of me;*
> *no refuge remains to me;*
> *no one cares for my soul.*

I cry to you, O LORD;
*   I say, "You are my refuge,*
*   my portion in the land of the living."*
Attend to my cry,
*   for I am brought very low!*
Deliver me from my persecutors,
*   for they are too strong for me!*
Bring me out of prison,
*   that I may give thanks to your name!*
The righteous will surround me,
*   for you will deal bountifully with me.* (**Ps 142:1-7**)

PSALM 146

Put not your trust in princes,
*   in a son of man, in whom there is no salvation.*
When his breath departs he returns to the earth;
*   on that very day his plans perish.*
Blessed is he whose help is the God of Jacob,
*   whose hope is in the LORD his God,*
who made heaven and earth,
*   the sea, and all that is in them,*
*   who keeps faith forever.* (**Ps 146:3-6**)

John Mark Hicks recalls how lament brought him to a comforting communion with the Lord. His son, Joshua, had a terminal condition of premature aging. As a boy, Joshua had looked forward to riding the school bus. When he was old enough to ride the bus, one day he didn't want to get on the bus. Hicks urged him to get on the bus, but as the bus drove off, it was obvious why Joshua was reluctant. The older students mocked him, calling him names and ridiculing him for wearing diapers. Seeing his son humiliated in this way filled Hicks with anger. He wished those kids knew what it felt like to be mocked.

While thinking of what course of action to take Hicks took his lament to God.

> Finally, I took my anger and hurt to God. I went to my office and poured my heart before him. I held nothing back. I complained bitterly, and then I complained some more. There was plenty to complain about. Why was my son born with this condition? Why are others permitted to inflict pain upon the innocent? Why hadn't God answered our prayers for a healthy son? Why couldn't Joshua ever fulfill the dreams we had for him and honor the name which we gave him as a

leader among God's People? Why hadn't the sovereign God of the universe blessed him with health?

Somewhere in the middle of that complaint, in the middle of that lament, I became intensely aware that my complaint had been heard. I did not hear a voice or a whisper. I did not have a vision or feel the wind blow across my face. Rather, I sensed God's presence, and I came to understand his own pain. In the middle of my lament over my own son, I became aware that God understood. God empathized with me. It was as if God had said to me, "I understand—they treated my Son that way, too." In that moment God provided a comfort that I cannot yet explain but one that I still experience in my heart. (*Trust*, 184)

"They treated my Son that way, too."

He said he gained a new appreciation for God's pain in watching the death of His Son on the cross. Aware of being in God's presence, Hicks said his "lament turned to praise not because I had received an answer to my 'why' questions, but because God gave me the answer I needed . . . God's presence" (**ibid., 185**).

We need to be honest with God in our prayers as we face suffering and difficulties in life. Taking our deepest hurts to the Lord and trusting Him with them, often results in a transformed attitude enabling us to deal with the suffering. I know when I have experienced suffering, I have expressed my deepest feelings and concerns more completely to our heavenly Father than to any other. I, too, can testify that I experienced God's presence in a deeper way when I poured my heart out to Him. I believe the deeper the hurt, the closer God is.

PSALMS OF THANKSGIVING

Psalms of thanksgiving express gratitude to God for an act of deliverance such as healing from illness (*30; 32; 116*), deliverance from enemies (*18; 92; 118; 138*), receiving a needed good harvest (*67*), or simple rescue from trouble (*66:14*). The main theme is thanksgiving for deliverance. *"O LORD my God, I cried to you for help, and you have healed me"* (*Ps 30:2*).

"These psalms assume the presence of the congregation, which is gathered either for worship (*30:4-5; 34:5,8,9; 118:1-4,24,29*) or for instruction (*32:8-11; 34:11-14*) and who hear the story of the deliverance (*40:9-10; 66:16-19*)" (**Limburg, 5:532**).

Thanksgiving psalms usually include praise, description of past trouble, testimony, and exhortation. It is hard to distinguish between lament and thanksgiving at times because the thanksgiving psalms presuppose some trouble and give thanks for deliverance and offer praise to God. Individual psalms of thanksgiving include report of a crisis and thanks for deliverance Community psalms of thanksgiving report on a national crisis and subsequent deliverance.

Thanklessness is a terrible disregard of God's goodness. Shakespeare said, "How sharper than a serpent's tooth it is to have a thankless child" (*Lear*, I,iv,312). Ingratitude is a mark of unbelief which leads to a sinful lifestyle (*Rom 1:20-21*). Falling into a habit of grumbling jeopardizes one's relationship with God (*Num 14:26-29; 1Cor 10:10; Php 2:14; Jas 5:9*). Even in the direst of circumstances, we can find things for which to give thanks. The psalms of thanksgiving can help us in expressing thanksgiving even in the midst of suffering.

Psalms of Thanksgiving

Individual Psalms of Thanksgiving—
18, 30, 31, 32, 40, 66, 92, 116, 118, 120, and 138.
Community Psalms of Thanksgiving—
65, 66, 67, 75, 107, 118, 124, 129, and 136.

PSALM 40

Remembering past blessings from God helps us to face present trials. Having observed God's faithfulness keeps us trusting Him. This psalm recounts God's deliverance and ends with a plea for mercy.

PSALM 107

A series of psalms celebrates God's mighty acts: *Psalm 104*—the creation; *Psalm 105*—the Exodus; *Psalm 106*—from the Exodus to the return from Babylonian exile. Here we see God's redemptive activity in the life of Israel.

> Just as God responded to the cries of his people in Egypt and in the exile (*Psalm 106:44-45*), so God listens to the cries of his people in their personal crises. God's mighty works in

redemptive history provide the pattern of God's works in the lives of his people. They know God hears them because he has always acted to redeem his people and he has demonstrated that he is the Lord Almighty who remembers his covenant. (**Hicks, *Trust*, 148**)

"Oh give thanks to the Lord, for he is good, for his steadfast love endures forever!" (**Ps 107:1**) People cry to God for help (**Ps 107:6,13, 19,28**), and He hears their cries and spares them. God is praised for acting in the personal troubles in the lives of His people, delivering them from hunger, thirst, affliction, oppression, and other troubles. *"Let them thank the Lord for his steadfast love, for his wondrous works to the children of men! And let them offer sacrifices of thanksgiving, and tell of his deeds in songs of joy!"* (**Ps 107:21-22**). If we feel abandoned by God in a personal crisis, we need to remember our faithful God remains active in our lives today. This psalm concludes, *"Whoever is wise, let him attend to these things; let them consider the steadfast love of the Lord"* (**Ps 107:43**).

The psalmists can help us to offer prayers of trust, lament, and thankfulness. The Sufferer's Songbook can be an especially valuable resource in times of suffering.

Think about It

1. Why do you think that the book of Psalms is the most loved and widely read of the Old Testament books?

2. List and briefly define types of psalms.

3. Psalms of trust usually include what elements?

4. Summarize *Psalm 73*.

5. Describe a psalm of lament.

6. What common questions sufferers ask are found frequently in the psalms of lament?

7. Describe John Mark Hicks's experience with lament when his son was ridiculed.

8. How do the psalms of thanksgiving relate to suffering?

9. Summarize *Psalm 107*.

CHAPTER FIVE

THE PROPHETS ASK WHY

*The LORD declares, "When your people say,
'Why has the LORD our God done all these things to us?'
you shall say to them, 'As you have forsaken me and served foreign gods
in your land, so you shall serve foreigners in a land that is not yours.'"*
Jeremiah 5:19

God raised up prophets, who were special persons to be his divinely inspired spokesmen to declare His word to His people. They received and declared a message from God. God put the words in the prophet's mouth and he spoke what God commanded (*Deu 18:18*). Peter tells us, *"For no prophecy was ever produced by the will of man, but men spoke from God as they were carried along by the Holy Spirit"* (*2Pet 1:21*). The prophets suffered with the people of God and often suffered personal persecution because people hated the truth of God that they declared. This chapter will focus on Habakkuk and Jeremiah as they both wrestled with the problem of suffering and evil.

INSIGHTS FROM THE PROPHETS

Even though the prophets received messages of truth from God, sometimes they questioned God about what was happening. Habakkuk asks, *"Why do you make me see iniquity, and why do you idly look at wrong?"* (*Hab 1:3*). Jeremiah questions God, *"Why have you struck us down so that there is no healing for us?"* (*Jer 14:19*). They also dealt with the "why" and "how long" questions that people raise against God.

I. Insights from the Prophets
II. Habakkuk
III. Jeremiah

The prophets received communications from God, but humanly, at times, they found it difficult to understand and accept the message. Peter says they did not always understand the message they delivered (*1Pet 1:10-11*). We have God's word

The prophets can help us in knowing the sovereign Lord of history.

in the Bible, but at times we have difficulty in understanding and accepting what God says. A study of the prophets can help us in knowing the sovereign Lord of history. While at times we may identify with their questions, it is important that we learn from their strong trust and faithfulness to God even through difficult situations.

From the books of Job, the Psalms, and the prophets we gain a better knowledge of the greatness of God. In our efforts to emphasize meeting people's felt needs, we may have neglected to teach on the greatness of God.

HABAKKUK

A contemporary with the prophet Jeremiah, Habakkuk wrote in the final years of Judah (after 605 BC). The literary form of his book is unusual. It is a dialogue between the prophet and God. Habakkuk could not understand why God was acting as He was.

Twice the prophet openly complains to God and God answers him. Habakkuk questions God about why He allows evil to go unchecked and how long He will permit it. God says He will use the Chaldeans (Babylonians) to punish the evildoers. A perplexed Habakkuk asks how He could use such an evil power to punish a less wicked people. God responds that the wicked will perish but the righteous person will live by his faithfulness to God. The book ends with the prophet's prayer expressing joy and confidence in the Lord.

Donald Gowan says the book of Habakkuk:

> speaks to some of the deepest needs of men and women who are oppressed and depressed by the ways of this world. Those who have asked, "Why, in a world governed by a good God, does wickedness so often triumph?" will find Habakkuk wrestling with the same question. Those who do not understand why they see the righteous suffering beyond anything they could be thought to deserve, while the wicked prosper, will find their bewilderment echoed in the stirring pleas of this prophet. (**10**)

Raymond Calkins writes, "There is no Old Testament book that is able to do more for the burdened souls of men or to raise them to higher levels of hope and confidence than the brief prophecy of Habakkuk. . . . Here is a man with a soul sensitive to evil, yet firm in his faith in an omnipotent God" (**Quoted in Gowan, 10**).

Habakkuk teaches us that we can persevere through the difficulties in life, trusting God in spite of some missing answers. The key to the book is its most famous text: *"The just shall live by his faith"* (**2:4, KJV**). We may not understand God's ways, but we can always trust Him.

After condemning the sins of Judah, both Habakkuk and Jeremiah declare that God is going to use an emerging world power to punish Judah. Habakkuk is exasperated with the sins of his people—injustice, violence, and ignoring the Law. He is also distressed with the apparent silence of God ignoring his prayer and tolerating these conditions. Impatient, he takes his concern directly to God.

> *O LORD, how long shall I cry for help, and you will not hear?*
> *Or cry to you "Violence!" and you will not save?*
> *Why do you make me see iniquity, and why do you idly look at wrong?*
> *Destruction and violence are before me; strife and contention arise.*
> *So the law is paralyzed and justice never goes forth.*
> *For the wicked surround the righteous; so justice goes forth perverted.*
> (**Hab 1:2-4**)

He asks the Lord why violence rules when there should be justice.

God responds by pointing out that things would get worse. He is using a ferocious formerly insignificant people, the Babylonians (Chaldeans), to execute judgment on God's people (**Hab 1:5-11**). This would be a work so great that no one would believe it at that time. The Babylonians were at that time not yet a world power.

The prophet asks the Lord how He could send someone so cruel and evil to punish His people (**Hab 1:12-17**). While Habakkuk waited in the watchtower, the Lord responded that the wicked will meet their end, but *"The righteous shall live by his faith"* (**Hab 2:4**).[1] Woes are pronounced against the Babylonians for various kinds of oppression: plunder, arrogance, greed, cruelty, drunkenness, and idolatry. In spite of these evils, *"The LORD is in his holy temple; let all the earth keep*

---

[1] This verse is quoted in **Romans 1:17; Galatians 3:11; and Hebrews 10:38** emphasizing the importance of faith in regard to righteousness and life.

> **The key to enduring suffering is to reverence and trust the Lord of heaven.**

silence before him" (**Hab 2:20**). The punishment of Israel is not the end of the story. Babylon is not supreme. God will bring Babylon down at the proper time. The key to enduring suffering is to reverence and trust the Lord of heaven.

Samuel J. Schultz summarizes Habakkuk's response:

> These thoughts evoke a psalm of praise from the prophet's lips. Known to him are the mighty works of God in times past. With an appeal that God will remember mercy in his wrath, Habakkuk implores him to make known once more his mighty acts. God manifested his glory and used nature to bring salvation to his people Israel when he brought them through the wilderness and established them in the promised land. Habakkuk is willing to endure present adversities in the knowledge that God's day of trouble will come upon the aggressor. Were the fields and the flocks to fail in their material provisions, he would still rejoice in the God of his salvation. Through a living faith in God the prophet gathers strength to face the uncertain future. (**408**)

Habakkuk strongly affirms the power and majesty of God as the sovereign Lord over all the earth. He affirms that God's justice will prevail over the oppressors (**Hab 3:16**). His book concludes with one of the most beautiful expressions of trust found in the Scriptures. He did not say, "You bless me, and then I will bless you." Rather on the basis of God's faithfulness in the past, Habakkuk affirms his unconditional trust and delight in God.

> *Though the fig tree should not blossom, nor fruit be on the vines,*
> > *the produce of the olive fail*
> > *and the fields yield no food,*
> *the flock be cut off from the fold*
> > *and there be no herd in the stalls,*
> *yet I will rejoice in the LORD;*
> > *I will take joy in the God of my salvation.*
> *GOD, the Lord, is my strength;*
> > *he makes my feet like the deer's;*
> > *he makes me tread on my high places.* (**Hab 3:17-19**)

His complaint against God has now turned to praise of God.

Laetsch says, "The book was intended as an urgent call to repentance for the wicked, as a message of consolation for the little flock of believers, and as an admonition for the latter to continue steadfast in their trust and confidence in the promised salvation and Savior" (317).

Kaiser says Habakkuk addresses the problem "of squaring the goodness and justice of God with the presence of what seems like unbridled evil and wickedness among men and nations." He was frightened,

> But balancing his outward fear and realistic assessment of the fact that his whole nation and its temple, army, and citizens, and all that he held dear, were to be lost to one of the most despicable, godless, and unmerciful conquerors known on earth to that time, he had a peace in his heart that passed all understanding. . . . Habakkuk, then, will teach us how to live by faith in a God who is alive and active in the current affairs of life, distasteful and unappealing as those affairs seem at times. (*Mastering*, 142)

For centuries Assyria and Babylon dominated the region. The Chaldeans from the vicinity of Babylon and southern Macedonia were a rising power who formerly played only a minor role in world history. The Chaldeans with the help of the Medes in 612 BC destroyed Nineveh, the capital of Assyria. They defeated the Egyptians at Carchemish in 605 BC. (**Laetsch, 314; Gowan, 16**)

> What had seemed unbelievable had become an incontrovertible fact. A Chaldean was the world ruler, and his son, the Chaldean Nebuchadnezzar, became God's instrument to punish wicked Judah and Jerusalem (*Dan. 1:1ff.; 2 Kings 24-25; Jeremiah 27-29; 36-44; 52*). God's word never fails. (*Cp. Habakkuk 2:3.*) (**Laetsch, 316**)

> Habakkuk's book was produced in the midst of all that. When we read it with the turmoil, terror, and tragedy of those years in mind we shall see that it is a response to such a time, but, . . . the prophet chose a way of speaking which would give his words a universal appeal so that they might speak with a peculiar directness time after time to those of other ages and places who find themselves in deep trouble. (**Gowan, 17**)

James Russell Lowell wrote:

> Careless seems the great Avenger; history's pages but record
> One death-grapple in the darkness 'twixt old systems and the Word;
> Truth forever on the scaffold, Wrong forever on the throne,—

Yet that scaffold sways the future, and, behind the dim unknown,

Standeth God within the shadow, Keeping watch above his own. **(128)**

JEREMIAH

God called Jeremiah, a priest, to be a prophet. God told him,

> *Before I formed you in the womb, I knew you, and before you were born I consecrated you; I appointed you a prophet to the nations. . . . for to all to whom I send you, you shall go, and whatever I command you, you shall speak. Do not be afraid of them for I am with you to deliver you, declares the LORD. (Jer 1:5,7-8)*

Misunderstood by his family, mistreated by priests, prophets, and kings, rejected by his people, his life was filled with tragedy. Jeremiah is called the "weeping prophet." He saw much suffering. He experienced much suffering. He spoke much about suffering.

Jeremiah's forty-year ministry began about 627 BC. During the last years before the fall of Jerusalem in 586 BC, he repeatedly warned Judah of its impending doom at the hands of the Babylonians. Schultz points out,

> Since he ministered to an apostate nation with godless leadership he was subjected to persecution by his own people. A martyr's death undoubtedly would have been a relief compared to the constant suffering and anguish that Jeremiah endured as he continued his ministry among a people whose national life was in the process of disintegration. Instead of obeying God's message as delivered by the prophet they persecuted the messenger. (325)

The accompanying chart lists several of the sufferings of Jeremiah. At times Jeremiah was overwhelmed with his suffering and complained to the Lord. He asks, *"Why is my pain unceasing?"* (*Jer 15:18*). He cursed the day he was born and wished he had died in his mother's womb. He asks, *"Why did I come out from the womb to see toil and sorrow, and spend my days in shame?"* (*Jer 10:18*). He was so miserable he thought he would prefer to be dead or better yet, never born. He asks, *"Why does the way of the wicked prosper? Why do all who are treacherous thrive?"* (*Jer 12:1*). In his despair and exhaustion, he even feels misled by the Lord, *"O LORD, you have deceived me, and I was deceived; you are stronger than I, and you have prevailed. I have become a laughingstock all the day; everyone mocks me" (Jer 20:7).* Pushed to the limit by his enemies, he calls upon God to bring divine vengeance upon them *(Jer 18:19-23).* Jeremiah be-

Jeremiah wanted to see God's righteousness vindicated.

lieved his message was God's message and his enemies were God's enemies. He wanted to see God's righteousness vindicated.

Even though he sometimes was pushed to anger and despair, his basic character was one of tender sympathy for his people. Contemplating the ruin awaiting Judah, he said, *"My anguish, my anguish! I writhe in pain! Oh the walls of my heart! My heart is beating wildly; I cannot keep silent, for I hear the sound of the trumpet, the alarm of war"* *(Jer 4:19).* He grieves for his people: *"My joy is gone; grief is upon me; my heart is sick within me"* *(Jer 8:18).* He prays for understanding, affirming confidence in God's power and steadfast love in dealing with His people *(Jer 32:17-22).*

Jeremiah's Sufferings²

Jeremiah experienced deep inner conflict and grief because his people rejected the warnings and would experience God's terrible punishments (9).

People from his hometown threatened to kill him if he did not stop prophesying in the name of the Lord (11).

His family dealt treacherously with him (12).

He was arrested in the temple, beaten by the priest, and put in stocks for the night (19–20).

He sank to the depths of depression as he faced persecution (20).

When proclaiming in the court of the temple its destruction, the priests and prophets demanded his execution (26).

When Jeremiah was portraying the Babylonian captivity by wearing a yoke, a false prophet, Hananiah, broke the yoke and denied the message (28).

Other false prophets in Jerusalem and Babylon opposed Jeremiah and his message (23, 28, 29).

One of the false prophets who was a captive wrote to Jerusalem to get Zephaniah and priests to rebuke and imprison Jeremiah (29).

---

² Chapters in the book of Jeremiah are in parentheses.

When Jeremiah's scribe read God's warning to Jehoiakim, he
defied the message, burned the scroll, and ordered the
arrest of the prophet and the scribe (*36*).
When the Babylonian siege temporarily stopped, Jeremiah was
arrested and charged with being a traitor and
Babylonian sympathizer; he was beaten and imprisoned
(*37*).
When the battle resumed, Zedekiah asked Jeremiah's advice. The
king disliked being rebuked, so he put Jeremiah under
guard and had him thrown into a cistern where he sank
in the mire (*38*).
After the fall of Jerusalem, the leaders asked to learn God's will.
He said to stay in Jerusalem, but they disobeyed and
went to Egypt, taking the prophet with them (*42–43*).

Jeremiah wrestled with God through the rough reality of the times, and he was made stronger. It is hard to find a person who experienced more undeserved suffering and opposition, made more unceasing intercession for his people, and showed greater sincerity and fearless proclamation of God's message than this man of God. With clarity and power he thundered the word of God showing both God's wrath against sin and His steadfast love for His people.

Jeremiah lived in a day of idol worship (*1:16; 11:13; 32:29*). He addressed the kings, priests, and prophets who said to an image cut from *"a tree, 'You are my father' and to [one carved from] a stone 'You gave me birth.'"* When suffering and trouble came, they called out to these idols, *"Arise, and save us!"* (*Jer 2:27-28*). The Israelites did not trust in the Lord. Jeremiah said, *"They have spoken falsely of the LORD and have said, 'He will do nothing; no disaster will come upon us, nor shall we see sword or famine'"* (*Jer 5:12*). Practical atheism leaves people ill-prepared for suffering.

Practical atheism leaves people ill-prepared for suffering.

Suffering exposes the utter defenselessness and helplessness of those who have forsaken God. Those who put their ultimate trust in money and material things, medical science and human power, fame and pleasure will find these gods useless when they face a terrible tragedy, a terminal illness, or death itself. It was Jeremiah's deep personal faith and commitment to God that enabled him to survive spiritually the tragedies of his tumultuous life. We must speak Jeremiah's message today warning that those who forsake God will face His wrath.

When religion becomes organized hypocrisy divorced from godly living, people are left without resources to endure suffering or to minister to the hurting. Jeremiah delivers God's message that they were not to boast in wisdom, might, or riches, *"but let him who boasts boast in this, that he understands and knows me, that I am the LORD who practices steadfast love, justice, and righteousness in the earth"* (*Jer 9:24*). God wants his people to have wholeness and hope. *"Then you will call upon me and come and pray to me, and I will hear you. You will seek me and find me. When you seek me with all your heart, I will be found by you"* (*Jer 29:13-14*).

God gave Judah a chance to repent, *"Amend your ways and your deeds, and I will let you dwell in this place"* (*Jer 7:3*). Since Judah refused to repent, they would be sent into exile in Babylon as a punishment for their sins (*Jer 7:1–8:3*). They had rejected God, worshiping idols instead, living lives of hatred, immorality, and ungodliness. *"Therefore thus says the Lord GOD: behold, my anger and my wrath will be poured out on this place"* (*Jer 7:20*). Even later the

> **Even though He punishes them, God loves and yearns for His people.**

Lord offered Judah other opportunities to repent and avoid punishment but they contemptuously refused (*Jer 26:1ff.; 36:9ff.*). *"Because your guilt is great, because your sins are flagrant, I have done these things to you"* (*Jer 30:15*). Even though He punishes them, God loves and yearns for His people. He seeks their restoration: *"And you shall be my people, and I will be your God"* (*Jer 30:22*).

Isaiah names the Persian king, Cyrus, through whom God would redeem His people from bondage (*Isa 44:45; Jer 6:22; 51:1,11; Ezra 1:1*). The hand of the Lord was moving in world history. *"Who has performed and done this, calling the generations from the beginning? I, the LORD, the first, and with the last; I am he"* (*Isa 41:4*). God punished Judah by Babylon and then used Persia to punish Babylon. Jeremiah predicted the land of Judah would be desolate (*Jer 4:23-26*) and also predicted the redemption of the land (*Jer 31:5-19; 33:12-13*).

Jeremiah promises God's people will be restored to their land (*Jer 24:6; 30:10*). The Lord says, *"I will give them a heart to know that I am the LORD, and they shall be my people and I will be their God, for they shall return to me with their whole heart"* (*Jer 24:7*). God will enter into a new spiritual covenant with His people: *"I will be their God, and they shall be my people"* (*Jer 31:33*). This promise finds fulfillment in Christ (*Heb 8:7-13; 10:15-18*). In the tenderest of terms, God declares His love for His people (*Jer 33:3,20*). Even in the darkest night, believers can see forward to the light of a new day because we have a loving, all-powerful God. Even in tragic times, following Jeremiah's example, we can put our trust and hope in God, who will give us inner strength to faithfully continue serving Him.

In answer to the question, "Why do bad things happen to good people?" Jeremiah responds, "There are no 'good people.' The puzzle should rather be why good things happen to bad people! We are good people only by the standards of bad people" (*Sense*, 115). Jeremiah speaks God's Word, *"From the least to the greatest of them, everyone is greedy for unjust gain; and from prophet to priest, everyone deals falsely. They have healed the wound of my people lightly, saying, 'Peace, peace,' when there is no peace"* (*Jer 6:13-14*; cp. *Isa 64:6*).

Peter Kreeft says, "According to Jeremiah, all the prophets, and all the Bible, sin is not just a few baddies committed by goodies, bad deeds done by basically good people. Yet that is what nearly all modern psychology tells us. By biblical standards, that is nothing less than a false religion" (**ibid.**). Thankfully we have Christian psychologists and counselors who take the biblical view of human nature seriously. Humanistic psychology has fostered a cult of self-worship (**Vitz**). Human nature is assumed to be essentially good, and evil is considered a mistake of society. Absorption with self characterizes much of our culture. Views which deny the biblical teaching of human beings as sinners cannot deal with the problem of suffering.

The question "Why do bad things happen to good people?" makes a false assumption—that we are good people. This is false. The Bible emphatically teaches that all men are sinners. One must acknowledge the terribleness of his or her personal sinfulness before beginning to learn the meaning of suffering.

The question makes a false assumption—that we are good people.

In the book of Lamentations, Jeremiah mourns the loss of the nation and the fall of Jerusalem to Babylon (586 BC). He graphically describes the sorrow and suffering of people experiencing the horrors of war (*Lam 2:20-22*). Arnold and Beyer describe the scene:

> The author wept as he saw Jerusalem's suffering. Little ones starved to death in their mothers' arms while enemies mocked the city's downfall. The dead became food for the living due to the extreme food shortage! Jerusalem's fall meant God had fulfilled his word, for the people had failed to heed his persistent warnings. The prophet challenged the people to pray for God's compassion. (**404**)

The righteousness of God is affirmed in punishing Judah for her disobedience. Hope can be found in confession of sin and trust in the God who brought judgment upon them. They are reminded God's mercies are *"new every morning"* (*Lam 3:23*) and great is His faithfulness even to a people who have been unfaithful to Him. When we suffer to the extent we feel God has abandoned us, we need to remember our only hope is to trust in our faithful God.

Throughout his ministry Jeremiah knew he was God's messenger. God providentially supported him as he faithfully declared God's truth regardless of how unpopular or dangerous it was. Jeremiah is a sterling example and inspiration for God's messengers to witness faithfully to God's truth no matter the cost.

God, as creator and ruler over the world, acts in human history according to His own purpose. "Nothing is arbitrary with him. He permits evil in the world, and he uses it to punish, deter, test, and educate. But he also acts to punish, deter, test, educate, and, most importantly, to redeem. What God seeks is holy fellowship with his people. Everything God does is related to that single desire and intent . . . to have a people who are his own" (**Hicks, *Trust*, 150**). Evil cannot defeat God's purpose. God in His infinite wisdom and eternal love has His reasons for what He permits in this world.

Knowing God is the most important knowledge. It is the knowledge that really matters for understanding life. It is impossible to find a reason for human existence without recognition of God. For those who do not know whose world this is and who runs it,

> The world becomes a strange, mad, painful place, and life in it a disappointing and unpleasant business, for those who do not know about God. Disregard the study of God, and you

sentence yourself to stumble and blunder through life blind-
folded, as it were with no sense of direction and no understanding of what surrounds you. This way you can waste your
life and lose your soul. (**Packer, 14-15**)

As in the days of the prophets, so it is today that people's greatest
need is to know the great God of the universe. John Piper reported
that one January he preached on the vision of God's holiness from
Isaiah 6.

> So I preached on the holiness of God and did my best to dis-
> play the majesty and glory of such a great and holy God. I
> gave not one word of application to the lives of the people.
> Application is essential in the normal course of preaching, but
> I felt led that day to make a test: Would the passionate por-
> trayal of the greatness of God in and of itself meet the needs
> of people?
>
> I didn't realize that not long before this Sunday one of the
> young families of our church discovered that their child was
> being sexually abused by a close relative. It was incredibly
> traumatic. They were there that Sunday morning and sat
> under that message. I wonder how many advisers to us pastors
> today would have said: "Pastor Piper, can't you see your peo-
> ple are hurting? Can't you come down out of the heavens and
> get practical? Don't you realize what kind of people sit in
> front of you on Sunday?" Some weeks later I learned the story.
> The husband took me aside one Sunday after a service.
> "John," he said, "these have been the hardest months of our
> lives. Do you know what has gotten us through? The vision of
> the greatness of God's holiness that you gave me the first week
> of January. It has been the rock we could stand on."
>
> The greatness and the glory of God are relevant. It does not
> matter if surveys turn up a list of perceived needs that does
> not include the supreme greatness of the sovereign God of
> grace. That is the deepest need. Our people are starving for
> God. (*Supremacy*, **10-11**)

A strong, deep confidence in the loving and mighty God who rules
this world is the solid rock foundation that will strengthen us to work
through all the "whys" and "how longs" that we may ask. In the
prophets we see that at least some suffering is punishment for sin. We
also see that even those faithfully serving the Lord will experience suffering. The key to it all is trust in our Heavenly Father.

Think about It

1. What is the central problem addressed in Habakkuk?

2. Quote the verse from Habakkuk which is quoted three times in the New Testament.

3. Does God still punish nations with other nations? If so, how can we know?

4. Summarize Habakkuk's prayer at the end of the book.

5. Is it appropriate to raise questions to God?

6. List several ways Jeremiah suffered.

7. How can we account for Jeremiah's complaint to God and his deep trust in God?

8. Discuss how forsaking God leaves one defenseless in the face of suffering and how knowing God is the essential key to enduring suffering.

CHAPTER SIX

CHRIST–THE SUFFERING SERVANT

He was despised and rejected by men;
a man of sorrows, and acquainted with grief.
Isaiah 53:3

Jesus came to this earth as a Suffering Servant and as a man acquainted with grief. The sufferings He experienced were intensified during the final days of His life. His sufferings provided the basis for our redemption and provide an example for believers as we face suffering.

The New Testament teaching recognizes the purposes of suffering stated in the Old Testament, but Christ's redemptive suffering places suffering in a new light. The New Testament has fewer references to suffering as punishment, but it is not without solemn warnings of God's wrath against sin and promised future punishment for the unrepentant.

Jesus did not speak of the origin and causes of suffering. However He rejected the view that every instance of suffering is a direct result of a specific sin (*Jn 9:3; Lk 13:2-5*). Sickness is faced realistically and is to be combated. Jesus healed all manner of sickness and made the people whole. Jesus had compassion on the suffering: the sick (*Mt 14:14; Mk 1:41*), the hungry (*Mt 15:32*), and the helpless (*Mt 9:36*). He was willing to identify Himself with those rejected by society (*Mt 25:35-40*).

In examining the sufferings of Christ, the Old Testament messianic prophecies, especially those pertaining to His sufferings, will be considered. Next Jesus' own predictions about His sufferings will be highlighted. A review of the recorded sufferings of Jesus will be made. The chapter will conclude with a summary of New Testament teaching concerning the meaning of the cross.

THE PROPHETS FORETOLD
THE MESSIAH'S SUFFERINGS

The New Testament highlights the importance of Jesus' suffering and states that His suffering and death is a divine necessity in fulfillment of the Old Testament prophecies (*Mt 26:54; Mk 14:49; Lk 24:25-26,45-46; Jn 19:24,28; Acts 3:18; 17:2-3; 26:22-23; 1Cor 5:3*). In several instances New Testament authors document the sufferings of Christ that were predicted in the Old Testament (*Mk 9:12; Lk 24:26; Acts 3:18; 1Pet 1:11*). The Old Testament has many prophetic statements concerning the Messiah's suffering (e.g., *Gen 3:15; Pss 2:2; 22:1,6-8,12-18; 69:21; Isa 50:6; 52:12–53:12; Zech 9:9-10; 12:10; 13:7*).

The New Testament Scriptures clearly and consistently present the case that Jesus of Nazareth is in fact the Christ, the Messianic prophet, priest, and king promised in the OT Scriptures. The sufferings and sorrow of Jesus did not cancel His role as the Son of Man in glory, the judge of all the nations, triumphant King of kings and Lord of lords. In His sufferings, death, and resurrection, His greatest glory is demonstrated (*Jn 17:1-5*).

Psalm 22 and *Isaiah 53* are the two Old Testament chapters containing the most specific details concerning the sufferings of the promised Messiah. *Psalm 22*, written by David about 1,000 years before Christ, reads like a script for the events at the cross: the cry of being forsaken by God (*22:1*); the very words of some of the mockers (*22:7-8*); hands and feet pierced (*22:16*); garments parted and lots cast for His clothing (*22:18*). David also predicts other details: betrayal by a friend (*41:9*); vinegar offered for His thirst (*69:21*); prayer committing His spirit to the Father (*31:5*); no bones broken (*34:20*); resurrection from the dead (*16:10*).

The prophet Isaiah, writing in the eighth century BC, made many predictions about the coming Messiah. *Isaiah 53* details these facts about the Messiah: rejected by His own people (*53:3*); physically wounded and bruised and spit upon (*53:5-6*); did not answer His accusers (*53:7*); killed with thieves yet interceded for the transgressors (*53:12*); buried in a rich man's tomb

(*53:9*); would be a substitute sacrifice (*53:3-5,6,8-9,10-12*); anticipated His final victory (*53:11*). Isolated, despised, rejected, the Messiah would bear the sins, sorrows, and diseases of all men so that they could have spiritual healing and health.

The New Testament clearly identified Jesus as the Suffering Servant of *Isaiah 53* (*Acts 8:26-35*). Matthew quotes *Isaiah 53:4* as fulfilled in Jesus (*Mt 8:14-17*). Jesus says *Isaiah 53:12* was fulfilled in Him (*Lk 23:37*). Peter refers to Jesus as Servant (*Acts 3:13,26; 4:27,30*; cf. *Mt 12:18*) and in his letter describes the sufferings of Christ in terms used by Isaiah (*1Pet 1:19; 2:22-25; Isa 53:6-7*). Alan Richardson comments, "The whole passage, *Isa. 52.13–53.12*, including almost every phrase of it, echoes through the New Testament—the Synoptists, John, Acts, Paul, Heb. and I Peter" (*135*).

William Barclay says,

> The Suffering Servant is the figure the picture of whom finds its highest point in *Isaiah 53*. No interpretation of Jesus has been more precious to, and more influential on, Christian thought than the conception of Jesus as the Suffering Servant. . . . The picture is the picture of one who suffered terribly and undeservedly, of one whose contemporaries regarded him as outcast by man and God alike, of one whose sufferings came to be seen to have in some way a redemptive value for his fellowmen, and of one who in the end was vindicated by God. (*Jesus*, 163)[1]

In Peter's Pentecost sermon, he states, *"But what God foretold by the mouth of all the prophets, that his Christ would suffer, he thus fulfilled"* (*Acts 3:18*). In his first letter Peter says, *"The prophets who prophesied about the grace that was to be yours searched and inquired carefully, inquiring what person or time the Spirit of Christ in them was indicating when he predicted the sufferings of Christ and the subsequent glories"* (*1Pet 1:10-11*).

Chapter 6
The Suffering Servant

---

[1] See *Isa 52:13–53:12; 42:1-4; 49:1-6; 50:4-9*.

Prophecies Related to the Messiah's Sufferings

Reference	Prophecy	Fulfillment
Gen 3:15	Satan would bruise His heel	Mt 27, Mk 15, Lk 23, Jn 19
Ps 2:1-2	Rulers oppose the Lord's Anointed	Acts 4:25-26
Ps 22:1	Cry as one forsaken by God	Mt 27:46
Ps 22:7-8	Words of mockers	Mt 27:31,39-41
Ps 22:16	Feet and hands pierced	Lk 23:33; Jn 19:18; 20:25
Ps 22:18	Lots cast for garments	Mt 27:35; Jn 19:23-24
Ps 31:5	Committed spirit to Father	Lk 23:46
Ps 35:11	Accused by false witnesses	Mt 26:59-61
Ps 41:9	Betrayed by a friend	Mt 10:4; Jn 13:18-21
Ps 69:4	Hated without cause	Jn 15:24-25
Ps 69:8	Rejected by brethren	Jn 7:3,5
Ps 69:21	Vinegar for thirst	Mt 27:34
Ps 118:22	Rejected by rulers	Mt 21:42
Isa 53:3	Rejected by own people	Jn 1:11; 7:5,48
Isa 53:5-6	Wounded and spit upon	Mt 26:67
Isa 53:7	Silent before accusers	Mt 26:63; 27:12-19
Isa 53:12	Killed with thieves	Mt 27:38,50
	Numbered with transgressors	Mk 15:27-28
	Interceded for transgressors	Lk 23:34
Zec 11:12	Sold for 30 pieces of silver	Mt 26:15
Zec 11:13	Money thrown into Temple	Mt 27:3-5
	Money purchased potter's field	Mt 27:7
Zec 12:10	Side pierced	Jn 19:34,37

Jesus' fulfillment of these and other Messianic prophecies constitutes an important evidence that Jesus of Nazareth is the Messiah of God predicted in the Old Testament Scriptures. Paul *"powerfully refuted the Jews in public, showing by the Scriptures that the Christ was Jesus"* (**Acts 18:28; cf. Acts 9:22; 17:3; 18:5**).

Lee Strobel interviewed Louis Lapides who testified of the persuasive power of these prophecies. Lapides grew up in a Jewish family, but their faith didn't affect their life much. In Los Angeles in 1969, Lapides, while involved in the drug scene, found a challenge when some Christians engaged him in a spiritual discussion. They encouraged him to read the OT and look for the prophecies and see if he could find Jesus in there. He said he would read the OT but not the NT because he felt it was just a primer on anti-Semitism for Christians. When he came to *Isaiah 53* he was amazed. He felt Christians must have twisted Isaiah's words, so he read the text from a Hebrew OT and found it the same. He decided to read the NT and his excitement grew. He became a Christian because he was convinced that Jesus of Nazareth

Louis Lapides became a Christian because he was convinced that Jesus was in fact the predicted Messiah.

was in fact the predicted Messiah. Lapides now urges others to read the Scriptures and ask God to show them whether or not Jesus is the Messiah, "That's what I did—and without any coaching it became clear to me who fit the fingerprint of the Messiah" (*Christ*, 171-185).

CHRIST FORETOLD HIS SUFFERINGS

The idea of God becoming flesh and suffering was scandalous to Greek thinking. Completely misreading these messianic prophecies, a dead Messiah was also unthinkable to the Jews (*1Cor 1:23*). However, Christ's sufferings were not meaningless accidents. To the believer, His sufferings constitute the *"power of God and the wisdom of God"* (*1Cor 1:24*).

The Gospels' predictions of the sufferings and death of Jesus are general at first but become very specific as Christ's suffering approaches. Simeon told Mary, *"A sword will pierce through your soul also"* (*Lk 2:35*). *"Destroy this temple, and in three days I will raise it up"* (*Jn 2:19*). *"As Moses lifted up the serpent in the wilderness, so must the Son of Man be lifted up"* (*Jn 3:14*). *"The bridegroom is taken away from them"* (*Mk 2:20*). *"So will the Son of Man be three days and three nights in the heart of the earth"* (*Mt 12:40*). *"And the bread that I will give for the life of the world is my flesh"* (*Jn 6:51*).[2]

Jesus saw His sufferings as necessary in the will of God (*Mt 16:21; Mk 8:31; 9:12; Lk 13:33; 17:25; 24:26*). It was not a meaningless accident of history. It was not a final resort after all else had failed. It was the plan of God. He *must* suffer and die. He chose to suffer and die for mankind. Motivated by love, Jesus says, *"I lay down my life that I may take it up again. No one takes it from me, but I lay it down of my own accord"* (*Jn 10:17-18*). As His death approached, He identified this as

[2] Cf. *Mt 17:22; 20:18; Mk 10:32-34; Lk 9:31; 12:50; 20:13-15; 22:15; Jn 10:11; Mt 20:28; Jn 12:24; 15:13; 12:32-33.*

Chapter 6
The Suffering Servant

His purpose for coming into the world (*Jn 12:27*). Jesus' journey to glory went through suffering (*Lk 24:26; Jn 12:23*).

Repeatedly Jesus foretold His sufferings and His death in Jerusalem (*Mk 8:31; 9:12,31; 10:33,45; 14:21; Mt 17:22; 20:18-19*). After Peter's confession that Jesus was the Christ, the Son of God, Jesus plainly told the disciples, *"The Son of Man must suffer many things and be rejected by the elders and the chief priests and the scribes and be killed, and after three days rise again"* (*Mk 8:31;* cf. *Mt 16:21; Lk 9:22*). Peter objected to Jesus' prediction of His suffering and death. Jesus corrected him with a stinging rebuke. *"Get behind me. Satan! You are a hindrance to me. For you are not setting your mind on the things of God, but on the things of men"* (*Mt 16:23*). The only way to restore the lost relationship between God and man was through Jesus' death on a cross.

Jesus' journey to glory went through suffering.

On the Mount of Transfiguration, Jesus spoke with Moses and Elijah about his "departure" (*Lk 9:31*). He told the disciples, *"He must suffer many things and be rejected by this generation"* (*Lk 17:25*). Later he told the disciples,

> See, we are going up to Jerusalem, and everything that is written about the Son of Man by the prophets will be accomplished. For he will be delivered over to the Gentiles and will be mocked and shamefully treated and spit upon. And after flogging him, they will kill him, and on the third day he will rise. (*Lk 18:31-33*)

Note the detail in Jesus' prediction of the treatment He would receive.

The risen Christ told the two dejected travelers on the road to Emmaus,

> *"O foolish ones, and slow of heart to believe all that the prophets have spoken! Was it not necessary that the Christ should suffer these things and enter into his glory!"* And beginning with Moses and all the prophets, he interpreted to them in all the Scriptures the things concerning himself. (*Lk 24:25-27*)

Later, He told the disciples,

> *"These are my words that I spoke to you while I was still with you, that everything written about me in the Law of Moses and the Prophets and the Psalms must be fulfilled."* Then he opened their minds to understand the Scriptures, and said to them, *"Thus it is written that the Christ should suffer and on the third day rise from the dead, and that repentance and forgiveness of sins should be proclaimed in his name to all nations, beginning from Jerusalem."* (*Lk 24:44-47*)

THE SUFFERINGS OF CHRIST

Jesus experienced physical and emotional suffering: hunger, exhaustion, beating, crucifixion, grief, sadness, alienation. He suffered physical pain and emotional agony.

Ways Jesus Suffered

Herod tried to kill him when he was a baby (*Mt 2:13-15*).

His family tried to seize him declaring, "He is out of his mind" (*Mk 3:21*).

His brothers did not believe in Him (*Jn 7:5*).

Tempted by the devil (*Mt 4:1-8; Lk 4:1-9; Mk 1:13*).

Hated by the world (*Mt 2:13; Jn 1:10; 3:20; 7:7; 15:18-20; 1Cor 2:8*).

Rejected by his own people (*Jn 1:11; Isa 53:1; Mt 23:37; Lk 19:41-42; 24:20; Jn 18:40; Acts 2:36; 3:13; 4:10; 1Th 2:14-15*).

Disciples' dullness (*Mk 8:17-21; Mt 16:8-11*) and failure (*Mk 14:40; Mt 26:56; Mt 16:22; 26:40,74-75; Lk 18:34*).

Unbelieving response of crowds (*Mk 9:19; Mt 17:17; Lk 9:41; Mt 12:39; Lk 11:29; Mk 8:11-12*).

Opposed by the religious leaders (*Mt 12:14; Mk 3:6; Lk 6:11; Jn 5:18; 7:1; 8:48*).

Suffered empathetically with the sufferings of others (*Lk 19:41; Mk 7:34; Lk 7:13; Jn 11:33-35*).

His soul was sorrowful and troubled (*Mt 26:36-42; Mk 14:32-39; Lk 22:40-44; Jn 12:27; 13:21*).

Betrayed by Judas (*Mt 26:21-25,47-49; Mk 14:17-21,43-45; Lk 22:21-23,47-48; Jn 13:18-30; 18:2-5*).

Humiliated and beaten (*Mt 26:67-68; 27:26; Mk 14:65; 15:15-20; Lk 22:63-65; 23:11,21*).

Crucified (*Lk 23:33; Mt 27:35; Mk 15:25; Jn 19:18*).

Suffered separation from God (*Mt 17:46; Mk 15:34; Lk 23:46; Ps 22:1*).

When Jesus, as a baby, was presented to the Lord in the temple at 40 days of age, the grandfatherly Simeon blessed the child. He then told Mary, *"Behold, this child is appointed for the fall and rising of many in Israel, and for a sign that is opposed (and a sword will pierce through your own soul also), so that thoughts from many hearts may be revealed"* (*Lk 2:34-35*). Opposition began early in Jesus' life with Herod the Great's murders of the babies in Bethlehem in an attempt to eliminate a potential rival to his power (*Mt 2:13-15*).

One of the worst kinds of suffering one can face is misunderstanding and opposition from one's own family. When Jesus was busy teaching, being thronged by crowds, His family tried to interfere saying, *"He is out of his mind"* (**Mk 3:21**). Even His own brothers did not believe His claims (**Jn 7:5**).

Immediately after Jesus' baptism, He was fasting in the wilderness and was tempted by Satan (**Mt 4:1-11; Lk 4:1-13**). Mark notes that He was with the wild beasts (**Mk 1:12-13**). This was not His only confrontation with the devil. Luke says, *"And when the devil had ended every temptation, he departed from him until an opportune time"* (**Lk 4:13**). When Peter rejected Jesus' prediction of His death, Jesus rebuked him as speaking for Satan (**Mt 16:23**). Judas allowed Satan to enter into his heart as he plotted to betray Jesus (**Lk 22:3; Jn 13:27**).

> **Even His own brothers did not believe His claims, and He was disappointed in the disciples' slowness to believe.**

He was disappointed in the disciples' slowness to believe (**Mk 8:17-21; Mt 16:8-11**) and their inability to stay awake and watch and pray with Him (**Mk 14:40; Mt 26:56**; cf. **Mt 16:22; 26:40,74-75; Lk 18:34**).

Being moved with compassion, He suffered empathetically with the sufferings of others (**Lk 19:41; Mk 7:34; Lk 7:13; Jn 11:33-35**). Several of His miracles involved healing various diseases and physical ailments. He wept at Lazarus's tomb (**Jn 11:35**).

A very sad verse states, *"He came to his own [world], and his own [people] did not receive him"* (**Jn 1:11**). His hometown of Nazareth rejected His message and tried to kill Him by casting Him off a cliff (**Lk 4:16-30**). Later, he again was rebuffed by unbelief in Nazareth (**Mk 6:1-6**). During the last week before His death, Jesus lamented over Jerusalem, *"O Jerusalem, Jerusalem, the city that kills the prophets and stones those who are sent to it! How often would I have gathered your children together as a hen gathers her brood under her wings, and you would not!"* (**Mt 23:37**; cp. **Lk 19:41-42**). When Pilate wanted to release Jesus, the Jews demanded the robber, Barabbas, be released instead (**Jn 18:40**). To the Jews present on the Day of Pentecost, Peter said, *"This Jesus . . . you crucified and killed by the hands of lawless men"* (**Acts 2:23**; cp. **Acts 3:13; 4:10; 1Th 2:14-15**).

Jesus said the reason the world hated Him was because He testified that its works were evil (**Jn 7:7**; cp. **Jn 3:20; 15:18-20**). The world failed to realize who Jesus actually was (*Jn 1:10; 1Cor 2:8*). He called the crowds a *"faithless and twisted generation"* (*Mt 17:17; Lk 9:41;* cf. *Mk 9:19*) and *"an evil and adulterous generation"* (*Mt 12:39;* cf. *Mk 8:11-12; Lk 11:29*). He said, *"How long am I to bear with you?"* (*Mk 9:19*).

Early in His ministry the Jews were seeking to kill Him (*Jn 5:18*). The Jews suggested that he was a Samaritan and had a demon (*Jn 8:48*). During His Galilean ministry, *"The Pharisees went out and immediately held counsel with the Herodians against him, how to destroy him"* (*Mk 3:6;* cf. *Mt 12:14*). After Jesus healed the man with the withered hand, the Pharisees *"were filled with fury and discussed with one another what they might do to Jesus"* (*Lk 6:11*). Motivated by envy (*Mk 15:10*), the high priest and chief priests plotted and engineered His execution.

The night before Jesus' death He prayed with the disciples in the Garden of Gethsemane. He *"began to be greatly distressed and troubled. And he said to them, My soul is very sorrowful, even to death"* (*Mk 14:33-34;* cf., *Mt 26:36-42; Mk 14:32-39; Lk 22:40-44; Jn 12:27; 13:21*). When worse came to the worst, He pled, *"Father, if you are willing remove this cup from me. Nevertheless, not my will, but yours, be done . . . And being in agony he prayed more earnestly; and his sweat became like great drops of blood falling down to the ground"* (*Lk 22:42,44*). Dr. Alexander Metherell describes this condition as hematidrosis, "What happens is that severe anxiety causes the release of chemicals that break down the capillaries in the sweat glands. As a result, there's a small amount of bleeding into these glands, and the sweat comes out tinged with blood" (**Strobel, Christ, 195**).

Even though humanly Jesus shrank from His upcoming death, He offered His request in humility, trust, and submission to the Father's will, *"My Father, if it be possible, let this cup pass from me; nevertheless, not as I will, but as you will"* (*Mt 26:39*). When we wrestle with God in prayer, we must remember to pray *"Nevertheless, not my will, but yours be done."* R.C. Sproul observes, "We are astonished that in the light of such clear biblical records anyone would ever have the audacity to suggest that it is wrong for the afflicted in body or soul to couch their prayers for deliverance in terms of 'If it be thy will'" (32).

> **When we wrestle with God in prayer, we must remember to pray "not my will."**

Jesus was betrayed by Judas, one of His twelve disciples (*Mt 26:21-25; Mk 14:17-21; Lk 22:21-23; Jn 13:18-30; Mt 26:47-49; Mk 14:43-45; Lk 22:47-48; Jn 18:2-5*).

He was humiliated.

> Then the soldiers of the governor took Jesus into the governor's head-quarters, and they gathered the whole battalion before him. And they stripped him and put a scarlet robe on him and twisting togeth-er a crown of thorns, they put it on his head and put a reed in his right hand. And kneeling before him, they mocked him, saying, "Hail, King of the Jews!" and they spit on him and took the reed and struck him on the head. And when they had mocked him, they stripped him of the robe and put his own clothes on him and led him away to crucify him. (*Mt 27:27-31;* cf. *Mk 15:16-19*) (*Mt 26:67-68; Mk 14:65; Lk 22:63-65*) (*Mt 27:26; Mk 15:15; Lk 23:33*) (*Lk 23:11*).

"Then Pilate took Jesus and flogged him" (*Jn 19:1;* cf. *Mt 27:26; Mk 15:15*). This scourging was harsh. A whip was used with leather thongs imbedded with pieces of metal and bone. Jesus would have been stripped and His hands tied to an upright post. The Roman soldiers repeatedly struck Him on the back, leaving lacerations cutting deep into the flesh and underlying muscles. The excruciating pain and the loss of blood left Jesus in weakened condition (**Edwards, Gabel, Hosmer, 1457; Strobel,** *Christ,* **195-196**).

After the beating, *"The soldiers twisted together a crown of thorns and put it on his head and arrayed him in a purple robe. They came up to him saying, 'Hail, King of the Jews!" and struck him with their hands"* (*Jn 19:2-3*).

Jesus carried his cross outside the city walls to Golgotha where He was crucified (*Lk 23:33; Mt 27:35; Mk 15:25; Jn 19:18*). Crucifixion was a form of government-sponsored sadism. The public humiliation added to the prolonged agony and pain made this one of the most terrible and degrading ways to die. When we have been shielded from such cruel torture, it is hard for us to realize the horrible, excruciating pain experienced when one was crucified. "Although the Romans did not invent crucifixion, they perfected it as a form of torture and capital punishment that was designed to produce a slow death with maximum pain and suffering. It was one of the most disgraceful and cruel methods of execution" (**Edwards, Gabel, Hosmer, 1458**).

Crucifixion was a form of government-sponsored sadism.

He faced the cross in utter loneliness. *"Then all the disciples left him and fled."* (*Mt 26:56*). In spiritual anguish, while on the cross, He cried, *"My God! My God! Why have you forsaken me?"* (*Mk 15:34*; cf. *Mt 27:46; Lk 23:46; Ps 22:1*). It is impossible for us to comprehend the suffering involved in this Godforsakenness He experienced. He felt the full force of God's displeasure and wrath against sin. "In perfect harmony with the purpose of God He passed into the place of separation from God, and in the awful cry which expresses His loneliness, there is revealed the most stupendous sorrow that has ever been witnessed through the ages" (**Morgan, 300**).

> # He felt the full force of God's displeasure and wrath against sin.

Even more than His physical sufferings His spiritual sufferings were beyond our comprehension. James Stalker pictures the scene:

> Looking on that Face, we see the shadow of a deeper woe than smarting wounds and raging thirst and a racking frame—the woe of slighted love, of a heart longing for fellowship but overwhelmed with hatred; the woe of insult and wrong, and of unspeakable sorrow for the fate of those who would not be saved. Nor is even this the deepest shadow. There was then in the heart of the Redeemer a woe to which no human words are adequate. He was dying for the sin of the world. He had taken on Himself the guilt of mankind, and was now engaged in the final struggle to put it away and annihilate it. (**100**)

We will never understand the magnitude of the terrible horror of carrying the weight of all sins ever committed in human history.

In a crucifixion, when the wrists were nailed to the crossbar and the feet to a support on the post, it often caused very painful nerve damage. As the body hung on the cross, breathing became difficult. In order to exhale the victim pushed on the feet and flexed the elbows, causing additional pain along the damaged nerves. Dr. Metherell explains,

> Crucifixion is essentially an agonizingly slow death by asphyxiation. The reason is that the stresses on the muscles and diaphragm put the chest into the inhaled position; basically, in order to exhale, the individual must push up on his feet so the tension on the muscles would be eased for a moment. (**Strobel, *Christ*, 195-196**)

Rapid heart beat, muscle cramps, dehydration, and exhaustion added more pain to the ordeal. The soldiers did not break his legs which would make breathing almost impossible, thus hastening death, because they concluded He was already dead. When blood and water came out from the spear thrust in the side, it confirmed to them that death had occurred (*Jn 19:31-34*).

How did Jesus respond to suffering? Jesus willingly submitted to suffering (*Mt 17:46; Mk 15:34; Isa 53:7,11; Lk 23:46; Heb 5:7-8; 12:2*). He did not retaliate. *"When he was reviled, he did not revile in return; when he suffered, he did not threaten him who judges justly"* (*1Pet 2:23*; cf. *Mt 27:12-14; Mk 15:3-5*). To those crucifying Him, Jesus said, *"Father, forgive them, for they know not what they do"* (*Lk 23:34*). *"In the days of his flesh, Jesus offered up prayers and supplications, with loud cries and tears, to him who was able to save him from death, and he was heard because of his reverence. Although he was a son, he learned obedience through what he suffered"* (*Heb 5:7-8*). He was made *"perfect through suffering"* (*Heb 2:10*).

"For because he himself has suffered when tempted, he is able to help those who are being tempted" (*Heb 2:18*), and *"For we do not have a high priest who is unable to sympathize with our weaknesses, but one who in every respect has been tempted as we are, yet without sin"* (*Heb 4:15*). How He faced suffering is a model and example for how we should deal with suffering (*1Pet 2:21; Heb 13:12f.*).

How He faced suffering is a model and example for how we should deal with suffering.

"In the days of his flesh, Jesus offered up prayers and supplications, with loud cries and tears, to him who was able to save him from death, and he was heard because of his reverence" (*Heb 5:8*). His attitude was one of trusting obedience and patiently accepting and enduring the suffering.

The Gospels are amazingly brief in describing the physical aspects of Jesus' sufferings. The New Testament places the emphasis on the significance and meaning of His sufferings.

THE MEANING OF
THE CROSS

The death of Christ on a cross stands at the center of human history. James Stalker says,

> The spot to which we have come is the center of all things. Here two eternities meet. The streams of ancient history converge here, and here the river of modern history takes its rise. The eyes of the patriarchs and prophets strained forward to Calvary, and now the eyes of all generations and of all races look back to it. This is the end of all roads. The seeker after truth, who has explored the realms of knowledge, comes to Calvary and finds at last that he has reached the center. The weary heart of man, that has wandered the world over in search of perfect sympathy and love, at last arrives here and finds rest. **(96)**

Our understanding of the nature and purposes of God and of the nature and destiny of human beings hinges on our understanding of the meaning of the cross of Christ. McGrath asks, "The very existence of the cross, and of the crucified Christ, forces us to make a crucial decision: Will we look for God somewhere else, or will we make the cross; and the crucified Christ, the basis of our thought about God?" (*Mystery*, 13)

| **The death of Jesus displays the love of God.**

The death of Jesus displays the love of God. If Jesus were merely a man, then the cross represents only human love. Knowing the divine Son of God died gives power and meaning to the cross. Jesus' resurrection assures us that He is God.

The cross was essential to His purpose of coming *"to seek and to save the lost"* (**Lk 19:10**). He did not come to condemn, but to save the world (*Jn 3:17*). John the Baptist identified Jesus as *"the Lamb of God who takes away the sins of the world"* (*Jn 1:35*). Jesus compared Himself to a good shepherd who willingly lays down his life for his sheep (*Jn 10:11,18*).

ESTABLISHED THE NEW COVENANT

Jesus' sacrificial death established the covenant. As believers we enter into this new covenant with God, accepting the terms He laid down. At His last meal Jesus instituted the Lord's Supper, *"This is my blood of the covenant, which is poured out for many for the forgiveness of sins"* (**Mt 26:28**).

When we partake of the Lord's Supper, we *"proclaim the Lord's death until he comes"* (**1Cor 11:27**). Leon Morris says, "We proclaim to others and to ourselves our deep conviction that the Lord's death is central. It is by that death alone that our sins are put away and that we are brought into right relationship with God. Our participation is a pledge that we, whose covenant with God has been established at such cost, will live in a manner befitting the covenant" (***Atonement*, 42**)

RESTORES OUR RELATIONSHIP WITH GOD

Sin puts up a barrier and alienates us from God. As sinful human beings we could never remove our guilt. God does not wish that any should perish (**2Pet 3:9**). However, a righteous God could not overlook sin saying a sinner has not sinned. Payment must be made to satisfy His wrath against sin. The world takes sin lightly; God does not. We could not solve the problem because sinful humans could never make an appropriate sacrifice.

God acted to remove the barrier alienating man from God, thus making possible peace and friendship again with God. Because of His love for us, God became a man to suffer as a God-man and die as our substitute sacrifice on the cross, thus paying for our sins.

Graciously God offered forgiveness based on Christ's death as a propitiation, the putting away of God's wrath against sin. *"For all have sinned and fall short of the glory of God, and are justified by his grace as a gift, through the redemption that is in Christ Jesus, whom God put forward as a propitiation by his blood, to be received by faith. This was to show God's righteousness, because in his divine forbearance he had passed over former sins"* (**Rom 3:23-25**).

Modern translations often avoid the word, "propitiation." However Paul uses this word that denotes "the means of averting God's wrath" (**ibid., 168-170**). Seth Wilson says, "God cannot simply say a sinner has not sinned. He cannot ignore sin. It is absolutely morally impossible for God simply to forget about and overlook the sins of men" (**496**). The penalty for sin had to be paid. Christ

The good news is that the wrath of God has been removed.

died to pay our penalty. *"It was to show his righteousness at the present time, so that he might be just and the justifier of the one who has faith in Jesus"* (**Rom 3:26**). The good news is, that for the believer in Christ, the terrible wrath of God against sin has been removed.[3]

PROVIDES FORGIVENESS OF SINS

Love motivated God to act.

> *God shows his love for us in that while we were still sinners, Christ died for us. Since, therefore, we have now been justified by his blood, much more shall we be saved by him from the wrath of God. For if while we were enemies we were reconciled to God by the death of his Son, much more, now that we are reconciled, shall we be saved by his life. More than that, we also rejoice in God through our Lord Jesus Christ, through whom we have now received reconciliation.* (**Rom 5:8-11**)

People have wrongly assumed that if God had been there, He wouldn't have let Jesus die. But in fact, *God was in Christ reconciling us to Himself,* the Sinless One became the sin offering for sinners (**2Cor 5:19-21**). He became our substitute sacrifice, taking our rightful penalty. He died *"for our trespasses"* (**Rom 4:25**), *"for our sins"* (**1Cor 15:3**). Because of Jesus' *"suffering of death"* by God's grace He *"taste[d] death for everyone"* (**Heb 2:9**).

While Jesus' death was a heinous, murderous crime, God was working in this event at the centerpiece of human history to make salvation available to us. While not comprehending all that Jesus experienced, we can trust that *"He himself bore our sins in his body on the tree"* (**1Pet 2:24**).

"Christ loved us and gave himself up for us, a fragrant offering and sacrifice to God" (**Eph 5:2**). Believers have been made holy *"through the offering of the body of Jesus Christ once for all"* (**Heb 10:10**). Jesus suffered outside the gate of Jerusalem as did the Old Testament sin offering (**Heb 13:11-13; Lev 16:27**). Christ *"offered for all time a single sacrifice for sins"* (**Heb 10:12**). His sacrifice was offered "once for all" for "all time." No other sacrifice for sin will ever be needed (**Heb 7:17; 10:14,18**; cf. **1Pet 3:18**). Forgiveness can be found only through the death of the Son of God.

---

[3] See **Rom 1:18; 2:5,8; 3:4-5,20,24,28; Eph 1:7; Heb 10:17-18; 13:12; 1Pet 2:21**.

In the old covenant, the act of putting your animal on the altar, placing your hand on its head, and killing it had significance. It was a means of seeking cleansing from sin. This action must have conveyed the idea that sin is serious business with God. How much more does the sacrifice of Jesus mean that sin is not to be trifled with, but can only be forgiven through the death of the Son of God. Our salvation is free, but it is not cheap. In

Our salvation is free, but it is not cheap.

response we should be giving our lives as living sacrifices, giving our all in surrender to the lordship of Christ.

PROVIDES ACCESS TO THE PRESENCE OF GOD

Through Christ's death we gain access to the very presence of God.

> Therefore, brothers, since we have confidence to enter the holy places by the blood of Jesus, by the new and living way that he opened for us through the curtain, that is, through his flesh, and since we have a great priest over the house of God, let us draw near with a true heart in full assurance of faith, with our hearts sprinkled clean from an evil conscience and our bodies washed with pure water. (**Heb 10:19-22**)

Immediately after Jesus *"yielded up his spirit" "the curtain of the temple was torn from top to bottom"* (**Mt 27:50-51**; cf. **Mk 15:38; Lk 12:45**) signifying our direct access to God. We need no earthly mediator. Every day we have open access to God and live our lives completely in His presence. *"For Christ also suffered once for sins, the righteous for the unrighteous, that he might bring us to God, being put to death in the flesh but made alive in the spirit"* (**1Pet 3:18**). We live in His presence.

DELIVERS FROM SLAVERY TO SIN

Redemption in the first-century world meant that the captive was freed by a ransom, money paid to secure this release. *"The Son of Man came not to be served but to serve, and to give his life as a ransom for many"* (**Mt 20:28; Mk 10:45**). Morris says, "His word 'ransom' is the technical term used of the money paid to release a prisoner of war or a slave. To release the slaves of sin he paid the price. We were in captivity. We were in the strong grip of evil. We could not break free. But the price was paid and the result is that we go free. 'Sin shall not be your master' (**Rom. 6:14**)" (*Atonement*, 121).

We "*are justified by his grace as a gift, through the redemption that is in Christ Jesus*" (**Rom 3:24**). "*In him we have redemption through his blood, the forgiveness of our trespasses, according to the riches of his grace*" (**Eph 1:7**). By means of shedding His own blood, our Lord "*secured an eternal redemption*" (**Heb 9:12**). Paul reminded the Ephesian elders that Christ bought the church of God "*with his own blood*" (**Acts 20:28**).

Paul says, "*Christ, our Passover also has been sacrificed*" (**1Cor 5:7**, NASB).[4] The image of Christ as Passover suggests the deliverance from the power of the enemy and sin. We have a wonderful freedom in Christ.

We have a suffering Savior. "He went to His death with no outward evidence of any known disease. But the cumulative pain of every disease was laid upon him. He bore in His body the ravages of every evil, every sickness, every pain known to the human race" (**Sproul, 28**). The work of Christ delivers us from suffering, corruption, and death (**Rom 8:21; 1Cor 15:26**), as well as from sin (**Mt 1:21**).

DEFEATS THE DEVIL AND DEATH

The death of Jesus defeated the devil and death. "*Through death he might destroy the one who has the power of death, that is, the devil, and deliver all those who through fear of death were subject to lifelong slavery*" (**Heb 2:14-15**). Through Christ's death and resurrection "*'Death is swallowed up in victory.' 'O death, where is your victory? O death, where is your sting?' The sting of death is sin, and the power of sin is the law. But thanks be to God, who gives us the victory through our Lord Jesus Christ*" (**1Cor 15:54-57**).

Human wisdom would have never dreamed up the idea of the cross of the Savior. His sufferings, however, were necessary for our salvation (**Lk 24:26-27,46-47; Acts 3:18; 17:3; 26:23**). Christ's death gives us assurance of freedom from the ultimate suffering problem—hell. He suffered that we might not suffer forever. Through suffering Jesus was made the author of our salvation (**Heb 2:9ff.**). Divine suffering puts a new face on

> **Human wisdom would have never dreamed up the idea of the cross of the Savior.**

---

[4] Both the NIV and ESV insert the word "lamb" after Passover, but "lamb" is not in the Greek text.

human suffering. Sin is the ultimate cause of human suffering, and the cross is the ultimate solution to our sin problem. It does not remove our suffering and grief, but it does defang it. If the sinless Son of God experienced suffering, why do we think we should be exempt from suffering in this life?

GIVES NEW LIFE

Seth Wilson explains how we gain new life through accepting Jesus' death:

> God declares that Christ died for my sins. I must accept His death as the evidence of God's love. I must accept His death as God's provision for my own death as the sentence I deserve and turn my own life over to Jesus. If Jesus gave me His death and I give Him my life, then it is a fair exchange. If I accept His death as mine so that my death is past, then He died my death, and it is no more my life that I live, but Christ lives in me. I am united with Him so that God sees Him in me, because He now lives in me, and sees me in Him. Then you can see how God is just and the justifier of those who have faith in Jesus. (**497**)

In Paul's words, *"It is no longer I who live, but Christ who lives in me. And the life I now live in the flesh I live by faith in the Son of God, who loved me and gave himself for me"* (**Gal 2:20**). The believer who has accepted Christ's death as his own, who has been buried in baptism into His death, and been raised to walk in newness of life is able to view personal suffering from a new perspective (**Rom 6:1-6**).

Benefits Brought by the Death of Jesus

Atonement—a sacrifice that brings forgiveness and cleansing from sin

Justification—God's justice is preserved because the penalty for sin is paid, but the believer is declared "not guilty"

Reconciliation—restoration of friendship with God after being alienated by sin

Redemption—freedom gained in being released from the slavery caused by the guilt and power of sin

Propitiation—offering that turns away the wrath of God against the sinner

---

> New Life—characterized by righteousness as Christ lives in us
> Defeat of the Devil and Death—basis for hope and eternal life
> beyond the grave

THE RELEVANCE OF THE CROSS TO HUMAN SUFFERING

Christ's death was not only redemptive, but it also provides an example and inspiration for us in our suffering. How does the cross speak to our suffering?

1. Through obedience Jesus was made perfect through suffering, so through our obedient faith we can be matured in holiness through suffering (*Heb 2:10; 5:8-9; Rom 5:3-5; Jas 1:2-4*). The maturing effect is not in the pain and suffering itself but in how we allow it to shape us.

2. We should follow Christ's example of nonretaliation and perseverance as we face any suffering (*1Pet 2:18-23; Heb 12:1-3*).

Jesus considers what is done to us is done to Him.

Jesus experienced broken relationships, betrayal, abuse, mistreatment, culminating with the excruciating pain of the cross. He identifies and sympathizes with us in whatever suffering we face. He considers what is done to us is done to Him (*Mt 25:40*).

3. Christ's service even through suffering motivates us to serve even if it means suffering. We must take up the cross daily and follow Him (*Lk 9:23; Mt 20:22; Mk 13:9*). Serving Christ requires being willing to suffer persecution for the sake of the gospel (*Mt 5:4,10-12*). Stott says,

> The greatest single secret of evangelistic or missionary effectiveness is the willingness to suffer and die. It may be a death to popularity (by faithfully preaching the unpopular biblical gospel), or to pride (by the use of modest methods in reliance on the Holy Spirit), or to racial and national prejudice (by identification with another culture), or to material comfort (by adopting a simple lifestyle). But the servant must suffer if he is to bring light to the nations, and the seed must die if it is to multiply. (*Cross*, 322)

Suffering is a necessary part of unselfish, fruitful service.

4. As Christ endured the cross seeing *"the joy set before him"* (*Heb*

The road to future glory goes through suffering.

12:2), looking forward to ultimate glory makes our suffering bearable. *"For this slight momentary affliction is preparing for us an eternal weight of glory beyond all comparison"* (**2Cor 4:17**). *"If we endure, we will also reign with him"* (**2Tm 2:12**). Jesus said that those who share His suffering will eat and drink at his table in glory (**Lk 24:26; Jn 12:23**). The road to future glory goes through suffering. All human suffering does not lead to eternal reward. But the believer has a solid hope of future reward. Anticipating this future glory makes it possible to rejoice even in our present sufferings.

5. The self-giving God of the cross assures us He is trustworthy. *"He who did not spare his own Son but gave him up for us all, how will he not also with him graciously give us all things?"* (**Rom 8:32**). The cross does not answer all our questions we ask while suffering, but it provides the basis for trusting God's perspective on our suffering. The cross is the Christian's apologetic to the problem of suffering.

6. The cross shows us that God is not indifferent to our sufferings, but in His suffering He identifies with us because He loves us. God did not prevent the cross. His willingness to suffer and die on the cross is proof positive of His love for us. Even when God does not remove our suffering, we can know He still loves us.

7. Jesus found victory through suffering because He submitted to the will of the Father. He did not negotiate but willingly drank the bitter cup. *"Nevertheless, not my will, but yours, be done"* (**Lk 22:42**). When this spirit of "nevertheless" guides us, we too will find ultimate victory through suffering.

In 1518, Martin Luther wrote these wise words:

> The cross teaches us to believe in hope even when there is no hope. The wisdom of the cross is hidden deeply in a profound mystery. In fact, there is no other way to heaven than taking up the cross of Christ. On account of this we must beware that the active life with its good works, and the contemplative life with its speculations, do not lead us astray. Both are most attractive and give peace of mind, but for that very reason hide real dangers, unless they are tempered by the cross and disturbed by adversaries. The cross is the surest path of all. Blessed is the man who understands this truth. (**McGrath, Mystery**, 9)

Alister McGrath shows the powerful relevance of the cross as a symbol of Christianity:

> It declares that any outlook on life which cannot cope with the grim realities of suffering and death does not deserve to get a hearing. This symbol of suffering and death affirms that Christianity faces up to the grim, ultimate realities of life. It reminds us of something we must never be allowed to forget. God entered into our suffering and dying world in order to bring it newness of life. Those outside Christianity need to learn—need to be *told about*—its relevance and power for the tragic situation of humanity. It is a sign of a glory which is concealed. It confronts the worst which the world can offer, and points to—and makes possible—a better way. It stands as a symbol of hope which transfigures, in a world which is too often tinged with sadness and tears.
>
> So consider the cross. A symbol of death? No. A symbol of suffering? No. A symbol of a world of death and suffering? Not quite. A symbol of hope in the midst of a world of death and suffering? Yes! A symbol of a God who is with us in this dark world, and beyond? Yes! In short, the cross stands for a hope that is for real, in a world that is for real. But that world will pass away, while that hope will remain for eternity. (**What**, 117-118)

Through Christ we can have a confident hope of ultimate victory over whatever suffering we experience in this life. Thanks be to God for sending His Suffering Servant.

Think about It

1. What two chapters in the Old Testament have the most predictions concerning the sufferings of the Messiah? What were some of the things they predicted?

2. What evidence convinced Louis Lapides that Jesus was the Messiah?

3. Give evidence that Jesus taught the necessity of His sufferings and death.

4. Quote a passage where Jesus predicts clearly His sufferings and death.

5. List several ways Jesus suffered even before the final week before His death.

6. How did Jesus suffer from His own family and His hometown of Nazareth?

7. Describe the brutality involved in the flogging or scourging.

8. List several aspects of the pain experienced by one who was crucified.

9. Briefly define: atonement, justification, reconciliation, redemption, and propitiation.

10. Show how Jesus handled suffering providing a model for us in dealing with our suffering.

11. How is the cross of Christ a symbol of hope?

CHAPTER SEVEN

THE APOSTLES–
SUFFERERS FOR CHRIST

I will show him [Paul] how much he must suffer for the sake of my name.
Acts 9:16

C hrist's chosen apostles faced much persecution and suffering. This chapter will survey the sufferings of the Twelve, especially Peter, James, and John, the martyrdom of Stephen (even though he was not an apostle, he was an important early leader in the church), and the sufferings of Paul.

THE TWELVE

Jesus tells the apostles that persecution will come.

> *Behold, I am sending you out as sheep in the midst of wolves, so be wise as serpents and innocent as doves. Beware of men, for they will deliver you over to courts and flog you in their synagogues, and you will be dragged before governors and kings for my sake, to bear witness before them and the Gentiles. When they deliver you over, do not be anxious how you are to speak or what you are to say, for what you are to say will be given to you in that hour. For it is not you who speak, but the Spirit of your Father speaking through you. Brother will deliver brother over to death, and the father his child, and children will rise against parents and have them put to death, and you will be hated by all for my name's sake.* (**Mt 10:16-22**)

The night before His death Jesus reminds the apostles,

> *If the world hates you, know that it has hated me before it hated you. If you were of the world, the world would love you as its own; but because you are not of*

121

the world, but I chose you out of the world, therefore the world hates you. Remember the word that I said to you: "A servant is not greater than his master." If they persecuted me, they will also persecute you. If they kept my word, they will also keep yours. But all these things they will do to you on account of my name, because they do not know him who sent me. (*Jn 15:18-21;* cf. *Jn 17:14-16*)

The Sadducees, the ruling Jewish party, were angry and disturbed because the apostles preached the resurrection of Jesus. They considered the resurrection impossible and felt threatened by the growing numbers of followers of Christ. Peter and John were arrested and imprisoned overnight. The next day they were questioned, threatened, and released (*Acts 4:1-22*).

The growing impact of the Christian movement motivated the rulers to again question and imprison the apostles. God intervened by sending an angel to release them. The authorities found them again publicly preaching in bold defiance. They were beaten and released. They left *"rejoicing that they were counted worthy to suffer dishonor for the name"* (*Acts 5:41*).

After the death of Stephen, *"There arose on that day a great persecution against the church in Jerusalem, and they were all scattered throughout the regions of Judea and Samaria, except the apostles"* (*Acts 8:1*). Luke does not give us the details of these hostile actions. We are curious as to why the apostles were not driven out. Donald Guthrie explains that it was probable "the officials decided as a matter of policy to refrain from arresting the apostles again in view of the earlier failure to silence them by this means. They presumably thought that a more effective method would be the scattering of the rank and file members. Leaders without followers would be reduced to ineffectiveness" (*Apostles*, 63). F.F. Bruce thinks that the apostles again became a target of attack after Peter's fraternizing with the Gentiles, (*Acts 10*), an action approved by the other apostles (*Peter*, 27-28).

King Herod Agrippa I, grandson of Herod the Great, wanting the approval of the Jews, took violent action against the church. He beheaded the apostle James, brother of John (*Acts 12:1-3*). Eusebius, an early church historian, reports the following incident based on a record in Clement of Alexandria. "The man who led him [James] to the judgment seat, seeing him bearing his testimony to the faith, and moved by the fact, confessed himself a Christian. Both therefore, says he, were led away to die" (**Eusebius, 2.9; Clement of Alexandria,** *Hypotyposes,* **7**).

When Agrippa saw that the execution of James *"pleased the Jews,"* he imprisoned Peter, his next intended victim, with four squads of guards. While Christians prayed, God supernaturally enabled Peter to escape the chains, the guards, and the prison (*Acts 12:3-11*). God in His faithful persistence regularly overrules the designs of men. After reporting to the brethren meeting at John Mark's

> **God in His faithful persistence regularly overrules the designs of men.**

mother's house, he departed for an unknown destination (*Acts 12:12-17*). After Herod's death (AD 44) Peter came out of hiding and moved about in Jerusalem.

Jesus told Peter that he would die a death glorifying Christ (*Jn 21:18-19*; cf. *2Pet 1:14-15*). Tradition is early and strong that Peter died as a martyr and was buried in Rome. Eusebius says, "Thus Nero publicly announcing himself as the chief enemy of God, was led on in his fury to slaughter the apostles. Paul is therefore said to have been beheaded at Rome, and Peter to have been crucified under him" (**2.25**). Everett Ferguson states, "Literary and archaeological evidence do confirm a ministry in Rome by both Paul and Peter and their separate deaths there under Nero" (**292**).

The apostle John was in exile on *"the island of Patmos on account of the word of God and the testimony of Jesus"* (*Rev 1:9*). Most likely John was in exile for the same reason the saints under the altar had been killed: *"for the word of God and for the witness they had borne"* (*Rev 6:9*).

STEPHEN

The church chose Stephen and six other men to serve the needs of the Hellenistic widows. Luke described him as *"full of the Spirit and of wisdom . . . full of faith and of the Holy Spirit . . . and full of grace and power . . . doing great wonders and signs among the people"* (*Acts 6:3,5,8*). His preaching evoked strong opposition from certain Jews who *"rose up and disputed with Stephen."* Apparently underestimating him, they proved no match for Stephen's inspired speaking (*Acts 6:10*).

Defeated in debate they enlisted individuals to misrepresent Stephen as saying *"blasphemous words against Moses and God"* (*Acts 6:11*). They incited the people and the elders and the scribes who brought Stephen before the Council. They had false witnesses say that

Stephen spoke against the temple and the law. They claimed they heard him say that Jesus said he would destroy the temple and change the customs of Moses (*Acts 6:13-14*). Jesus had taught that both the temple and the law would be fulfilled and superseded in Himself. As Stephen stood before the Council, his face had a radiance and brilliance as an angel (*Acts 6:15*).

Opposition to Stephen included misrepresentation and false accusation in which his words were twisted to mean something different from what he had stated (*Acts 6:13*). This reminds us of the false witnesses recruited to testify against Jesus (*Mt 26:60*). When these methods were not defeating Stephen's message, the persecutors turned to violence. Stephen's example stands as a model for how we should respond when we face mistreatment for our faith. Too often Christians respond to opposition with much less grace than did Stephen.

In Stephen's defense he said the great figures of the OT never thought God was confined to a building (*Acts 7:1-53*). Stott summarizes Stephen's speech:

> What Stephen did was to pick out four major epochs of Israel's history, dominated by four major characters. First he highlighted Abraham and the patriarchal age (*7:2-8*); then Joseph and the Egyptian exile (*9-19*); thirdly Moses, the Exodus and the wilderness wanderings (*20-44*); and lastly David and Solomon, and the establishment of the monarchy (*45-50*). The connecting feature of these four epochs is that in none of them was God's presence limited to any particular place. On the contrary, the God of the Old Testament was the living God, a God on the move and on the march, who was always calling his people out to fresh adventures, and always accompanying and directing them as they went. (*Acts*, 130-131)

Boldly Stephen called the rulers "stiff-necked" always resisting the Holy Spirit (*Acts 7:51*). Their persecution was in the same line of earlier generations that opposed the prophets of God.

The anger of his accusers boiled forth in grinding of their teeth, refusing to listen to him by covering their ears, and yelling at the top of their voices. They then dragged him out of the city. Following the laws against blasphemy, they stoned him (*Acts 7:54-60: Lev 24:16*). The Romans had prohibited the Jews from using capital punishment. F.F. Bruce states that in the area of "offences against the sanctity of the temple" the Sanhedrin council "was allowed to pronounce and execute the death sentence" (*Peter, 52-53; Paul, 68*). Nevertheless, it was more of a lynch mob mentality rather than any fair-minded judicial treatment. Stephen's testimony was made more powerful when sprinkled with his blood. They silenced his voice, but his testimony lives on.

Stephen was guided by the mind of Christ. He had a vision of the Son of Man standing at the right of God. As he was stoned he said, *"Lord Jesus, receive my spirit"* (*Acts 7:59* cf. *Lk 23:46*). Before he died, he fell to his knees and cried out, *"Lord, do not hold this sin against them"* (*Acts 7:60*; cf. *Lk 23:34*).

> **They silenced his voice, but his testimony lives on.**

One may die mistakenly for a cause, but Stephen and later the apostles died for what they knew to be true. Throughout the history of Christianity the death of martyrs has powerfully confirmed the truth of the gospel. Tertullian said "The blood of the martyrs is the seed of the church." Stephen died as a faithful witness.

A specific influence of Stephen's death can be seen in Saul of Tarsus who approved of the execution of Stephen. Later, eyewitness Paul confessed to Jesus, *"And when the blood of Stephen your witness was being shed, I myself was standing by and approving and watching over the garments of those who killed him"* (*Acts 22:20*). This practice followed Mosaic law (*Deu 17:7*). Jesus had asked Saul, *"Saul, Saul, why are you persecuting me? It is hard for you to kick against the goads"* (*Acts 26:14*). No doubt the memory of the killing of Stephen was a goad in Paul's mind and conscience.

Stott observes, "The church was shocked, even stunned, by the martyrdom of Stephen and by the violent opposition which followed. But, with the benefit of hindsight, we can see how God's providence used Stephen's testimony, in word and deed, through life and death, to promote the church's mission" (*Acts, 143*). The scattering of Christians dispersed the influence of the gospel as far north as Antioch and as far southwest as Alexandria in Egypt.

Church historians record that some of the pagans who killed Christians later became Christians because they were so impressed by the martyrs' courage (**Latourette, 91**).[1]

---

[1] See also *The Martyrdom of Polycarp*, 1:2; 2:2; 2:3 and Justin Martyr, *Second Apology*, II, 12.

The Greek word for "martyr" means a legal witness. In NT uses it refers to faithful testimony for Christ, often in the face of hostile persecution or death. The meaning of martyrdom as death is more evident in the early Christian writers than in the NT. The prophets in the old covenant often were killed for their testimony to the Word of God (*Mt 23:35; Acts 7:52*).

Josef Ton, a Romanian, lost his faith from communist teaching but regained it from the testimony of Christians. He lost it again from liberalism taught at a Baptist seminary. Again he regained his faith through the witness of Richard Wurmbrand and others. After study at Oxford University, he was warned not to return to Romania for fear he would be killed. In 1972, he returned to Romania, prepared to suffer as he evangelized. During Ceausescu's reign of terror, Ton was the pastor of a 1400-member Baptist church.

Ton was arrested and imprisoned. When the officials threatened to kill him, he responded,

> Your supreme weapon is killing. My supreme weapon is dying. . . . You know that my sermons on tape have spread all over the country. If you kill me, those sermons will be sprinkled with my blood. Everyone will know I died for my preaching. And everyone who has a tape will pick it up and say, "I'd better listen again to what this man preached, because he really meant it; he sealed it with his life."
>
> "So, sir, my sermons will speak ten times louder than before. I will actually rejoice in this supreme victory if you kill me."
>
> His interrogator sent him home. (**Fisher, 267-268**)

He was exiled in 1981 and began a radio ministry. In 1990 he relocated back in Romania working training people for ministry.

PAUL

Saul of Tarsus, as a ringleader in the persecution of believers, *"was ravaging the church, and entering house after house, he dragged off men and women and committed them to prison"* (*Acts 8:3*). Luke uses a word depicting a wild beast destroying its victim. Guthrie notes, "The idea seems to be that he was like a wild beast tearing apart the Church as a body until nothing recognizable would remain of it. . . . All he succeeded in doing was to fill the Jerusalem dungeons with people who would rather die than renounce their faith and to plant innumerable witnesses to the Gospel through Judea and Samaria" (*Apostles, 63-64*).

Paul later says, *"I am the least of the apostles, unworthy to be called an apostle, because I persecuted the church of God"* (*1Cor 15:9*). He tells the Galatians, *"You have heard of my former life in Judaism, how I persecuted the church of God violently and tried to destroy it"* (*Gal 1:13*). Luke describes the persecutor, *"But Saul, still breathing threats and murder against the disciples of the Lord, went to the high priest and asked him for letters to the synagogues at Damascus, so that if he found any belonging to the Way, men or women, he might bring them bound to Jerusalem"* (*Acts 9:1-2*).

After having persecuted the church, he was converted and became the target of Jewish opposition and plots (*Acts 9:23-24; 20:19; 23:12-14*). Frequently he mentions the persecution he experienced at the hands of the Jews (*Rom 15:31; 2Cor 11:24,26; Gal 5:11; 1Th 2:14-16*). Several reasons account for the Jews' persecution of Paul: he preached the faith he once sought to destroy (*Gal 1:23*); he regarded cherished elements of Judaism as rubbish (*Php 3:4-8*); he opposed requiring Gentile converts to keep the Mosaic Law (*Gal 2:11-21*); and he did not preach circumcision (*Gal 5:11*).

Paul faced opposition from non-Jews as well. Angered at their economic loss, the Gentile slave owners of the demonized girl had Paul and Silas beaten and imprisoned (*Acts 16:22-23*). The charge against Paul and Silas before the magistrates in Philippi was that they

> **Paul was persecuted because he preached the faith he once sought to destroy.**

were teaching things unlawful for Romans (*Acts 16:20-21*). Beaten, secured in stocks in an inner prison, they could have had self-pity, but rather they were praying and singing. After God intervened in a terrifying way, the jailer became a believer in the God who could deliver these two men (*Acts 16:25-34*).

His sufferings in Philippi did not keep him from coming to Thessalonica where he was opposed as well (*1Th 2:2*). There, Paul was opposed by Gentile unbelievers and was driven from the city by non-Christian Jews (*1Th 2:15-17; Acts 17:1-10*). Paul's converts were harassed by their fellow Gentiles who viewed their new lifestyle as exclusive and offensive (**Still, 287**). Their suffering severely tested their faith. His endurance of suffering became a model for them (*1Th 1:6-7*).

Paul's suffering did not invalidate his ministry, as was alleged, but rather verified it. He was not motivated by greed and characterized by guile as were some of his contemporaries. His willingness to suffer demonstrated his integrity and genuineness and showed he was empowered by the Spirit (*1Th 1:6*).

Paul confronted the superiority and snobbery of intellectualism in Athens. His mention of the resurrection and judgment brought a mocking response (*Acts 17:16-32*). In Ephesus, the silversmiths' guild opposed Paul because the gospel was affecting their economic trade of cult shrines, but the angry mob was prevented from doing harm to Paul (*Acts 19:23-41*).

Suffering is a part of Paul's call to be a witness for Christ (*Acts 22:15*). The Lord spoke to Ananias about Paul, *"I will show him how much he must suffer for the sake of my name"* (*Acts 9:16*; cf. *2Tm 1:11-12*). Paul said, *"I die every day"* (*1Cor 15:31*). He considers suffering as a distinguishing credential of his apostleship (*Gal 6:17; 1Cor 2:1-5; 2Cor 11:23-25; Php 1:30; 2:9*). He rejoices in his sufferings and even boasts about them (*2Cor 11:30; 12:10; Php 1:19-26*).

> ## Suffering is a part of Paul's call to be a witness.

Paul does not view his suffering as mere circumstance or fate but God's plan *"to destroy the wisdom of the wise"* (*1Cor 1:19*) and to show the power of God in the cross. Paul comments on his suffering as an apostle,

> For I think that God has exhibited us apostles as last of all, like men sentenced to death, because we have become a spectacle to the world, to angels, and to men. We are fools for Christ's sake, but you are wise in Christ. We are weak, but you are strong. You are held in honor, but we in disrepute. To the present hour we hunger and thirst, we are poorly dressed and buffeted and homeless, and we labor, working with our own hands. When reviled, we bless; when persecuted, we endure; when slandered, we entreat. We have become and are still, like the scum of the world, the refuse of all things. (*1Cor 4:9-13*)

"His suffering reminded his hearers that the glory and power belonged to God rather than Paul" (**Schreiner, 94**). God's power is demonstrated through the sufferings of the apostles. Not the wisdom of the world nor personal skill and knowledge, but the cross of Christ was their source of wisdom and power (*1Cor 1:17-18,24; 2:1-5*). Both the cross and the apostles' suffering demonstrate the foolishness of the wisdom of the world. The tyranny of man is futile against the power of God.

> **The cross was the witnesses' source of wisdom and power.**

God demonstrated the reality of the power of the cross and resurrection of Christ through the sufferings Paul encountered in his life. Depending upon the same divine power God displayed in raising Jesus from the dead, Paul endured suffering and found deliverance from it. Hafemann says, "The wisdom and power of God first made known through the cross and resurrection of Christ were therefore now being further manifest and revealed publicly through Paul's own suffering as an apostle" (**Suffering, 919-920**). God's power shown through the cross works in the midst of suffering in this world.

Paul accepted the fact that his work as an apostle meant that God would lead him through suffering. The most extensive discussion of his sufferings is found in *2 Corinthians*. Paul describes the affliction experienced in Asia, *"For we were so utterly burdened beyond our strength that we despaired of life itself. Indeed we felt that we had received the sentence of death. But that was to make us rely not on ourselves, but on God who raises the dead. He delivered us from such a deadly peril, and he will deliver us. On him we have set our hope that he will deliver us again"* (*2Cor 1:8-10*). He says, *"For we who live are always being given over to death for Jesus' sake, so that the life of Jesus also may be manifested in our mortal flesh"* (*2Cor 4:11*).

Paul pictures his own suffering as being led as a slave to his death which conveys a fragrant aroma of sacrifice testifying to the glory, wisdom, and power of God (*2Cor 2:14-15*). "Rather than calling his apostolic ministry into question, it is precisely Paul's suffering which therefore commends him to the Corinthians within the church, as well as defending him from the attacks of his opponents from outside the church" (**Hafemann, *Suffering*, 226**). Hafemann also states,

> The suffering of the apostle does not serve as a disconfirmation of his ministry, but is rather an integral part of it. For Paul's suffering not only provides the occasion for the manifestation of God's power/glory as the one who rescues the apostle from his suffering, but also ensures that the power thus displayed is recognized to be God's alone. (**ibid., 65**)

Schreiner believes Paul's suffering had spiritual benefits for the kingdom: "As God led Paul to death, the fragrant aroma of the gospel was spread through the world. The death working in Paul led to life for others (*2 Cor 4:12*)" (**99**).

Some of Paul's opponents boasted of their knowledge and strength and criticized Paul's weaknesses. D.A. Black says, "Paul takes up their charges about his 'weakness' and turns it to his own purpose of defending his gospel and ministry" (**966**). Weakness makes people realize their dependence on God (*1Cor 2:3*) and recognize their inability to gain God's favor by their own accomplishments (*1Cor 9:22*). Weakness becomes a channel through which God manifests His power as was shown in Christ (*1Cor 1:25–2:6*).

> **Weakness becomes a channel through which God manifests His power.**

God does not depend on human strength. God can transform those weak and without spiritual resources into willing vessels through whom His strength is expressed. Persons who acknowledge their need and identify with Christ live *"by the power of God"* (*2Cor 13:4*). When we are weak, we cannot claim credit for any success but only depend upon God. Paul knew what he accomplished was because of God's power working through a very limited vessel.

As Christ *"was crucified because of weakness, but lives because of the power of God"* (*2Cor 13:4*), so this characterized the apostles as well.

> But he said to me, 'My grace is sufficient for you, for my power is made perfect in weakness.' Therefore I will boast all the more gladly of my weaknesses, so that the power of Christ may rest upon me. For the sake of Christ, then, I am content with weaknesses, insults, hardships, persecutions, and calamities. For when I am weak, then I am strong" (*2Cor 12:9-10*).

Paul also had to contend with opposition from Satan. When he wanted to return to Thessalonica and encourage his converts, he says, *"But Satan hindered us"* (*1Th 2:18*). He calls his *"thorn in the flesh"* *"a messenger of Satan"* (*2Cor 12:7*). He says, *"For we do not wrestle against flesh and blood, but against the rulers, against the authorities, against the cosmic powers over this present darkness, against the spiritual forces of evil in the heavenly places"* (*Eph 6:12*).

Paul refers to hardships as *"tools in the hand of God"* (*2Cor 4:7–5:10*). Paul does not wallow in self-pity but puts things in context looking at the big picture. *"For this slight momentary affliction is prepar-*

Paul refers to hardships as "tools in the hand of God."

ing for us an eternal weight of glory beyond all comparison" (*2Cor 4:17*; see *6:4ff.; 11:23ff.*). "There is no hint anywhere in this epistle [*2 Corinthians*] that he resents or questions the wisdom of God in allowing suffering" (**Stott,** *Acts,* **143**).

Paul describes his sufferings:

> *As servants of God we commend ourselves in every way: by great endurance, in afflictions, hardships, calamities, beatings, imprisonments, riots, labors, sleepless nights, hunger; by purity, knowledge, patience, kindness, the Holy Spirit, genuine love, by truthful speech, and the power of God; with the weapons of righteousness for the right hand and for the left; through honor and dishonor, through slander and praise. We are treated as impostors, and yet are true; as unknown, and yet well known; as dying, and behold, we live; as punished, and yet not killed; as sorrowful, yet always rejoicing; as poor, yet making many rich; as having nothing, yet possessing everything.* (*2Cor 6:4-10*)

He endures suffering through God's power being delivered from his afflictions.

Here Paul gives a more extensive listing of his sufferings:

> *Are they servants of Christ? I am a better one—I am talking like a madman—with far greater labors, far more imprisonments, with countless beatings, and often near death. Five times I received at the hands of the Jews the forty lashes less one. Three times I was beaten with rods. Once I was stoned. Three times I was shipwrecked; a night and a day I was adrift at sea; on frequent journeys, in danger from rivers, danger from robbers, danger from my own people, danger from Gentiles, danger in the city, danger in the wilderness, danger at sea, danger from false brothers; in toil and hardship, through many a sleepless night, in hunger and thirst, often without food, in cold and exposure. And, apart from other things, there is the daily pressure on me of my anxiety for all the churches.* (*2Cor 11:23-28*)

Paul honestly confesses that his afflictions have caused him distress (*2Cor 1:8-9*) and affirms that it was God's power, not his own strength, that enabled him to endure (*2Cor 12:9-10*). Paul writing to Timothy in what was undoubtedly his last letter, says, *"You, however, have followed my teaching, my conduct, my aim in life, my faith, my patience, my love, my steadfastness, my persecutions and sufferings that*

Chapter 7
The Apostles

happened to me at Antioch, at Iconium, and at Lystra—which persecutions I endured; yet from them all the Lord rescued me" (*2Tm 3:10-11*). What an example of grace and peace—after all he had been through!

Paul says, *"Now I rejoice in my sufferings for your sake, and in my flesh I am filling up what is lacking in Christ's afflictions for the sake of his body, that is, the church"* (*Col 1:24*). Paul did not consider his own suffering as a payment for sin. Christ's atoning sacrifice was all-sufficient (*Col 1:20; 2:13-14; Gal 1:4; 1Cor 1:18-31; 2Cor 5:16-21; Rom 3:21-26*). But Christ's sufferings through His body, the church, continued in the process of bringing the gospel to the lost. Hafemann said:

> Paul completes what is "lacking" in Christ's afflictions on behalf of the church in the sense that his ministry *extends* the knowledge and reality of the cross of Christ and the power of the Spirit to the Gentile world (*Col 1:23*; cf. *Eph 3:13*). Paul's suffering also functioned to make it clear, therefore, that the power and knowledge of the gospel was God's and not his own, so that those who encountered Paul would place their faith in the power of God and not in the person of the apostle (*1 Cor 2:1-5; 2 Cor 4:7; 12:9-10*). Whatever Paul's much debated (and still unclear) "thorn in the flesh" actually was, it too functioned in this way by keeping him from boasting in the abundance of the revelations that he had received (*2 Cor 12:7*). (Suffering, 920)

Clearly Paul did not see his sufferings as a repeat atonement, but rather they highlighted the significance of the death of Jesus (*2Cor 1:3-11; 4:7-12*).

Opponents of Paul

Physical Persecution:

In Jerusalem, the Hellenistic Jews *"were seeking to kill him"* (*Acts 9:29*).

In Antioch of Pisidia, *"The Jews incited the devout women of high standing and the leading men of the city, stirred up persecution against Paul and Barnabas, and drove them out of their district"* (*Acts 13:50*).

In Iconium, both Gentiles and Jews, with their rulers attempted to mistreat and stone Paul and Barnabas (*Acts 14:5*).

At Lystra, Jews came from Antioch and Iconium *"persuaded the crowds, they stoned Paul and dragged him outside the city, supposing that he was dead"* (*Acts 14:19*).

At Philippi, *"The crowd joined in attacking them, and the magistrates tore the garments off them and gave orders to beat them with rods."* They were beaten and fastened in stocks in the inner prison (*Acts 16:22-23*; cf. *1Th 2:2*).

In Corinth, The Jews *"made a united attack on Paul and brought him before the tribunal"* (*Acts 18:12*).

In Jerusalem, *"All the city was stirred up. . . . They seized Paul and dragged him out of the temple . . . they were seeking to kill him . . . when they saw the tribune and the soldiers, they stopped beating Paul"* (*Acts 21:30-32*).

After being rescued from the mob, they interrupted Paul when he spoke to them, *"They raised their voices and said, 'Away with such a fellow from the earth! For he should not be allowed to live'"* (*Acts 22:22*).

When he was before the council, *"And when the dissension became violent, the tribune, afraid that Paul would be torn to pieces by them, commanded the soldiers to go down and take him away from among them by force and bring him into the barracks"* (*Acts 23:10*).

The Jews made a plot and took an oath not to eat or drink until they had killed Paul (*Acts 23:12-22*).

Transferred to prison in Caesarea and then taken to prison in Rome (*Acts 23:23-35; 27; 28*).

Second and final imprisonment in Rome and death as a martyr.

(For Paul's listings of his sufferings, see *1Cor 4:9-13; 2Cor 4:8-9; 6:4-5; 11:23-29; 12:10*).

Doctrinal Opposition:

False apostles (*2Cor 11:13-15*) and super apostles (*2Cor 11:4; 12:11*)—Palestinian Judaizers who tried to bring new converts under the Law of Moses (*2Cor 11:13-15; 3:6-7*). They claimed to be servants of Christ, Paul saw them as *"servants of Satan"* (*2Cor 11:14,23*).

False Jewish brethren in Galatia taught circumcision was essential to salvation and wanted to require Gentile converts to be circumcised (*Gal 2:3-5; 3:6-14; 6:12,16*).

Outsiders who came to Corinth *"peddlers of God's word"* with *"letters of recommendation,"* claiming superiority over Paul (*2Cor 2:17; 3:1; 11:5,23*).

In Athens faced the snobbery of intellectualism and when Paul mentioned the resurrection they mocked (*Acts 17:32*).

> *"Those who create dissensions and difficulties in opposition to the doctrines you have been taught"* (***Rom 16:17***).
>
> Those who *"slanderously charge"* Paul with saying, *"Why not do evil that good may come?"* (***Rom 3:8***; cf. ***Rom 6:1; Gal 2:17***).
>
> Jewish Gnostics in Colossae characterized by circumcision, asceticism, observance of days, mysticism, and worship of angels (***Col 2:8-23***).
>
> In Philippi, Judaizers who preached Christ because of envy of Paul (***Php 1:15,17; 3:2***).
>
> In *1 & 2 Timothy* and *Titus*, the opponents seem to be apostate former coworkers, unscrupulous men following myths (***2Tm 3:1-9; 4:3-5***).
>
> Satan and spiritual forces of evil (***2Cor 11:13-15; 12:7; 1Th 2:18; Eph 6:12***).

When Paul despaired of life itself, he came to rely on God rather than on himself (*2Cor 1:8-9*). While dealing with his thorn in the flesh he learned from the Lord that the power of Christ is made perfect in human weakness (*2Cor 12:8-9*).

Experiencing suffering can prepare one to be more sensitive to the needs of others who are suffering.

Even when God does not heal the sick believer, He still strengthens and comforts. Paul's sufferings led him to experience God's comfort which enabled him to be more effective in comforting others (*2Cor 1:3-7*). Experiencing suffering can prepare one to be more sensitive to the needs of others who are suffering.

Paul had a physical ailment which he came to view as a blessing instead of a curse:

> So to keep me from being too elated by the surpassing greatness of the revelations, a thorn was given me in the flesh, a messenger of Satan to harass me, to keep me from being too elated. Three times I pleaded with the Lord about this, that it should leave me. But he said to me, "My grace is sufficient for you, for my power is made perfect in weakness." (*2Cor 12:7-9*)

This was "a distressing, indeed humiliating, physical ailment which he feared at first might be a handicap to his effective ministry but which in fact, by giving his self-esteem a knock-out blow and keeping him constantly dependent on the divine enabling, proved to be a help, not a handicap" (**Bruce,** *Paul***, 135**).

Whatever the bodily ailment was, Paul said it was a "trial" to the Galatians. He says, *"You did not scorn or despise me, but received me as an angel of God, as Christ Jesus. What then has become of the blessing you felt? For I testify to you that, if possible you would have gouged out your eyes and given them to me"* (***Gal 4:12-15***). God did not remove it or deliver Paul from the ailment, rather he gave him the necessary grace to bear it—not simply to live with it but to be thankful for it. If his ministry was so effective despite this physical weakness, then the transcendent power was manifestly God's not his own.

Paul knew he must travel to Rome and suffer (***Acts 20:22-23; 21:4,12; 23:11; 25:12,25; 26:32; 17:1,24; 28:14,16***). Paul's imprisonment was for Christ. He called himself a *"prisoner for Jesus Christ"* (***Eph 3:1; Phm 1,9***) and *"a prisoner for the Lord"* (***Eph 4:1***). He tells Timothy *"Therefore do not be ashamed of the testimony about our Lord, nor of me his prisoner, but share in suffering for the gospel by the power of God"* (***2Tm 1:8***). Because of preaching the risen Christ, Paul is *"suffering, bound with chains as a criminal"* (***2Tm 2:8-9***). Apparently when Paul was imprisoned for the final time, nearly all his former supporters forsook him (***2Tm 1:15***). He begs Timothy to come soon. Companionship can help one deal with suffering.

> **Companionship can help one deal with suffering.**

Stott says, "He may be the emperor's prisoner in the eyes of men; he is the Lord's prisoner in reality, his willing captive, and held in prison by man only by Christ's permission and for Christ's sake" (*2 Timothy*, **32**). "His imprisonment is for no other reason than that he serves the Lord" (**Knight, 373**). Paul used his imprisonment as a platform for being an *"ambassador in chains"* (***Eph 6:20***). He appreciates the fellowship of the Philippians saying, *"You are all partakers with me of grace, both in my imprisonment and in the defense and confirmation of the gospel"* (***Php 1:7***) He says, *"My imprisonment is for Christ"* (***Php 1:13***). Paul says it is because of declaring the mystery of Christ that *"I am in prison"* (***Col 4:3,18***).

The leaders of the early church faced the danger of imprisonment or death by the Jews or the Romans. Guthrie says, "The messengers of the crucified Christ were conditioned to expect suffering in His service, and some of the most heroic epics of Christian courage have come from prison cells" (*Apostles*, **141**).

Paul instructs Timothy *"Therefore do not be ashamed of the testimony about our Lord, nor of me his prisoner, but share in suffering for the gospel by the power of God"* (*2Tm 1:8*). God would give him strength to endure it. The gospel arouses opposition, which in turn means the messengers are also opposed. Since Paul has suffered for preaching Christ, he does not ask Timothy to do what he was not willing to do himself (*2Tm 1:12*).

Paul was executed under Nero. Among his last written words, Paul states,

> For I am already being poured out as a drink offering, and the time of my departure has come. I have fought the good fight, I have finished the race, I have kept the faith. Henceforth, there is laid up for me the crown of righteousness which the Lord, the righteous judge, will award to me on that Day, and not only to me but also to all who have loved his appearing. (*2Tm 4:6-8*)

In the words of Clement of Alexandria, "So he departed from the world and was taken up into the holy place—the greatest example of endurance" (*I Clement*, **5.7**).

After a lifetime of study on Paul, F.F. Bruce summarizes Paul's response to suffering:

> Paul would not have interpreted his sustaining of trouble and danger in terms of toughness; in his eyes all this was part of the life of faith, not to be endured as something one would rather be spared but to be embraced with joy as a sure token of acceptance by God and as a strengthening of Christian hope. This attitude belonged to the reversal of all conventional values implicit in the cross of Christ. Paul welcomed such hardships the more gladly as a sharing in the sufferings of Christ and as a means of absorbing in his own person afflictions which would otherwise fall to the lot of his fellow-Christians. As the hardships wore down the outer man, they were at the same time used by God for the renewal of the inner man and the augmenting of his heritage of glory. (*Paul*, **462**)

Schreiner states, "Suffering was not a side effect of the Pauline mission; rather it was at the very centre of his apostolic mission" (**87**).

Why do those who proclaim the gospel have to suffer? The gospel offends the nonbeliever because he does not want to admit his guilt and sin and total inability to save himself. Sinful pride makes it difficult to admit the absolute necessity of God's grace and Christ's death on the cross. Many minimize the cross. Stott says, "They preach man and his merit instead of Christ and his cross, and they substitute the one for the other 'in order that they

> "Suffering was not a side effect of the Pauline mission . . . it was at the very centre."

may not be persecuted for the cross of Christ' (*Gal. 6:12*; cf. *5:11*). No man can preach Christ crucified with faithfulness and escape opposition, even persecution" (*2 Timothy*, 42-43).

We are to *"share in suffering as a good soldier of Christ Jesus"* (*2Tm 2:3*). Soldiers in frontline duty do not expect a life of ease. Duty demands hardship, risk, and suffering for a soldier at war. An early Christian writer, Tertullian, says, "No soldier comes to the war surrounded by luxuries, nor goes into action from a comfortable bedroom, but from the makeshift and narrow tent, where every kind of hardness and severity and unpleasantness is to be found" (*2.3*). Faithful servants of Christ will experience opposition and hardship.

In this call to suffering Paul gives the example of Jesus, himself, and all believers (*2Tm 3:3,8,9-10,11-13*). George Knight says,

> Each of these three provides a reason for suffering and enduring. In the case of Jesus the unstated by implicit reason is that only through his suffering was redemption accomplished and death vanquished. Even he had to suffer. Paul suffers (*v. 9*) and is willing to endure all things so that "the chosen" "may obtain the salvation in Christ Jesus with eternal glory." In the case of all Christians, enduring is part of their calling, and the result of their endurance is that they "reign with Christ." (*396-397*)

Remembering Christ is the key to enduring suffering. "Keep remembering Jesus Christ, risen from the dead, descended from David, according to my gospel, for which I am suffering hardship in bonds as an evildoer. But the word of God is not bound. Therefore I endure all things on account of the chosen ones in order that they may obtain salvation in Christ Jesus with eternal glory" (*2Tm 2:8*, original translation; cf. *Heb 12:3*).

```
┌─────────────────────────────────────────────────┐
│   Principles Gained from the Sufferings          │
│          of the Apostles and Stephen             │
│                                                   │
│  1) Leaders are not exempt from opposition and    │
│     suffering; in fact they are often the target. │
└─────────────────────────────────────────────────┘
```

2) Opposition is to be expected because the world does not like the message of truth or a life of righteousness.
3) Faithful witness in response to persecution and suffering can be a means of evangelism.
4) Persecution is to be endured with grace and a forgiving spirit.
5) God does not always heal when we pray for healing of a physical illness.
6) Trust in God's strength because, when we are weak, His power is demonstrated.
7) Remember the crucified and risen Jesus who will give you ultimate victory.

Think about It

1. Why do you think the apostles were able to rejoice when they suffered dishonor for Christ?

2. What do we know about the deaths of the apostles James, Peter, and John?

3. What similarities do you see in comparing the deaths of Stephen and Jesus?

4. Why was Josef Ton willing to die at the hands of the communists?

5. How did Paul relate his suffering to the cross and resurrection of Jesus?

6. What did Paul mean by *"I am filling up what is lacking in Christ's afflictions for the sake of his body, the church"* (**Col 1:24**)?

7. Give examples of the kinds of opposition that Paul faced.

8. Would your faith withstand the kinds of suffering the apostles faced?

9. What does this mean in your life? *"For when I am weak, then I am strong."*

10. What did Paul mean when he said that he was *"a prisoner for Jesus Christ"*?

11. Why do those who proclaim the gospel suffer?

12. What principles or insights can leaders draw from the kinds of sufferings the apostles faced and how they handled suffering?

CHAPTER EIGHT

SUFFERING AS A CHRISTIAN

All who desire to live a godly life in Christ Jesus will be persecuted.
2 Timothy 3:12

hy do we believers think it strange when we suffer, when the NT repeatedly tells us we will suffer as Christians? Perhaps we should be more surprised and amazed when we are not suffering. Recently we have heard a lot about "God wants you well and wealthy" and that "the church will take care of all your felt needs." The NT does not instruct us to seek suffering and persecution. But it certainly tells us to expect it and endure it trusting in the Lord for strength. This chapter will explore the teaching of the NT concerning the sufferings of believers.

THE GOSPELS

Jesus "never promised an unrealistic trouble-free existence, since he knew that in the present imperfect world this would be impossible" (**Guthrie,** *New Testament,* **900**). The beatitude *"Blessed are those who mourn, for they shall be comforted"* (*Mt 5:4*) places an importance on suffering.

PERSECUTION

Christians are told they will face opposition because of their faith. In the last of the Beatitudes in the Sermon on the Mount, Jesus says, *"Blessed are those who are persecuted for righteousness' sake, for theirs is the kingdom of heaven. Blessed are you when others revile you and persecute you and utter all kinds of evil against you falsely on my account. Rejoice and be glad, for your reward is great in heaven, for so they persecuted the prophets who were before you"* (**Mt 5:10-12**). "Jesus takes it for granted that those who display the qualities of the previous beatitudes will not escape persecution" (**ibid., 902-903**).

We are not blessed for being persecuted when we are foolish, obnoxious, or overly zealous. The blessings come when we're persecuted *for righteousness' sake.* It is persecution for being like Jesus. In His message to the disciples about the destruction of Jerusalem and the end times, Jesus predicted,

> *But be on your guard. For they will deliver you over to councils, and you will be beaten in synagogues, and you will stand before governors and kings for my sake, to bear witness before them. . . . And brother will deliver brother over to death, and the father his child, and children will rise against parents and have them put to death. And you will be hated by all for my name's sake. But the one who endures to the end will be saved.* (**Mk 13:9,11-13**)

Jesus said,

> *If the world hates you, know that it has hated me before it hated you. If you were of the world, the world would love you as its own; but because you are not of the world, but I chose you out of the world, therefore the world hates you. Remember the word that I said to you: A servant is not greater than his master. If they persecuted me, they will also persecute you.* (**Jn 15:18-20**)

> *You will be hated by all for my name's sake.* (**Mt 10:22**)

Jesus told the disciples, *"In the world you will have tribulation. But take heart; I have overcome the world"* (**Jn 16:33**). Jesus did not come to make life easy but to save us and give us the things in life that really matter.

Even if it means persecution, the church must speak the truth.

Even if it means persecution, the church must speak the truth.

Where there is good the Church must praise; where there is evil the Church must condemn—and inevitably men will try to silence the troublesome voice of conscience. It is not the duty of the individual Christian to find fault, to criticize, to condemn, but it may well be that his every action is a silent condemnation of the unchristian lives of others, and he will not escape their hatred. (**Barclay,** *Matthew,* **114**)

Christians must oppose certain practices, trades, and professions because they are sinful. Therefore believers will suffer opposition for their faith.

Jesus did not follow the world's method for winning friends and influencing people. "The world will offer a man roses, roses all the way, comfort, ease, advancement, the fulfillment of his worldly ambitions. Jesus offered His men hardship and death" (**ibid., 385**). He says, *"In the world you will have tribulation. But take heart; I have overcome the world"* (*Jn 16:33*).

Church history records a long list of those persecuted for Christ's sake, for example, Polycarp, John Hus, and Adoniram Judson. Genuine believers face persecution from religious people as well as outsiders. *"Woe to you, when all people speak well of you, for so their fathers did to the false prophets"* (*Lk 6:26*).

Suffering for Christians may mean physical violence or death. It may be cruel whispers and lies told about us. It may be ridicule or sneering at us. It may mean loss of a job because you refuse to be dishonest or carry out orders that compromise your Christian values. This happens because believers are fundamentally different with a new nature and different values. Our supreme loyalty belongs to Christ. Persecution may be social, political, or religious. We are not to retaliate (*1Pet 2:21-23*) but leave the vengeance to the Lord (*Rom 12:14-21*).

> **Suffering for Christians may mean anything from death to ridicule or sneering.**

How can we rejoice when we are unjustly persecuted? We can rejoice in view of our reward in heaven. Jesus endured suffering *"for the joy that was set before him"* (*Heb 12:2*).

SICKNESS AND HEALING

Jesus supernaturally healed sick people, including blindness (*Mt 9:27-31; Mk 8:22-26*); lameness (*Jn 5:1-5*); leprosy (*Lk 5:12-16; 17:11-19*), fever (*Mk 1:19-31; Jn 4:43-53*); hemorrhage (*Mk 5:23-34*); withered hand (*Mk 3:1-6*); severed ear (*Lk 22:51*) and many other unnamed diseases. He healed with a word, a touch, even at long distance.

Craig Blomberg states,

> Sometimes Jesus heals an individual in response to that per-

son's faith. Both Jairus' daughter and the woman with the hemorrhage are explicitly declared to be healed as a result of their faith or of the faith of their loved ones (*Mk 5:34,36*). Sometimes lack of faith prevents Jesus from healing as at his hometown of Nazareth (*Mt 13:58*). Jesus similarly explains that his disciples were unable to exorcise a demon-possessed epileptic because of their lack of faith (*Mt 17:20*). Many Christians deduce from accounts like these that if a person could only generate enough faith, healing would always occur. But this does not follow. There is a balancing theme which pervades the Gospels as well. Frequently healings occur where there is little or no faith in order to try to instill belief in Jesus as the Son of God. All of the healings in John have this as one purpose (*Jn 20:31*). . . . So it is clear that miracles may be designed to produce faith where there is none; once that faith has developed, healings may be less necessary. (**300-301**)

In the Great Commission given after His resurrection when Jesus sent the apostles out to evangelize the world (*Mt 28:18-20*), no mention is made of healing the sick as was given in the earlier commission to the apostles in *Matthew 10:7-8*.

On only two occasions in the Gospels Jesus is said to heal because of compassion (*Mt 14:14; 20:24*). Blomberg comments,

> If compassion were a dominant motive [for Jesus' healings], then presumably all sick people in his day (or in any other day) would have been healed, and this was patently not the case (cf. *Jn 5:3-5* in which Jesus singles out only one of the many disabled people lying near the Bethesda pool). Jesus undoubtedly had compassion for all the sick, but the broader testimony of Scripture is that God's power may be demonstrated at least as dramatically through people's suffering as through their health. (**ibid., 301**)

ACTS

The book of Acts gives the greatest attention to the ministries of Peter and Paul. While it does not give an exhaustive history of persecutions from AD 30 to AD 62, it gives some indication of sufferings experienced by believers.

God exercised divine punishment on Ananias and Sapphira for lying to Him. This brought the fear of God upon the church and outsiders as well (*Acts 5:1-13*). The death of Herod Agrippa and the blindness of Elymas are attributed to God (*Acts 12:20-23; 13:6-13*). Other sicknesses and deaths in the book Acts apparently are due to natural means.

The healings described in Acts are cases where an apostle or a messenger heals a person through a word or prayer (*Acts 3:1-10; 8:7; 9:34,36-41; 14:10; 16:18; 19:11; 20:10; 28:5,8*). This healing was done in the name of Jesus and by His power. These healings attested to the divine authority of the messenger.

Luke records persecutions brought against Christians by Jews and Gentiles. Saul arrested and imprisoned believers (*Acts 8:3; 9:2; 22:4-5*); Stephen was stoned to death (*Acts 7:54-60*). Saul cast his vote for their death (*Acts 26:10*). Christians were forced to flee homes and relocate (*Acts 8:1,4; 11:19*). They were beaten (*Acts 18:17*). Believers were displaced from synagogues (*Acts 9:2; 22:19; 26:22; 18:7*; cf. *Acts 18:17*) and expelled from cities (*Acts 13:50*).

Roman laws in some cases helped the spread of the gospel (*Acts 17:1-9; 18:12-17; 19:23-41; 21:30-32; 23:12-35*). Some political officials were fair-minded toward Christians (*Acts 12:4-12; 19:23-41; 26:30-31*). Initially the Roman authorities did not distinguish between Judaism and Christianity, so Christians enjoyed legal protection afforded to the Jews. Jewish objections against Christianity were viewed as an internal matter (*Acts 18:12-17*). Later the Jews made definite distinction between themselves and Christians (*Acts 13:50; 14:2,19; 17:5-6,13; 18:12; 24:1-2; 25:1-3*).

Ferguson observes,

> **Suffering frequently both follows and empowers ministry.**

> Christianity started with several legal liabilities. It took its name from and was founded on a man who had been executed by Roman authority on a charge that amounted to treason. This was sure to provoke suspicion if not hostility in official circles. And then everywhere the teaching went it seemed to provoke disturbances and riots, something neither Rome nor the local establishments could view kindly. (**602**)

Suffering frequently follows ministry, and this gives rise to new opportunities for ministry. Others look to the person who has endured suffering for inspiration and support. Having experienced suffering can make one more sensitive to the hurts of others and more diligent in prayer for the needs of others. Knowing what helped you through suffering, gives you more practical wisdom in helping others who hurt.

Persecution promoted the spread of the gospel (*Acts 8:1-4; 13:48-52; 14:5-6,19-20; 16:25-40; 17:10,13-15*). As believers suffered they identified with Jesus' role as Suffering Servant (*Acts 8:32-33; 26:23*). Jesus Himself suffers as His people suffer.

The Jews expelled from Rome by Claudius about AD 49 may have included Priscilla and Aquila who were apparently already Christians. Claudius died in AD 54 and by then the expulsion edict was a dead letter. The Christian community was flourishing in Rome when they received Paul's letter in AD 57.

PAUL'S LETTERS

William Barclay opens his commentary on *2 Corinthians* with these words,

> Paul writes to his friends in Corinth, as a man who knows trouble to those who are in trouble. . . . In the early years of Christianity the man who chose to become a Christian chose to face trouble. There might well come to him abandonment by his own family, hostility from his pagan neighbours, and persecution from the official powers. . . . It is always a costly thing to be a real Christian, for Christianity is not true Christianity without the cross. (**202**)

Paul says, *"Indeed, all who desire to live a godly life in Christ Jesus will be persecuted"* (*2Tm 3:12*). *"For the sake of Christ you should not only believe in him but also suffer for his sake"* (*Php 1:29*; cf. *2Tm 1:18*).

Unlike the martyrdom theology of some writers of the 2nd and 3rd centuries, Paul does not teach that all believers are *called* to suffer in the same way that he suffered as an apostle nor that all believers are to expect martyrdom. Rather, Paul recognizes that all Christians simply *will suffer* as a result of identifying themselves with Christ (*Rom 8:17; Php 1:29-30; 2Tm 3:12*). Of course some suffering is not due to our Christian faith, but comes because we live in a fallen world (*1Cor 7:28; 12:26; 1Tm 5:23*).

Paul asked the churches to follow his unselfish example which would lead to undue suffering (*1Cor 4:8-13; 6:7; 9:1-27*). Believers who remain faithful through sufferings find it a confirmation of their standing with Christ, as sufferings were a validating credential for Paul's

Believers who remain faithful through sufferings find confirmation of their standing.

apostleship (*Gal 4:12-15; Php 1:3-7; 4:14-15; 1Th 1:6; 3:1-5; 2Tm 1:8*). We enter the kingdom through tribulation (*Acts 14:22; Jn 16:21*). Following Christ means self-denial and daily cross-bearing (*Lk 9:23*).

Partnership with the community of believers is a strong source of support for the sufferer. Members of the body of Christ share in the sufferings of Christ (*2Cor 1:5ff; Php 3:10; Mk 10:39; Rom 8:17*). Paul tells the Philippians, *"You are partakers with me of grace, both in my imprisonment and in the defense and confirmation of the gospel"* (*Php 1:7*). He appreciates their *"partnership . . . in giving and receiving"* (*Php 4:15*). Paul exhorts Timothy, *"Therefore do not be ashamed of the testimony about our Lord, nor of me his prisoner, but share in suffering for the gospel by the power of God"* (*2Tm 1:8*).

Hardships and afflictions do not hurt Christians any less, but believers have a divine perspective of seeing God's hand producing in them endurance and hope. For this reason we can rejoice in suffering. Christians know their sufferings are not meaningless, but can be a means by which God strengthens their faith and endurance (*Rom 5:3-5; 8:12-39; 2Cor 1:6*). Through adversities and suffering, faith can be increased and love deepened as believers experience the power of God. Identifying with the Christ of the cross and His resurrection power enables us to endure the trials that come into our lives (*2Cor 4:14; 2Th 1:6-7*).

God gives comfort to help us endure suffering. Paul writes,

> Blessed be the God and Father of our Lord Jesus Christ, the Father of mercies and God of all comfort, who comforts us in all our affliction, so that we may be able to comfort those who are in any affliction, with the comfort with which we ourselves are comforted by God. For as we share abundantly in Christ's sufferings, so through Christ we share abundantly in comfort too. If we are afflicted, it is for your comfort, which you experience when you patiently endure the same sufferings that we suffer. Our hope for you is unshaken, for we know that as you share in our sufferings, you will also share in our comfort. (*2Cor 1:3-7*)

The comfort of God is not so much soothing sympathy as it is inner strengthening. His comfort gives us courage to cope with whatever challenges the day brings. God does not ask us to do anything that He does not give us the

God's comfort gives us courage to cope with whatever challenges the day brings.

strength to accomplish (*1Cor 10:13*). As we draw inspiration from the sufferings of Christ, we share in His sufferings.

When we are tempted to give up, we need to remember Paul's assurance that suffering cannot separate us from Christ:

> *Who shall separate us from the love of Christ? Shall tribulation, or distress, or persecution, or famine, or nakedness, or danger, or sword? As it is written, "For your sake we are being killed all the day long; we are regarded as sheep to be slaughtered." No, in all these things we are more than conquerors through him who loved us. For I am sure that neither death nor life, nor angels nor rulers, nor things present nor things to come nor powers, nor height nor depth, nor anything else in all creation, will be able to separate us from the love of God in Christ Jesus our Lord. (Rom 8:35-39)*

If we are faithful to Christ through suffering, we will be glorified with Christ (*Rom 8:17-18; Heb 12:1-2; Mt 5:10; 2Cor 4:10ff*). Our hope in Christ motivates us to faithfulness (*Rom 4:18-25; 8:18-25; 1Cor 15:20-34,58; 2Cor 4:16-18*). Those who refuse to identify with the sufferings of Christ have no such hope to sustain them (*2Th 1:6-10; Rom 2:9*).

We need to keep the difficulties of this life in perspective. The suffering we experience in this life is minimal when compared to the future glory awaiting us in heaven. *"For I consider that the sufferings of this present time are not worth comparing with the glory that is to be revealed to us"* (*Rom 8:18*).

> *So we do not lose heart. Though our outer nature is wasting away, our inner nature is being renewed day by day. For this slight momentary affliction is preparing for us an eternal weight of glory beyond all comparison, as we look not to the things that are seen but to the things that are unseen. For the things that are seen are transient, but the things that are unseen are eternal. (2Cor 4:17-18)*

These passages have been a great encouragement to me.

Christians learn to personalize the power of the cross and resurrection in their lives when experiencing suffering (*2Cor 8:1-2; 1Th 1:2-7; 2Th 1:3-5; Rom 12:12; 2Tm 4:5*).

HEBREWS

Paul may have been the author of Hebrews, however Hebrews will be treated separately because of the emphasis on suffering in the book. The strong emphasis of the book is that Christians should view suffering as discipline from God training us to be holy, therefore we must endure and be faithful through it all.

Christians should view suffering as discipline from God training us to be holy.

Jewish Christians were experiencing loss of some of their Jewish religious experiences and would soon, in a greater extent, suffer the loss of the temple and its accompanying religious festivals. They faced abandonment by family and friends, insults, imprisonment, and loss of property (*Heb 9:10; 10:32-34; 11:26,32-38; 13:3,9-10*).

As Christians *"you endured a hard struggle with suffering, sometimes being publicly exposed to reproach and affliction, and sometimes being partners with those so treated"* (*Heb 10:32-33*). They had stood courageously even though publicly scorned and taunted and even physically abused.

> You had compassion on those in prison, and you joyfully accepted the plundering of your property, since you knew that you yourselves had a better possession and an abiding one. Therefore do not throw away your confidence, which has a great reward. For you have need of endurance, so that when you have done the will of God you may receive what is promised. (*Heb 10:34-36*)

They had followed Jesus' teaching about rejoicing in persecution, realizing their treasures in heaven were more important then their treasures on earth (*Mt 5:12*). Sufferers for Christ must endure, making sure they are living in God's will. We must not be quitters who lose everything that matters, *"but of those who have faith and preserve their souls"* (*Heb 10:39*).

They gained strength from those who lived by faith before them and from one another as they dealt with these difficulties (*Heb 11:1-40; 13:3*). Jesus endured the violent and disgraceful death on the cross by focusing on the joy set before Him. The readers are reminded that they had not yet suffered a martyr's death among their number. Believers gain strength and resolve to endure and finish the race as we consider Christ's example (*Heb 12:2-4*).

Discipline expresses God's love, not His anger. Those suffering for Christ need to accept their lot as a loving discipline from the Lord validating their being genuine children of God. *"The Lord disciplines the one he loves"* (*Heb 12:6*; cf. *12:5-12; Prov 13:24*). Suffering is not viewed as a sign of God's disapproval, but as proof of His love. Suffering is necessary and valuable, for through it God expresses His care for us and establishes a meaningful relationship of father and son.

As an earthly father disciplines his children, helping them make a habit of good behavior, so God, as our father, trains his children by means of trials and difficulties to godly living. His discipline is wise and loving. *"He disciplines us for our good, that we may share his holiness. For the moment all discipline seems painful rather than pleasant, but later it yields the peaceful fruit of righteousness to those who have been trained by it"* (**Heb 12:10-11**). The school of suffering is a hard school, but wise is the believer who will learn from it.

> **The school of suffering is a hard school, but wise is the believer who will learn from it.**

No discipline is fun (**Heb 12:11**). "Yet it does help to know that there is light at the end of the tunnel, even if you cannot yet see it; to know that God is in control and is committed to his people's good, even though it still does not look like that to you. The suffering is no less real, but perhaps it is less debilitating when the larger perspective is kept in mind" (**Carson, How Long? 66**). Those enduring suffering *"according to God's will"* should *"entrust their souls to a faithful Creator while doing good"* (**1Pet 4:19**).

We have difficulty in determining what is done by God and what is done by Satan. Satan has a limited power to make men suffer (**2Cor 7:7; Job 1:12; 2:6**). The issue is made more complex because Paul says his *"thorn in the flesh"* is *"a messenger of Satan"* and sent by God Himself to keep Paul from becoming conceited (**2Cor 12:7-10**).

Is our suffering teaching us to repent of our sins, to strengthen us to deal with future hardships, to prepare us to be sympathetic and helpful to others? Or is it just part of living in a fallen world with thorns, thistles, accidents, disease, and death? We may never know if a specific affliction is a discipline of God, but we need to face the suffering with a trust and dependence upon God being open and willing to learn whatever we can from the experience.

Where is God when we suffer? Scripture does not fully explain God's role in our suffering. Scripture does teach us to know and trust God. We do know that God's love is pure and His will is perfect. In His providential care our heavenly Father will enable us to endure it and grow through it.

The NT does not share the modern notion that all suffering should be avoided. Suffering is put within the context of God's will. Guthrie comments,

> Although it is true that suffering is nowhere explained, there is enough evidence to show what the Christian attitude towards it should be. There is no suggestion that God is less than wise or good because suffering exists. Since the supreme example of suffering lies at the heart of God's redemptive activity in Christ, *it cannot be maintained that suffering is alien to the purpose of God.* It will always remain a mystery why God chose to redeem mankind the way he did, but this very fact must be taken into account in considering the NT view of God. (*New Testament,* 98)

"By his death Christ proved that God's weakness was stronger than human strength. This same Christ is now the example Christians are to follow. By living under the cross of Christ and dying daily with him, we participate in the weakness of Christ. This identification with our crucified Lord enables us not merely to endure our weaknesses but to glory in them" (**D. Black, Weakness, 966**). With God's help we will be able to endure suffering. *"For here we have no lasting city, but we seek the city that is to come"* (**Heb 13:14**). Like Abraham, we are *"looking forward to the city that has foundations, whose designer and builder is God"* (**Heb 11:10**).

JAMES

James begins his letter, *"Count it all joy, my brothers, when you meet trials of various kinds, for you know that the testing of your faith produces steadfastness. And let steadfastness have its full effect, that you may be perfect and complete, lacking nothing"* (**Jas 1:2-4**). This passage will be discussed in chapter 12.

James directs attention to the economic and social injustice experienced by the poor: discrimination and humiliation (**Jas 2:2-4**), legal exploitation of the working-class poor by the rich (**Jas 2:6; 5:1-6**), and inadequate food and clothing (**Jas 2:15**). Not all wealthy were oppressors, some members of the church were not impoverished (**Jas 2:16; 4:13**).

Christians facing economic mistreatment are urged to trust in their future hope when the ungodly rich will be dealt with by the eternal Judge (**Jas 1:9-11; 5:7-9**). The local community of believers is encouraged to avoid favoritism, being respectful and generous to the needy (*Jas 1:27; 2:1-26*; cf. *2Cor 8:1-5; Gal 2:10*).

James encourages those mistreated, *"As an example of suffering and patience, brothers, take the prophets who spoke in the name of the Lord. Behold, we consider those blessed who remained steadfast. You have heard of the steadfastness of Job, and you have seen the purpose of the Lord, how the Lord is compassionate and merciful"* (*Jas 5:10-11*). Men like Jeremiah and Job were examples of steadfastness.

James says of suffering and sickness,

> *Is anyone among you suffering? Let him pray. Is anyone cheerful? Let him sing praise. Is anyone among you sick? Let him call for the elders of the church, and let them pray over him, anointing him with oil in the name of the Lord. And the prayer of faith will save the one who is sick, and the Lord will raise him up. And if he has committed sins, he will be forgiven. Therefore, confess your sins to one another and pray for one another, that you may be healed. The prayer of a righteous person has great power as it is working.* (*Jas 5:13-16*)

At times anointing with oil had medicinal uses (*Isa 1:6; Jer 8:22; 46:11; 51:8; Lk 10:34*). The disciples *"anointed with oil many who were sick and healed them"* (*Mk 6:13*). Anointing with oil was also used ceremonially in rituals. One view is that the anointing with oil is a religious ritual because it is mentioned in conjunction with prayer. It seems more likely that James is advocating use of medicine and prayer when one seeks healing from sickness.

Whether healing comes through natural means in God's providence or by a miraculous intervention, all healing ultimately comes from God. Certainly the focus is on the fact that healing comes from the Lord. Contrary to what some people say, I believe our prayers for healing should be accompanied with the best available medical treatment. The sufferer prays for himself or herself (*Jas 5:13*) and asks for the elders to come and pray for them (*Jas 5:14*).

The author, apparently James, the Lord's brother, was martyred at the temple for his testimony for Christ. Eusebius says the scribes and Pharisees threw James off the temple wall, stoned him and one of their members beat his head with a club (**2.23**).[1]

All healing ultimately comes from God.

[1] Cf. Josephus, *Antiquities of the Jews* 20.9.1.

I PETER

Peter wrote his first letter to believers facing persecution. It was probably written from Rome around the time of Nero's persecution of Christians after the fire in Rome (*1Pet 4:12; 5:13*). Roman historian, Tacitus, tells how Nero shifted blame from himself to Christians. He had multitudes arrested for confessing to being Christian. "Mockery of every sort was added to their deaths. Covered with the skins of beasts, they were torn by dogs and perished, or were nailed to crosses, or were doomed to the flames. These served to illuminate the night when day light failed." Tacitus has no appreciation for Christianity, regarding it as "hideous and shameful" and "a deadly superstition" (**15.38-44**).

Suetonius, writing of the same event, says, "Punishment was inflicted on the Christians, a class of men given to a new and wicked superstition" (**16.2**). One is reminded of Peter's comment about the *"fiery trial"* believers would experience (*1Pet 4:12*).

Suffering for Christ will bring blessing. Trust in Christ will overcome the fear of men. One should respond with gentleness and respect when treated wrongfully. Those who suffer wrongfully find encouragement when they remember that Christ suffered unjustly. "His [Peter's] advice is threefold—be prepared; remember that a share in Christ's sufferings brings with it a share in His glory; and remember the contrast between suffering as a criminal and suffering for Christ's sake. Whatever happens Christians must glorify God" (**Guthrie,** *Apostles***, 370**). The suffering Christian will share the eternal glory of Christ (*1Pet 5:10*).

Christians will face persecution because they stand for the truth of God and because their godly life condemns the unholy lifestyle of non-Christians. Peter writes to Christians who as *"sojourners and exiles"* were living as outcasts and displaced persons in their hometowns. They lacked their former status and security, being subject to ridicule and social ostracism by those they dealt with in everyday life. They rejected the pagan activities and sought to do what was right (*1Pet 2:11-12,14-15,20; 4:3-4,14-15*). The church provided a new community of acceptance, support, and stability (*1Pet 2:4-10*).

Peter says careful living will not prevent persecution (*1Pet 4:12; 3:13*). Before conversion they were comfortable in the culture. Unexpectedly the new converts experienced hostility and isolation from their culture. Peter says they should not be shocked and surprised by this. Christ predicted this (*Mt 5:11-12; Mk 13:9-13; Jn 15:18-20*). God allows this suffering as a refining process that reveals the genuineness of their faith. Peter H. Davids says, "In Scripture suffering is never seen as good in itself or to be welcomed, but as an evil to be endured at times for a greater good" (*Peter,* 165, n.).

Peter writes,

> *Beloved, do not be surprised at the fiery trial when it comes upon you to test you, as though something strange were happening to you. But rejoice insofar as you share Christ's sufferings, that you may also rejoice and be glad when his glory is revealed. If you are insulted for the name of Christ, you are blessed, because the Spirit of glory and of God rests upon you. But let none of you suffer as a murderer or a thief or an evildoer or as a meddler. Yet if anyone suffers as a Christian, let him not be ashamed, but let him glorify God in that name. For it is time for judgment to begin at the household of God; and if it begins with us, what will be the outcome for those who do not obey the gospel of God? And "If the righteous is scarcely saved, what will become of the ungodly and sinner?" Therefore let those who suffer according to God's will entrust their souls to a faithful Creator while doing good.* (*1Pet 4:12-19*)

Believers can rejoice in suffering (*Mt 5:11-12; Lk 6:22-23; Heb 10:32-39; Jas 1:2; 1Pet 1:6*). Those who share in Christ's sufferings will share in His glory (*Lk 12:8; Rom 8:17; Heb 10:32-39; 11:26; 12:12-14; 1Pet 1:7; 5:4; Col 3:4*). Only those who suffer because they are Christian are blessed.

Suffering as a Christian brings honor to Christ.

Suffering as a Christian brings honor to Christ. Peter argues that if God is hard on Christians, how much harder will He be on those who reject Him. Christians are better off than some might think (*1Pet 4:17-18*).

Suffering tests our faith (*1Pet 1:6; 4:12; 5:8-9; 2Cor 13:5-7*). Suffering is within the providential will of God (*1Pet 1:6; 2:15; 3:17; 5:6*). God works in the lives of His people.

We follow God's will in our lives, entrusting ourselves to our faithful God regardless of earthly consequences (*Rom 9:6; 11:29; 2Cor 1:18; 2Tm 1:12; 2:13; Heb 10:23*).

"*Therefore let those who suffer according to God's will entrust their souls to a faithful Creator while doing good*" (*1Pet 4:19*). Because God is Creator, He can be trusted. "That God gives a person life is surely an indication of his ability to care for the person; God knows what he is doing. That God is faithful indicates that he has not changed nor will change and can therefore be trusted. This is the God in whom one is to rest, although physically threatened" (**Davids, Peter, 174**).

In helping fellow sufferers we must be "sympathetic" and "compassionate" (**1Pet 3:8**). We are to enter into the experience of other suffering Christians. *"Weep with those who weep"* (**Rom 12:15**). It must not just be a matter of understanding the feelings of others. We must care deeply for them so that their suffering becomes our suffering.

Christ's suffering as a servant provided an example for all believers (**1Pet 2:18-25**).

Christ's suffering as a servant provided an example for all believers.

Peter identifies difficult situations Christians faced: slaves suffering under harsh owners (**1Pet 2:18**) and believers facing undeserved suffering (**1Pet 2:19-20; 1:6; 3:14,17; 4:1,13,16,19; 5:9-10**). When believers suffer, it is important that they maintain a clear conscience (**1Pet 1:19; 3:16,21**) and exhibit good behavior (**1Pet 2:14-15,20; 3:6,17; 4:19**). Instead of retaliating, they bless (**1Pet 2:21-22; 3:9**).

"If you suffer for righteousness' sake, you will be blessed" (**1Pet 3:14**). A virtuous life will not necessarily prevent suffering. "Blessed" does not mean having happy feelings, but rather a deep joy and sense of well-being because life is seen from God's perspective. *"When you are slandered, those who revile your good behavior in Christ may be put to shame. For it is better to suffer for doing good, if that should be God's will, than for doing evil"* (**1Pet 3:16-17**).

When Christians suffer with a gracious spirit and good behavior, slanders are shown to be groundless. When suffering comes, we must make sure that it is for our stand as a Christian, remembering that God is in control of the universe and He seeks our best interest.

Believers exhibiting the fruit of the Spirit when suffering can have a redemptive effect on outsiders (**1Pet 2:12; 3:16**). W.J. Webb says, "A loving, non-retaliatory response to those inflicting the abuse (as well as the pursuit of what is good and commendable) should quiet, perplex, shame and possibly even bring about the salvation of unbelievers (**1 Pet 2:12,15; 3:1-2,9,16**; cf. **1 Pet 2:24-25; 3:18**). Suffering then produces an internal and external witness to the grace of God in the present" (**1136**).

Graciously enduring suffering has an evangelistic impact. *"The respectful and pure conduct"* of a wife may win an unbelieving husband (*1Pet 3:1-2*). The believer's response to mistreatment can *"silence the ignorance of foolish people"* (*1Pet 2:15*) and may put the attackers to shame (*1Pet 3:16*) making Christianity appealing (*1Pet 2:12; 3:8-9*).

Graciously enduring suffering has an evangelistic impact.

As Jesus was wounded so He could bring healing even to those who wounded Him, so sufferers can make Christ inviting to those who mistreat them.

Peter's Points on Suffering

Believing sufferers should keep in mind their future hope which is assured by the risen Jesus who is in heaven (*1Pet 3:18-22*).
The disobedient will ultimately face God's justice (*1Pet 1:7-8; 2:23; 4:17*).
Believers should continue to trust and obey God (*1Pet 2:23; 4:19*).
When suffering does not have present benefits, faith can be refined, verifying its genuineness, even yielding joy (*1Pet 1:6-9; 4:14,16*).
Suffering for righteousness' sake confirms the Spirit's presence in the believer (*1Pet 4:14*) and God's favor (*1Pet 2:20*).

Peter says, *"If you are insulted for the name of Christ, you are blessed, because the Spirit of glory and of God rests upon you"* (*1Pet 4:14*). It is not for being tough and enduring rude behavior. You are blessed when you are opposed *"for righteousness' sake"* and *"for the name of Christ."* "We can bring endless suffering upon ourselves, we can create difficulties for ourselves which are quite unnecessary, because we have some rather foolish notion of witnessing and testifying, because, in a spirit of self-righteousness, we really do call it down on our own heads" (**Lloyd-Jones,** *Sermon*, 1:130).

Conflicts often existed between non-Christian slave owners and Christian slaves (*1Pet 2:18-25*) and Christian wives with unbelieving husbands (*1Pet 3:1-6*). Peter exhorts Christians to do good even in the face of slander and threats (*1Pet 3:8-9*) following the example of Christ (*1Pet 2:22-23*), knowing that God will vindicate them (*1Pet 3:16-17; 4:5-6*) as He vindicated Christ (*1Pet 3:18-22*).

Recent studies have highlighted the importance of honor and shame in the NT world. In Roman society honor was the supreme goal in life. Christians and their contemporaries differed drastically on what they considered honorable and what they considered shameful.

J.R. Michaels explains this contrast:

> Honor to the Romans involved the praise and esteem of fellow citizens, usually with some kind of public recognition of their good deeds either within the household or on behalf of the larger community. Individual deeds of honor brought honor to the family, the state, the emperor and the gods. Shame was the result of antisocial behavior that tended to undermine or discredit these same institutions and consequently to disgrace in the eyes of the community those guilty of such behavior.
>
> According to *1 Peter*, honor and shame are determined not by public opinion, the emperor or the Roman gods but solely by the God of Israel, who is the Father of those who believe in Jesus and the universal Judge to whom all are accountable (*1 Pet 1:17; 4:5*). Not their acts of public service but their loyalty to God and faithful endurance of "various trials" are what Christians will example for "praise, glory and honor" at the future "revelation of Jesus Christ" (*1 Pet 1:6-7*). Jesus was slain as God's "faultless and flawless lamb," but God "raised him from the dead and gave him glory" (*1 Pet 1:19, 21*). Drawing on biblical language (*Is 28:16*), Peter compares Jesus to "a choice and precious stone, a cornerstone in Zion" and announces that "the person who believes in him will never be put to shame" (*1 Pet 2:6*). This honor (of never being put to shame) belongs to Christians (*1 Pet 2:7*), while to unbelievers Christ becomes "a stone for stumbling and a rock to trip over"—a fate to which they were "appointed" (*1 Pet 2:8*). The dualism of such texts is absolute: Christians are destined for honor and non-Christians for eternal shame. (**921-922**)

Answer attack with honorable behavior *"so that when they speak against you as evildoers, they may see your good deeds and glorify God on the day of visitation"* (*1Pet 2:12*), and those who slander you will be put to shame (*1Pet 3:16*). Christians seek to win converts who will also honor God. *"If you are insulted for the name of Christ, you are blessed, because the Spirit of glory and of God rests upon you. But let none of you suffer as a murderer or a thief or an evildoer or as a meddler. Yet if anyone suffers as a Christian, let him not be ashamed, but let him glorify God in that name"* (**1Pet 4:14-16**). Be careful that if you are accused, it is not because of wrongdoing on your part but only because of your Christian faith.

The devil as a "roaring lion" seeks to bring suffering into the lives of believers.

> *Resist him, firm in your faith, knowing that the same kinds of suffering are being experienced by your brotherhood throughout the world. And after you have suffered a little while, the God of all grace, who has called you to his eternal glory in Christ, will himself restore, confirm, strengthen, and establish you. To him be the dominion forever and ever. Amen.* (**1Pet 5:9-10**)

"Firm in faith" means deep, consistent, unshakable commitment and trust in God (**Acts 16:5; Col 1:23; 2:5; Rev 12:9-11**). They find consolation and strength in realizing they share the same kinds of sufferings as believers in other parts of the world. Peter assures his readers that their suffering will be temporary *"a little while,"* but experiencing the glory in Christ will be eternal. When their enemies intend evil for them, God is able to bring good out of it.

REVELATION

The book of Revelation deals with persecution with a view to helping believers stay faithful through opposition. For the original readers, as well as many Christians today, martyrdom was a very present danger (**Rev 6:9-11; 16:6; 17:6; 18:24; 19:2**). Rome is pictured as a woman drunk with the blood of the saints (**Rev 17:9**). Persecution forms the background for Revelation leading to the final vindication of believers (**Rev 19:11-21**) and their final destiny (**Rev 21:1–22:15**). The book of Revelation addresses the question, "Where is God when we suffer persecution?"

Persecution in the book of Revelation has religious, cultural, and political aspects. The Romans were not concerned with someone worshiping another god. They were more concerned about the threat to property and social order. They objected to the Christians' refusal to confess Caesar as Lord and sacrifice to the gods because they considered this a violation of the Roman sense of social order. Their refusal made them enemies of the empire.

The book of Revelation addresses the question, "Where is God when we suffer persecution?"

In Revelation believers are encouraged to endure suffering in the light of their future hope: coming of the righteous Judge (*19:11-16*), future reign with Jesus (*20:4-6*), the final judgment (*19:11-15*), and *"the new heaven and new earth"* (*21:1*). In heaven *"death shall be no more, neither shall there be mourning nor crying nor pain anymore"* (*21:4*). They could look forward to reigning with Christ (*20:1-6*). Through suffering, Christians give their witness (*1:2,9; 6:9; 12:17; 19:10; 20:4*). Willingness to die for one's faith was a strong witness, both rejecting the world and affirming the lordship of Jesus.

God allows persecution but sets limits on its extent (*Rev 6:9-11*). Diabolic powers may be involved in persecution (*Rev 2:10; 13:2,4,11; 16:13*). The dragon represents Satan (*Rev 20:2*). Persecution at Smyrna and Pergamum is attributed to Satan (*Rev 2:10,13*). The death of the two witnesses at the hand of the beast is the work of Satan (*Rev 11:3,7; 13:1-2*). The deaths of many martyrs are attributed to Satan (*Rev 12:11-12*).

A world of suffering calls for patient endurance by God's saints (*Rev 13:10*). Those martyred for the word of God cry out, *"O Sovereign Lord, holy and true, how long before you will judge and avenge our blood in those who dwell on the earth?"* (*Rev 6:10*).

Some faithful witnesses did not die as martyrs. Luter says,

It should not be assumed, however, that all who are faithful

Chapter 8 Suffering as a Christian

157

witnesses for "the word of God and the testimony of Jesus" die as a result. John, the writer, was alive in spite of persecution that saw him exiled to the island of Patmos (*Rev 1:9*). Only a relatively few believers in *Revelation 2–3* would die (*Rev 2:10, 13*). Even the "great multitude" standing before the heavenly throne in *Revelation 7:9, 14* are not all or necessarily martyrs. The comment about making their robes "white in the blood of the Lamb" may refer not to martyrdom but to Christ's redemptive death. (720)

Those who die in the Lord are blessed (*Rev 14:12-13; 20:4*). The message of Revelation is relevant to us all: Be faithful until death because victory comes to the overcomers (*Rev 2:10-11; 12:11; 21:7*).

> **Be faithful until death because victory comes to the overcomers.**

Think about It

1. What did Jesus say about the persecution of believers?
2. Why are Christians persecuted by the world?
3. Why didn't Jesus heal every sick person?
4. How did Roman officials treat Christian believers?
5. How does the community of believers minister to those suffering?
6. What kind of comfort does God give to the suffering?
7. What is the purpose of discipline?
8. What kind of suffering does James mention?
9. Describe the persecution experienced by Christians under Nero.
10. What kinds of suffering does *1 Peter* mention?
11. How should believers respond to suffering according to *1 Peter*?
12. Contrast the pagan and the Christian view of honor and shame.

CHAPTER NINE

THE BENEFITS OF PAIN AND SUFFERING

We rejoice in our sufferings, knowing that suffering produces endurance, and endurance produces character, and character produces hope.
Romans 5:3-4

Viktor Frankl spoke these words from his experience in a Nazi death camp:

> If there is a meaning in life at all, then there must be a meaning in suffering. Suffering is an ineradicable part of life. . . . I was struggling to find the *reason* for my sufferings, my slow dying. In a last violent protest against the hopelessness of imminent death, I sensed my spirit piercing through the enveloping gloom. I felt it transcend that hopeless, meaningless world, and from somewhere I heard a victorious "Yes" in answer to my question of the existence of an ultimate purpose. . . . Man's main concern is not to gain pleasure or to avoid pain, but rather to see a meaning in his life. That is why man is even ready to suffer, on the condition, to be sure, that his suffering has a meaning. **(106, 63-64, 179)**

Suffering has positive aspects as well as negative. In considering the matter of suffering it is important to keep the big picture in mind. We must admit we do not understand all the reasons for suffering in this life. It is possible that God has reasons which we do not understand which are necessary to produce eventual good. This chapter will discuss some positive benefits that can be seen in pain and suffering.

I. Biological Benefits of Pain
II. Adversity Produces Character
III. Reminder That This World Is Not Our Final Home

BIOLOGICAL BENEFITS
OF PAIN

The ability of the physical body to experience pain is a gift of God designed to protect us. Pain as an alarm warns us of impending danger which, if remedied, means a greater pain can be avoided. Pain functions as a communication network alerting us to danger, insisting that we seek treatment to remedy the matter. Insensitivity to pain is a horrible condition that results in much harm to the body. The physical condition of insensitivity to pain is a dangerous condition. A child who can feel no pain responds with abnormal indifference when burned or cut and when bones are broken or concussions occur. Pain is a warning, signaling that something has gone wrong in the body. Without the caution that pain provides, we harm ourselves without realizing it. Absence of pain does not equal happiness.

> **Pain functions as a communication network alerting us to danger.**

Dr. Paul Brand served his medical internship in London during World War II. Then he moved to India and served lepers (Hansen's disease) at the Vellore Christian Hospital in South India. He discovered that the ulcers, sores, blindness, and loss of limbs in lepers are secondary problems due to the loss of feeling.

Dr. Brand said when he came to America, "I encountered a society that seeks to avoid pain at all costs. Patients lived at a greater comfort level than any I had previously treated, but they seemed far less equipped to handle suffering and far more traumatized by it." He observes, "Most of us will one day face severe pain. I am convinced that the attitude we cultivate in advance may well determine how suffering will affect us when it does strike" (12).

After years of working with pain-deprived people, Dr. Brand says,

> I now regard pain as one of the most remarkable design features of the human body, and if I could choose one gift for my leprosy patients it would be the gift of pain. (In fact, a team of scientists I directed spent more than a million dollars in an attempt to design an artificial pain system. We abandoned the project when it became abundantly clear we could not possibly duplicate the sophisticated engineering system that protects a healthy human being.) My own encounters with pain, though, as well as the specter of painlessness, have produced

in me an attitude of wonder and appreciation. I do not desire, and cannot ever imagine, a life without pain. For that reason I accept the challenge of trying to restore balance to how we think about pain. (12-13)

Yancey states,

> Pain may have been intended as an efficiently protective warning system, but something about this planet has gone haywire and pain now rages out of control. We need another word for the problem: perhaps *pain* to signify the body's protective network and *suffering* to signify the human misery. After all, a leprosy patient feels no pain, but much suffering. (**Where, 62**)

Yancey admits, "The surprising idea of the 'gift of pain' does not answer many of the problems connected with suffering. But it is a beginning point of a realistic perspective on pain and suffering. Too often the emotional trauma of intense pain blinds us to its inherent value" (**ibid., 35**).

ADVERSITY PRODUCES CHARACTER

Suffering leads some people to reject God. Suffering leads others to a deeper faith in God. It is up to us how we respond to suffering. Suffering can cause us to acknowledge our dependence upon God. When we are forced to face our human limitations, we realize we are not masters of our own fate.

Adversity produces character and steadfastness. A coach who protects his football team from any scrimmage would not be preparing them for the rigors of the game. A child never taught to face obstacles and solve problems is unprepared for life.

Facing and overcoming difficulties and trials can make us strong. Suffering can produce endurance, character, and hope (**Rom 5:3-5**). Trials produce steadfastness (**Jas 1:2-4; 1Pet 1:6-9**). God disciplines us so that we may share His holiness (**Heb 12:10**). The only perfect life was not pain-free. Jesus was made "perfect through suffering" (**Heb 2:10**).

Carson says God's hand of providence is often dimly discerned. "For instance, prolonged suffering from

Suffering can produce endurance; trials, steadfastness; discipline, holiness.

chronic illness is certainly not a 'good' thing, yet rightly accepted it can breed patience, teach discipline of prayer, generate compassion for others who suffer, engender some reflection and self-knowledge that knocks out cockiness and the arrogance of condescending impatience" (*How Long?* 65).

When she was a teenager, Joni Eareckson Tada became a quadriplegic due to a diving accident. She has told her story with engaging honesty, how she had to work through anger, bitterness, and despair. With the help of her loving family and friends, she came to trust God to rebuild her life. Joni said it took three years after the accident to believe that she too could have fullness of life. (**Eareckson and Musser,** and **Tada and Estes**)

Through her books, paintings, speaking, songs, and her organization serving the handicapped, Joni and Friends, Joni Eareckson Tada has made a profound difference in many lives. My own brother who had cerebral palsy was a beneficiary of help from Joni and Friends. Out of her accident, which was certainly evil, God has brought much good through her life.

Lee Strobel tells of his friend Marc Harrienger. He had been shoveling snow from the driveway. When his wife backed the car up, their toddler was crushed beneath the car. Marc said he was paralyzed by the emotional pain. Through the process of grief he increasingly felt God's grace and comfort. Strobel states, "Having experienced God at his point of greatest need, Marc would emerge from this crucible a changed person, abandoning his career in business to attend seminary. Through his suffering—though it was life-shattering at the time—Marc has been transformed into someone who would devote the rest of life to bringing God's compassion to others who are alone in their desperation" (*Faith*, 53).

To those who scoff at the idea that God can bring good out of our pain, Marc responded,

> But I've watched it happen in my own life. I've experienced God's goodness through deep pain, and no skeptic can dispute that. The God who the skeptic denies is the same God, who held our hands in the deep, dark places, who strengthened our marriage, who deepened our faith, who increased our reliance on him, who gave us two more children, and who infused our lives with new purpose and meaning so that we can make a difference to others. (**ibid.**)

Strobel asked Marc, "Do you wish you had more answers about why suffering happens in the first place?" Marc answered, "We live in a broken world; Jesus was honest enough to tell us we'd have trials and tribulations. Sure, I'd like to understand more about why. . . . the ultimate answer is Jesus' presence. That sounds sappy, I know. But just wait—when your world is rocked, you don't want philosophy or theology as much as you want the reality of Christ. He *was* the answer for me. He was the very answer we needed" (**ibid., 54**).

John Mark Hicks was married in 1977 at age 19. His world was shaken in 1980 when his wife, Sheila, died from a blood clot while recovering from surgery. He wondered why God had not preserved her life when they had prayed for health and protection. He had formerly believed, "Christians should always wear a smile." His suffering led him to lament, appealing to God to help and rescue him (*Anchors*, **11-14**).

He said God renewed his joy, and in 1983 he married Barbara. They have three children . Their son, Joshua, was born in 1985. He was afflicted with a terminal genetic condition, Sanfilippo Syndrome, that would take his life by about age 16 after progressive physical and mental deterioration. Hicks says, "We still question, wonder, despair, cry, and doubt. Lament often turns to praise, but sometimes lament needs to continue to complain, question, and plead" (**ibid., 14-19**).[1]

Hicks says, "I confess with the psalmist that 'it was good for me to be afflicted' (*Ps. 119:71*)." Before his wife's death, he describes himself, "I was arrogant in my theology—I knew what was right, preached maliciously against error, and chastened everyone who left the 'old paths' of my tradition. . . . My spirit was contentious, my attitude was arrogant, my theology was perfect, and my goal was selfish" (**ibid., 15-16**).

Hicks comments about how suffering affected him,

> Sheila's death changed me. Scripture changed me. My encounter with the God of Scripture changed me. God changed me as I experienced his comforting presence and transforming power through suffering. The effect of that change was such that whereas I once had God so pegged that I knew what to expect from him and could plan out the course of my life without interruption, I now realized that my

[1] Joshua died May 21, 2001, at age 16.

attitude must be one of submission. Humility must replace arrogance, submission must replace pride, and gentleness must replace contentiousness. In other words, God's glory must replace my selfishness. Without that experience—at that moment—my heart may have hardened, and my path may have been set.

God used Sheila's death to change me. But was that fair? Why should Sheila suffer for my good? Why her instead of me? I was the problem, not her! I was filled with pride, but she was not. I wanted to move up the 'hierarchical' ladder of my church, but she just wanted to serve God. I wanted to be noticed, but that did not consume her. Why her instead of me? These questions have often plagued me. They are difficult questions, but in lament faith asks. But no matter how they are answered, I thank God for the change he worked in my life. Through my suffering—whatever the origin and reason for that suffering—God worked powerfully to effect good in my life. He opened my heart to his transforming presence. (**ibid., 16**)

Often the skeptics who object to God on the basis of suffering and evil, do so from situations of comfort. Many who have suffered incredible hardship have become examples of courage and faith.

> **Humility, submission, and gentleness must replace arrogance, pride, and contentiousness.**

A friend of mine, a Chinese Christian, was in charge of a business in Indonesia when riots broke out in 1998. The mobs destroyed, vandalized, burned, robbed, and looted businesses and homes. The only stores spared had "Owned by Muslim" signs. Women were brutally raped and families terrorized. The riots lasted three days and 2,244 burnt bodies were collected. He lost his business and livelihood. He is thankful his son and daughter were studying abroad so they did not experience this horrible nightmare. He and his wife came to America that fall. He testifies that his faith in God and Jesus has grown. He says God's grace and love helped him endure his loss. As he is serving Christ, he is finding joy out of his sorrow.

Some Uses of Suffering
as Listed by John Feinberg

1) "God sometimes allows affliction in the life of the righteous as a basis for some future work that demonstrates his power and glory." (*Jn 9:1-3*)

2) "God may use affliction to remove a cause for boasting." (*2Cor 12:7*)

3) "God still needs people today who will show others that even when life brings the unexpected and the tragic, they will continue to love and serve God, not because it pays to do so, but because he is worthy of devotion." (*1Pet 3:15*)

4) "Sometimes God uses affliction as an opportunity to demonstrate to believers and nonbelievers the concept of the body of Christ." (*1Cor 12:12-26*) Sufferers receive the compassionate care of other believers. Other believers have the opportunity to express Christian love to those in need.

5) "Afflictions have a way of driving believers away from committing specific acts of sin." (*1Pet 4:1-2*)

6) "Affliction promotes sanctification . . . by refining one's faith." (*1Pet 1:6-7*)

7) "Holiness is also promoted by suffering, when God uses it to educate believers in ways that cause them to grow closer to the Lord and to be more Christlike." (*Jas 1:3-4; Rom 5:3-5; 1Pet 5:10*)

8) "Through difficult experiences believers can also draw closer to the Lord by catching a glimpse of his sovereignty and majesty such as they have never seen before." (*Job 42:2-4*)

9) "Suffering also produces sanctification because it leads to intimacy with God." (*Job 42:5*).

10) "God may use it [affliction] to challenge the righteous to growth, instead of falling into sin." (*Jas 1:1-12*)

11) "A final way adversity promotes holiness is by offering sufferers the opportunity to imitate Christ." (*1Pet 3:17-18; 2:23; Mt 10:24-25*). (*Where*, 87-101)

Gerald Sittser lost his mother, wife, and daughter in a tragic accident when they were hit by a drunk driver. He describes his difficulty in dealing with his loss in *A Grace Disguised*. After all his struggles with the grief process and rebuilding his life, he affirms, "Despite the fact that I had been a Christian for many years before the accident, since then God has become a living reality to me as never before. My confidence in God is somehow quieter but stronger. I feel little pressure to impress God or prove myself to him; yet I want to serve him with all my heart and strength" (*Grace*, 116).

Yancey writes,

> Does God introduce suffering into our lives so that these good results will come about? . . . Questions about cause lie within God's domain; we cannot expect to understand those answers. . . . Instead, *response* is our assignment. . . .As we rely on God, and trust his Spirit to mold us in his image, true hope takes shape within us, "a hope that does not disappoint." We can literally become better persons because of suffering. Pain, however meaningless it may seem at the time, can be transformed. (*Where*, 109)

Where is God when we suffer? He is with us and works within us helping to bring good results out of bad situations.

In a discussion with Dr. Paul Brand about Christians who had undergone extreme suffering, Yancey says,

> I asked whether the pain had turned those people toward God or away from God. He thought at length, and concluded that there was no common response. Some grew closer to God, some drifted bitterly away. The main difference seemed to lie in their focus of attention. Those obsessed with questions about cause ("What did I do to deserve this? What is God trying to tell me? Am I being punished?") often turned against God. In contrast, the triumphant sufferers took individual responsibility for their own responses and trusted God despite the discomfort. (**ibid., 110**)

Aleksander Solzhenitsyn, famous author, found God while in a communist prison. He testifies,

> It was only when I lay there on rotting prison straw that I sensed within myself the first stirring of good. Gradually, it was disclosed to me that the line separating good and evil passes, not through states, nor between classes, nor between political parties either, but right through all human hearts. So bless you, prison, for having been in my life. (**Wright, *Life*, 34**)

The psalmist said,

> *Before I was afflicted I went astray,*
> *but now I keep your word. . . .*

It is good that I was afflicted,
That I might learn your statutes. (**Ps 119:67,71**)

REMINDER THAT THIS WORLD IS NOT OUR FINAL HOME

This fallen world is not fair or just. We must remember that the final reckoning is not in this life. In the final countdown God will work all things for good for Christians (**Rom 8:28**). Paul says, *"For this slight momentary affliction is preparing for us an eternal weight of glory beyond all comparison"* (**2Cor 4:17**).

God wants to liberate us from the false belief that we can live forever in this physical body and that this physical world is eternal. We will pass from this life and this world will pass away. Realizing that God is eternal and wants to have everlasting fellowship with us can prevent us from clinging to the values of this world. McGrath says, "Suffering strips away our illusions of immortality. It confronts us with the harsh facts of life and makes us ask those hard questions which have the power to erode falsehood and propel us away from the false security and transient rewards of the world toward our loving God" (**Suffering**, 33)

McGrath continues, "We are tied to this earth by sin, like gravity; something needs to be done to break its hold. Suffering, though

"Suffering strips away our illusions of immortality."

tragic, is not pointless. It is the pin which bursts the balloon of our delusions, and opens the way to an urgent and passionate wrestling with the reality of death and the question of what lies beyond" (**ibid., 34**).

J. Robertson McQuilkin, former president of Columbia Bible College, was approached by an elderly lady whose physical beauty had been diminished by sickness and the ravages of old age. She asked, "Why does God let us get old and weak? Why must I hurt so?"

He thought a while, then responded,

> I think God has planned the strength and beauty of youth to be physical. But the strength and beauty of age is spiritual. We gradually lose the strength and beauty that is temporary so we'll be sure to concentrate on the strength and beauty which is forever. It makes us more eager to leave behind the tempo-

rary, deteriorating part of us and be truly homesick for our eternal home. If we stayed young and strong and beautiful, we might never want to leave. (**Yancey, *Where*, 251**)

In this world God *"makes his sun to rise on the evil and on the good, and sends rain on the just and the unjust"* (**Mt 5:45**). But *"he has fixed a day on which he will judge the world in righteousness"* (**Acts 17:31**). *"Vengeance is mine, I will repay, says the Lord"* (**Rom 12:19**). In the final judgment God will administer perfect justice. Those who feel the suf-

> **The view from eternity will be far different from our view from the present.**

fering is unjustly distributed in this life need never fear about the final justice—each will go to an eternal destiny where he or she rightly should go.

Our omniscient God will take into account all relevant factors and His justice will be perfect. Keeping this fact in mind is tremendously important as we seek to think Christianly about suffering and evil. We live in faith and hope knowing that the view from eternity will be far different from our view from the present. We serve an all-knowing, just God whose promises never fail.

Lee Strobel asked Peter Kreeft, "Why doesn't God do something about evil people hurting people?" Kreeft answered,

> People *aren't* getting away with it. Justice delayed is not necessarily justice denied. There will come a day when God will settle accounts and people will be held responsible for the evil they perpetrated, and the suffering they've caused. Criticizing God for not doing it right now is like reading half a novel and criticizing the author for not resolving the plot. God will bring accountability at the right time—in fact, the Bible says one reason he's delaying is because some people are still following the clues and have yet to find him. He's actually delaying the consummation of history out of his great love for them. (***Faith*, 43**)

C.S. Lewis says we can ignore our pleasures but pain speaks with a louder voice.

> We can rest contentedly in our sins and in our stupidities; and anyone who has watched gluttons shovelling down the most exquisite foods as if they did not know what they were eating, will admit that we can ignore even pleasure. But pain insists upon being attended to. God whispers to us in our pleasures, speaks in our conscience, but shouts in our pains: it is His

megaphone to rouse a deaf world. A bad man, happy, is a man without the least inkling that his actions do not "answer", that they are not in accord with the laws of the universe. (***Problem*, 90-91**)

Understanding some of the benefits that can come from suffering does not answer all our questions. However it is important that we learn from suffering even if we do not understand all about it. As believers we do know that pain and suffering are part of the reality in this fallen world. We also know that God is loving and powerful. We want to be steadfast and faithful to Him regardless of the circumstances, knowing that someday we will claim the eternal victory.

Think about It

1. Why does suffering force us to think about meaning in life?

2. How does the ability to feel pain benefit the human body?

3. How has God brought good out of evil in Joni Eareckson Tada's life?

4. What did Marc Harrienger say to those who scoff at the idea of God bringing good out of evil?

5. Why did John Mark Hicks say it was good he was afflicted?

6. Yancey says questions about cause are God's domain, how we respond to suffering is our responsibility. Do you agree? Why?

7. In what ways does suffering remind us that this world is not our final home?

8. Summarize Peter Kreeft's answer to the question, "Why doesn't God do something about evil people hurting people?"

CHAPTER TEN

A SUMMARY OF THE BIBLE'S TEACHING ON SUFFERING[1]

All Scripture is breathed out by God and is profitable for teaching, for reproof, for correction, and for training in righteousness, that the man of God may be competent, equipped for every good work.
2 Timothy 3:16-17

1. Suffering is the common lot of human beings.
   But man is born to trouble as the sparks fly upward. (**Job 5:7**)
   For we know that the whole creation has been groaning together in the pains of childbirth until now. (**Rom 8:22**)
2. Suffering came to mankind as a result of sin.
   To the woman he said, "I will surely multiply your pain in child-bearing; in pain you shall bring forth children. Your desire shall be for your husband, and he shall rule over you." And to Adam he said, "Because you have listened to the voice of your wife and have eaten of the tree of which I commanded you, 'You shall not eat of it,' cursed is the ground because of you; in pain you shall eat of it all the days of your life; thorns and thistles it shall bring forth for you; and you shall eat the plants of the field. By the sweat of your face you shall eat bread, till you return to the ground, for out of it you were taken; for you are dust, and to dust you shall return." (**Gen 3:16-19**)
   Therefore, just as sin came into the world through one man, and death through sin, and so death spread to all men because all sinned. (**Rom 5:12**)
3. Suffering is not necessarily a penalty for the sufferer's sins.

---

[1] I am indebted to Willie W. White, *What the Bible Says about Suffering* (Joplin, MO: College Press, 1984) 280-290, for the questions and Scripture references in this chapter.

There were some present at that very time who told him about the Galileans whose blood Pilate had mingled with their sacrifices. And he answered them, "Do you think that these Galileans were worse sinners than all the other Galileans, because they suffered in this way? No, I tell you; but unless you repent, you will all likewise perish. Or those eighteen on whom the tower in Siloam fell and killed them: do you think that they were worse offenders than all the others who lived in Jerusalem? No, I tell you; but unless you repent, you will all likewise perish." (Lk 13:1-5)

As he passed by, he saw a man blind from birth. And his disciples asked him, "Rabbi, who sinned, this man or his parents, that he was born blind?" Jesus answered, "It was not that this man sinned, or his parents, but that the works of God might be displayed in him." (Jn 9:1-3)

4. Our suffering may be caused by the sins of others.

And as they were stoning Stephen, he called out, "Lord Jesus, receive my spirit."

And falling to his knees he cried out with a loud voice, "Lord, do not hold this sin against them." And when he had said this, he fell asleep. (Acts 7:59-60)

For our sake he made him to be sin who knew no sin, so that in him we might become the righteousness of God. (2Cor 5:21)

Five times I received at the hands of the Jews the forty lashes less one. Three times I was beaten with rods. Once I was stoned. Three times I was shipwrecked; a night and a day I was adrift at sea; on frequent journeys, in danger from rivers, danger from robbers, danger from my own people, danger from Gentiles, danger in the city, danger in the wilderness, danger at sea, danger from false brothers; in toil and hardship, through many a sleepless night, in hunger and thirst, often without food, in cold and exposure.

And, apart from other things, there is the daily pressure on me of my anxiety for all the churches. Who is weak, and I am not weak? Who is made to fall, and I am not indignant? (2Cor 11:24-29)

5. Christians are not immune to suffering.

Indeed, all who desire to live a godly life in Christ Jesus will be persecuted. (2Tm 3:12)

Then Jesus told his disciples, "If anyone would come after me, let him deny himself and take up his cross and follow me." (Mt 16:24)

For it has been granted to you that for the sake of Christ you should not only believe in him but also suffer for his sake, engaged in the

same conflict that you saw I had and now hear that I still have.
(*Php 1:29-30*)

6. God cares when we suffer.

   Casting all your anxieties on him, because he cares for you. (*1Pet 5:7*)

   For the Lord will not cast off forever, but, though he cause grief, he will have compassion according to the abundance of his steadfast love. (*Lam 3:31-32*)

7. God is with us in suffering.

   But now thus says the LORD, he who created you, O Jacob, he who formed you, O Israel: "Fear not, for I have redeemed you; I have called you by name, you are mine. When you pass through the waters, I will be with you; and through the rivers, they shall not overwhelm you; when you walk through fire you shall not be burned, and the flame shall not consume you. For I am the LORD your God, the Holy One of Israel, your Savior." (*Isa 43:1-3*)

   God is our refuge and strength, a very present help in trouble. Therefore we will not fear though the earth gives way, though the mountains be moved into the heart of the sea, though its waters roar and foam, though the mountains tremble at its swelling. (*Ps 46:1-3*)

   Who shall separate us from the love of Christ? Shall tribulation, or distress, or persecution, or famine, or nakedness, or danger, or sword? As it is written,

   > "For your sake we are being killed all the day long;
   > we are regarded as sheep to be slaughtered."

   No, in all these things we are more than conquerors through him who loved us. For I am sure that neither death nor life, nor angels nor rulers, nor things present nor things to come, nor powers, nor height nor depth, nor anything else in all creation, will be able to separate us from the love of God in Christ Jesus our Lord. (*Rom 8:35-39*)

   Keep your life free from love of money, and be content with what you have, for he has said, "I will never leave you nor forsake you." So we can confidently say, "The Lord is my helper; I will not fear; what can man do to me?" (*Heb 13:5-6*)

8. God does not cause suffering: God permits suffering.

   There was a man in the land of Uz whose name was Job, and that man was blameless and upright, one who feared God and turned away from evil.

And the LORD said to Satan, "Behold, all that he has is in your hand. Only against him do not stretch out your hand." So Satan went out from the presence of the LORD.

Now there was a day when the sons of God came to present themselves before the LORD, and Satan also came among them. (*Job 1:12; 2:6*)

9. God permits suffering for the good of the sufferer.

A. To bring us back when we stray.

Before I was afflicted I went astray, but now I keep your word. You are good and do good; teach me your statutes. . . . It is good for me that I was afflicted, that I might learn your statutes. (*Ps 119:67-68,71*)

B. To purify our lives.

Behold, I have refined you, but not as silver; I have tried you in the furnace of affliction. (*Isa 48:10*)

C. To make us steadfast.

More than that, we rejoice in our sufferings, knowing that suffering produces endurance, and endurance produces character, and character produces hope, and hope does not put us to shame, because God's love has been poured into our hearts through the Holy Spirit who has been given to us. (*Rom 5:3-5*)

D. To make our lives complete.

And after you have suffered a little while, the God of all grace, who has called you to his eternal glory in Christ, will himself restore, confirm, strengthen, and establish you. (*1Pet 5:10*)

E. To equip us for heaven.

But rejoice insofar as you share Christ's sufferings, that you may also rejoice and be glad when his glory is revealed. (*1Pet 4:13*)

10. God permits suffering for the good of others.

Blessed be the God and Father of our Lord Jesus Christ, the Father of mercies and God of all comfort, who comforts us in all our affliction, so that we may be able to comfort those who are in any affliction, with the comfort with which we ourselves are comforted by God. For as we share abundantly in Christ's sufferings, so through Christ we share abundantly in comfort too. If we are afflicted, it is for your comfort and salvation; and if we are comforted, it is for your comfort, which you experience when you patiently endure the same sufferings that we suffer. Our hope for you is unshaken, for we know that as you share in our sufferings, you will also share in our comfort. (*2Cor 1:3-7*)

But we have this treasure in jars of clay, to show that the surpassing power belongs to God and not to us. We are afflicted in every way, but not crushed; perplexed, but not driven to despair; persecuted, but not forsaken; struck down, but not destroyed; always carrying in the body the death of Jesus, so that the life of Jesus may also be manifested in our bodies. For we who live are always being given over to death for Jesus' sake, so that the life of Jesus also may be manifested in our mortal flesh. So death is at work in us, but life in you. Since we have the same spirit of faith according to what has been written, "I believed, and so I spoke," we also believe, and so we also speak, knowing that he who raised the Lord Jesus will raise us also with Jesus and bring us with you into his presence. For it is all for your sake, so that as grace extends to more and more people it may increase thanksgiving, to the glory of God. (**2Cor 4:7-15**)

11. God permits suffering that He might be glorified.

    As he passed by, he saw a man blind from birth. And his disciples asked him, "Rabbi, who sinned, this man or his parents, that he was born blind?" Jesus answered, "It was not that this man sinned, or his parents, but that the works of God might be displayed in him. (**Jn 9:1-3**)

    Truly, truly, I say to you, when you were young, you used to dress yourself and walk wherever you wanted, but when you are old, you will stretch out your hands, and another will dress you and carry you where you do not want to go." (This he said to show by what kind of death he was to glorify God.) And after saying this he said to him, "Follow me." (**Jn 21:18-19**)

    Beloved, do not be surprised at the fiery trial when it comes upon you to test you, as though something strange were happening to you. But rejoice insofar as you share Christ's sufferings, that you may also rejoice and be glad when his glory is revealed. If you are insulted for the name of Christ, you are blessed, because the Spirit of glory and of God rests upon you. But let none of you suffer as a murderer or a thief or an evildoer or as a meddler. Yet if anyone suffers as a Christian, let him not be ashamed, but let him glorify God in that name. (**1Pet 4:12-16**)

12. Jesus was made perfect (complete) through suffering.

    But we see him who for a little while was made lower than the angels, namely Jesus, crowned with glory and honor because of the suffering of death, so that by the grace of God he might taste death for everyone. For it was fitting that he, for whom and by whom all things exist, in bringing many sons to glory, should make the founder of their salvation perfect through suffering. (**Heb 2:9-10**)

13. Jesus is our example in suffering.

For to this you have been called, because Christ also suffered for you, leaving you an example, so that you might follow in his steps. He committed no sin, neither was deceit found in his mouth. When he was reviled, he did not revile in return; when he suffered, he did not threaten, but continued entrusting himself to him who judges justly. He himself bore our sins in his body on the tree, that we might die to sin and live to righteousness. By his wounds you have been healed. For you were straying like sheep, but have now returned to the Shepherd and Overseer of your souls. (**1Pet 2:21-25**)

14. Because Jesus suffered, He understands our suffering.

Therefore he had to be made like his brothers in every respect, so that he might become a merciful and faithful high priest in the service of God, to make propitiation for the sins of the people. For because he himself has suffered when tempted, he is able to help those who are being tempted. (**Heb 2:17-18**)

Since then we have a great high priest who has passed through the heavens, Jesus, the Son of God, let us hold fast our confession. For we do not have a high priest who is unable to sympathize with our weaknesses, but one who in every respect has been tempted as we are, yet without sin. Let us then with confidence draw near to the throne of grace, that we may receive mercy and find grace to help in time of need. (**Heb 4:14-16**)

15. Christians should rejoice in spite of suffering.

Blessed are those who are persecuted for righteousness' sake, for theirs is the kingdom of heaven. Blessed are you when others revile you and persecute you and utter all kinds of evil against you falsely on my account. Rejoice and be glad, for your reward is great in heaven, for so they persecuted the prophets who were before you. (**Mt 5:10-12**)

And when they had called in the apostles, they beat them and charged them not to speak in the name of Jesus, and let them go. Then they left the presence of the council, rejoicing that they were counted worthy to suffer dishonor for the name. (**Acts 5:40-41**)

And when they had inflicted many blows upon them, they threw them into prison, ordering the jailer to keep them safely. Having received this order, he put them into the inner prison and fastened their feet in the stocks. About midnight Paul and Silas were praying and singing hymns to God, and the prisoners were listening to them. (*Acts 16:23-25*)

*Therefore, since we have been justified by faith, we have peace with God through our Lord Jesus Christ. Through him we have also obtained access by faith into this grace in which we stand, and we rejoice in hope of the glory of God. More than that, we rejoice in our sufferings, knowing that suffering produces endurance. (**Rom 5:1-3**)*

16. Present sufferings are not comparable with future glory.

*The Spirit himself bears witness with our spirit that we are children of God, and if children, then heirs—heirs of God and fellow heirs with Christ, provided we suffer with him in order that we may also be glorified with him. For I consider that the sufferings of this present time are not worth comparing with the glory that is to be revealed to us. (**Rom 8:16-18**)*

17. Jesus invites us to suffering—and to fellowship—and to joy.

*And he said to all, "If anyone would come after me, let him deny himself and take up his cross daily and follow me. For whoever would save his life will lose it, but whoever loses his life for my sake will save it." (**Lk 9:23-24**)*

*Only let your manner of life be worthy of the gospel of Christ, so that whether I come and see you or am absent, I may hear of you that you are standing firm in one spirit, with one mind striving side by side for the faith of the gospel, and not frightened in anything by your opponents. This is a clear sign to them of their destruction, but of your salvation, and that from God. For it has been granted to you that for the sake of Christ you should not only believe in him but also suffer for his sake, engaged in the same conflict that you saw I had and now hear that I still have. (**Php 1:27-30**)*

*For his anger is but for a moment, and his favor is for a lifetime. Weeping may tarry for the night, but joy comes with the morning. (**Ps 30:5**)*

18. With God, we are more than conquerors.

*No, in all these things we are more than conquerors through him who loved us. (**Rom 8:37**)*

*Many are the afflictions of the righteous, but the LORD delivers him out of them all. (**Ps 34:19**)*

*I can do all things through him who strengthens me. (**Php 4:13**)*

19. A crown awaits the victor.

Do not fear what you are about to suffer. Behold, the devil is about to throw some of you into prison, that you may be tested, and for ten days you will have tribulation. Be faithful unto death, and I will give you the crown of life. (*Rev 2:10*)

And if children, then heirs—heirs of God and fellow heirs with Christ, provided we suffer with him in order that we may also be glorified with him. (*Rom 8:17*)

Then one of the elders addressed me, saying, "Who are these, clothed in white robes, and from where have they come?"

I said to him, "Sir, you know."

And he said to me, "These are the ones coming out of the great tribulation. They have washed their robes and made them white in the blood of the Lamb.

"Therefore they are before the throne of God, and serve him day and night in his temple; and he who sits on the throne will shelter them with his presence. They shall hunger no more, neither thirst anymore; the sun shall not strike them, nor any scorching heat. For the Lamb in the midst of the throne will be their shepherd, and he will guide them to springs of living water, and God will wipe away every tear from their eyes." (*Rev 7:13-17*)

20. The last word on suffering.

Then I saw a new heaven and a new earth, for the first heaven and the first earth had passed away, and the sea was no more. And I saw the holy city, new Jerusalem, coming down out of heaven from God, prepared as a bride adorned for her husband. And I heard a loud voice from the throne saying, "Behold, the dwelling place of God is with man. He will dwell with them, and they will be his people, and God himself will be with them as their God. He will wipe away every tear from their eyes, and death shall be no more, neither shall there be mourning nor crying nor pain anymore, for the former things have passed away."

And he who was seated on the throne said, "Behold, I am making all things new." Also he said, "Write this down, for these words are trustworthy and true." And he said to me, "It is done! I am the Alpha and the Omega, the beginning and the end. To the thirsty I will give from the spring of the water of life without payment. The one who conquers will have this heritage, and I will be his God and he will be my son." (*Rev 21:1-7*)

Part 2

Facing
Suffering
with
Faith, Joy
and
Hope

CHAPTER ELEVEN

WHEN OUR PRAYER REQUESTS ARE NOT GRANTED

If you ask anything in my name, I will do it.
John 14:14
Nevertheless, not as I will, but as you will.
Matthew 26:39

When I faced the real likelihood of death because of my pulmonary fibrosis, a minister told me they had many healings at their church through prayer. He told me they would pray for me and I would be healed. Nevertheless, I did not find healing until I received a double lung transplant. People prayed for our son Mark's safety, yet a truck accident claimed his life. Why doesn't God grant some of our prayer requests? God's silence led a frustrated Job to ask, "What profit do we get if we pray to him?" (*Job 21: 15b*) Left unanswered, such questions can lead to doubts in the minds of believers and become a rationale for unbelief on the part of others.

Some teach that whatever Christians request in prayer, they have an absolute guarantee that God will give them anything they ask. When their request is not granted, they feel God has let them down.

> **Jesus' promises have certain conditions.**

Some of Jesus' promises, if taken out of context, do sound like He will grant our every request. But Jesus' promises have certain conditions. They are not absolute unconditional guarantees.

J.I. Packer and Carolyn Nystrom say, it would be "sheer unbelief" to affirm that

Christians have unanswered prayers. They add this qualifier, "But . . . God, our heavenly Father, perfect as he is in wisdom, reserves the right to answer our pleas for help in the best way and at the best time" (55).

Philip Yancey contends, "Unanswered prayer poses an especially serious threat to the faith of trusting children." What are we to think about Yancey's drawer full of letters from Christians writing about their unanswered prayers? (*Prayer*, 216, 219)

Unanswered prayer may not be the best term. It may suggest an unwarranted implication that God is either unable or unwilling to respond to one's prayers. God may well answer in ways that we do not recognize. It may be better to speak of instances where our prayer requests are not granted. We need to study Jesus' promises to answer prayer requests in the light of the fact that sometimes our requests are not granted.

C.S. Lewis said he was not puzzled by the fact that God did not grant all prayer requests but he was puzzled by Jesus' sweeping promises to grant requests (*Reflections*, 148). What specifically did Jesus promise about granting prayer requests, and what did He mean by these promises? These promises should not be taken out of context. Context controls meaning. We need to read each promise in the light of the statements surrounding it. To whom was the promise given? Was it given only to the apostles? What in the context limits or qualifies the meaning? General statements should be understood in the light of specific statements and in agreement with what other relevant Scriptures teach. This chapter will focus on Jesus' promises to grant what is requested.

Context controls meaning.

UNDERSTANDING JESUS' PROMISES TO GRANT PRAYER REQUESTS

In the Sermon on the Mount, Jesus said, *"Ask, and it will be given to you; seek, and you will find; knock, and it will be opened to you. For everyone who asks receives, and the one who seeks finds, and to the one who knocks it will be opened"* (*Mt 7:7-8*, cp. *Lk 11:9-11*).

Jesus emphasizes that as human parents naturally want good for their children, our good and wise heavenly Father wants only to give good things to His children. As we continue to hunger and thirst after righteousness and ask for spiritual help, God will grant our request, including giving us the Holy Spirit (*Lk 11:13*). Jesus did not mean He would grant my every desire and wish, giving me exactly what I ask for. Only a bad father would grant a child's every request. The context deals with believers seeking for their actual basic needs and the good of the kingdom. The good things God gives pertain to seeking first His kingdom and its righteousness (*Mt 6:33*).

> **As we hunger and thirst after righteousness, God will grant our request.**

Darrell Bock states,

> The one who walks with God should be bold and diligent in asking for such [spiritual] benefits. As such, the passage is not simply a blank-check request, but a blank-check request for the necessities of the spiritual life, such as those mentioned in the Lord's Prayer and those related to spiritual well-being. (**1063**)

The "everyone" refers to believing disciples who seriously and persistently pray. "Divine delays do not indicate reluctance on God's part" (**Mounce, 65**). The Luke passage is preceded by the parable of the persistent neighbor. We will receive what will be for our ultimate good.

"Again I say to you, if two of you agree on earth about anything they ask, it will be done for them by my Father in heaven" (*Mt 18:19*). Jesus had just told the apostles, *"Whatever you bind on earth shall be bound in heaven, and whatever you loose on earth shall be loosed in heaven"* (*Mt 18:18*). The apostles would declare the terms of God's plan of salvation. The two or three probably refers to the "eyewitnesses" in *verse 16*. The context is about handling disagreements in the church and how to conduct church discipline. Unity and prayer are essential in acting according to God's will in seeking to bring about reconciliation and restoration of relationships.

Jesus does not give an unqualified guarantee that when any two people today agree on anything, perhaps even a foolish or sinful request, that God must grant it. Prayer is not a way to manipulate or control God. This view overlooks that fact that prayers must be expressed by believers who are submissive and obedient to God's will. This promise assures

> **Prayer is not a way to manipulate or control God.**

us of God's interest and involvement in the united efforts of believers bringing wayward persons back into fellowship with God. Jesus promises that discipline carried out as He teaches will have divine endorsement.

"And whatever you ask in prayer, you will receive, if you have faith" (**Mt 21:22**). *"Therefore I tell you, whatever you ask in prayer, believe that you have received it, and it will be yours"* (**Mk 11:24**). The apostles marveled at Jesus' withering of the fig tree. Jesus says if they have faith they could cast this mountain into the sea. We have no record in the Bible of Jesus or anyone else casting

Faith is a relationship of genuine trust in God.

a physical mountain into the sea. "Moving mountains" was a Jewish metaphor for doing something extremely difficult or seemingly impossible. Jesus explained to the apostles that just as they needed faith to work miracles, that prayer required faith on the part of the pray-er. Faith is not faith in "faith" or merely an affirmation of belief. It is not a momentary, "I believe God can fix everything." It is a relationship of genuine trust in God characterized by living in obedience to God's Word and His will.

David Garland says,

> Prayer is not imposing our will on God but opening up our lives to God's will. True prayer is not an endeavor to get God to change his will but an endeavor to release that will in our own lives. . . . So in prayer we should draw ourselves to God and not try to pull God down to us. . . . We must also guard against treating prayer as if it were a magic wand that allows us to get whatever we want. When Christians pray with confident faith that their prayers will have power, they can, like Jesus, overcome even the greatest opposition. Nothing is impossible. Prayer is not an engine by which we overcome the unwillingness of God. Jesus taught that God is ever ready to grant what is good for us. (**448**)

Jesus made promises in *John 14, 15, 16* to the apostles the night before His death. Some of these promises were limited to the apostles. He said the Holy Spirit would give them supernatural guidance in fulfilling their special mission. The apostles filled an unrepeatable role as Jesus' representatives in establishing His church.

Certainly not all promises Jesus gave to the disciples can be claimed by Christians today. Jesus told the apostles that the Holy

Spirit *"will teach you all things and bring to your remembrance all that I have said to you"* (*Jn 14:26*). Today we cannot "remember" what Jesus said because He has not physically spoken to us (at least, not to me). Just because God promised Abraham and Sarah a child in their old age, does not mean senior citizens today should (or would want to) claim that promise for themselves.

Even though Jesus was speaking to the apostles, in some cases, the context makes it clear that the promise has a broader application to believers in general. Whether these promises about prayer apply primarily to the apostles or to us as Christians in general, such prayers are subject to the qualifications Jesus mentioned. Rather than reading these promises as unqualified, attention must be given to the conditions listed. A general promise should not be interpreted as a universal guarantee when additional teaching gives qualifications or limitations.

We see this principle of interpretation in Jesus' teaching about divorce. Jesus' statement, *"Whoever divorces his wife and marries another*

> **Attention must be given to the conditions listed.**

commits adultery against her" (*Mk 10:11*), must be understood in the light of the exception Jesus gave, *"Whoever divorces his wife, except for sexual immorality, and marries another, commits adultery"* (*Mt 19:9*). Jesus' promises about answers to prayer must be understood in the light of qualifications stated with the promises or given elsewhere.

"Whatever you ask in my name, this I will do, that the Father may be glorified in the Son. If you ask me anything in my name, I will do it" (*Jn 14:13-14*). In **verse 12** Jesus says that *"whoever believes in me"* will do greater works than He did. Jesus tells the apostles He is going to the Father, which occurred through His death, resurrection, and ascension. His going to the Father is the reason He will do greater works through them. While physically here on earth, Jesus did marvelous miracles and deeds. After His glorification in the new covenant age His work will continue as He will perform greater works through His disciples' taking His saving message and mission throughout the world. Bringing another person to salvation in Christ is a greater work in eternal benefits than physical healings.

Leon Morris explains,

> Whatever the disciples ask in His name Christ will do. This does not mean simply using the name as a formula. It means

that prayer is to be in accordance with all that the name stands for. It is prayer proceeding from faith in Christ, prayer that gives expression to a unity with all that Christ stands for, prayer which seeks to set forward Christ Himself. And the purpose of it all is the glory of God. (*John,* **646**)

"If you abide in me, and my words abide in you, ask whatever you wish, and it will be done for you" (*Jn 15:7*). Abiding in Christ means surrender to Christ's spirit and will and living in obedience to His words and with all that Christ stands for. When we positively abide in Christ, His teaching energizes our spirit and controls our life. Christ shapes our thinking and character. Our obedience to Christ expresses our love for Him, resulting in spiritual vitality Far from assuring us that our every wish will be granted, being totally committed to Christ means we will desire that His will be done in our lives. Our prayers will be in agreement with God's will because we share the mind of Christ. Much fruit will be borne in our character, in our relationship with other believers, and in our outreach to those outside of Christ. Prayers in harmony with His Word and His mission will be answered and will glorify God.

> ## Christ's teaching energizes our spirit and controls our life.

"You did not choose me, but I chose you and appointed you that you should go and bear fruit and that your fruit should abide, so that whatever you ask the Father in my name, he may give it to you" (*Jn 15:16*). Jesus chose the apostles to be His representatives to lead in His evangelistic mission. The fruit of this work would be new converts for Christ. God would respond to their prayers in the accomplishment of this mission.

"Truly, truly, I say to you, whatever you ask of the Father in my name, he will give it to you. Until now you have asked nothing in my name. Ask, and you will receive, that your joy may be full" (*Jn 16:23-24*). Jesus' teaching in *John 14–16* shows that one remaining in His words, in His love, in His will, and in Him will bear fruit, find joy, and receive answers to their prayers. After Jesus finishes His work on earth, His disciples would have access to Him through prayer and would make their requests in Jesus' name. God would grant what they needed in their mission when they asked in Jesus' name. After His exaltation the disciples could no

longer ask Him direct questions for information, but they could pray in His name. They were to bear fruit through their evangelism.

Written to Christians obviously not limited to the apostles, John states, *"Beloved, if our heart does not condemn us, we have confidence before God; and whatever we ask we receive from him, because we keep his commandments and do what pleases him"* (**1Jn 3:21-22**) John makes it clear that our requests must be in accord with God's will. *"This is the confidence that we have toward him, that if we ask anything according to his will he hears us. And if we know that he hears us in whatever we ask, we know that we have the requests that we have asked of him"* (**1Jn 5:14-15**). God answers our requests according to His will. As we grow in Christ's likeness by keeping His commandments, our wills will become more aligned with His will.

> **God answers requests according to His will; as we grow, our wills are more aligned with His.**

J.W. Roberts states,

> In this context John is thinking particularly about our obedience to the new commandment of love and what it means ethically in our lives. But this answer to prayer is not that God responds to us because we have an inner conscience which is right or pure. He does so because such a conscience is proof that **we keep his commandments and do what pleases him.** The pure conscience and righteousness are the two sides of the coin. (**98**)

Scripture teaches that God hears the prayers of the righteous (***Prov 15:29; Ps 66:18f.; Job 27:8f.; Isa 1:11-15***). John Stott explains, "Obedience is the indispensable condition, not the meritorious cause, of answered prayer" (***John*, 152**). Obedience is the objective evidence that our wills are in harmony with God's will. Because of our communion with Christ we can pray with a confident boldness knowing our Father hears and will answer according to His will.

Stott says, "Prayer is not a convenient device for imposing our will upon God, or for bending his will to ours, but the prescribed way of subordinating our will to his. It is by prayer that we seek God's will, embrace it and align ourselves with it. Every true prayer is a variation on the theme 'your will be done'" (**ibid., 188**).

WHY SOME REQUESTS
ARE NOT GRANTED

Other passages explain why some prayer requests are not granted. James says, *"You do not have, because you do not ask. You ask and do not receive because you ask wrongly, to spend it on your passions"* (*Jas 4:2-3*). God withholds some gifts because we do not desire them enough to ask for them. Some requests are denied because the request is motivated by frivolous, selfish, or worldly desires.

Scripture teaches that our sin can thwart our prayer requests. *"If I had cherished iniquity in my heart, the Lord would not have listened"* (*Ps 66:18*). *"Even though you make many prayers, I will not listen; your hands are full of blood"* (*Isa 1:15*). *"Your iniqui-ties have made a separation between you and your God, and your sins have hidden his face from you so that he does not hear"* (*Isa 59:2*). *"Whoever closes his ear to the cry of the poor will himself call out and not be answered"* (*Prov 21:13*). Husbands are to honor and live considerately with their wives *"so that your prayers may not be hindered"* (*1Pet 3:7*).

Sin can thwart prayer requests.

When we seek to understand any statement, common sense and logic can be of assistance. Some prayers contradict each other— prayers for victory offered by players on opposite teams in a football game, two guys each praying that a certain girl will give her heart to him, four applicants for the same job all praying they will be chosen. God cannot grant all of these requests.

Did God intend to heal everyone who asks for healing and pre-vent every death in response to every prayer? If this were true, the earth could not contain all the persons. How long would we live? In Scripture, God does not promise to heal every illness and prevent every death and stop every suffering.

God certainly can and does heal supernaturally today. We have documented cases of miraculous healings. But He does not grant every request for healing. For Timothy's ailments Paul suggests medicinal wine (*1Tm 5:23*). Paul left Trophimus ill at Miletus (*2Tm 4:20*). While visiting Paul, Epaphroditus became so sick he almost died (*Php 2:25-27*). Paul's thorn in the flesh was not healed although Paul requested it in prayer. Rather God said, *"My grace is sufficient for you"* (*2Cor 12:10*). God did not grant what Paul requested, but he accepted what God gave. In a sense God had answered his prayer, but not in the way he had asked.

Augustine's mother prayed that he would not go to Rome because she feared he would go into a more ungodly lifestyle. He went to Rome in spite of her tears and prayers to the contrary. Later he gave his life to Christ. Augustine said to God, "Hearing afar the real core of her longing, You disregarded the prayer of the moment, in order to make me what she always prayed that I should be" (**V, viii, 15**).

Shadrach, Meshach, and Abednego, upon threat of being thrown in the fiery furnace, refused to worship the pagan gods. They told the king, *"Our God whom we serve is able to deliver us from the burning fiery furnace, and he will deliver us out of your hand, O king. But if not, be it known to you, O king, that we will not serve your gods or worship the golden image that you have set up"* (**Dan 3:17-18**). Even when our request is not granted, we will serve the Lord.

The "health and wealth" preachers misrepresent God. They say that, if you have faith, God will always heal and He will always make you prosperous. They create false expectations and leave many spiritually depressed. Scripture does not teach that God wills every believer to be healthy and wealthy all the time. Regardless of whether we are sick or well, poor or rich, God wills that we find salvation in Christ and grow in spiritual maturity. Our relationship with God is far more important than our physical circumstances.

> **Our relationship with God is far more important than our physical circumstances.**

If God granted every prayer request of ours exactly as we asked, it often would be the worst thing possible for us. Gerald Sittser lost three family members in a car accident and struggled with the fact his request for safety was not granted. Later he wrote, "We need unanswered prayer. It is God's gift to us because it protects us from ourselves. If all our prayers were answered, we would only abuse the power" (**Answer, 82**). We depend upon God to answer our requests according to His wisdom. As our loving heavenly Father, He gives what is best, often overlooking any folly or ignorance in our prayers.

In a short story entitled "Prayer," Tolstoy says, "God could satisfy all our prayers, but he knows that it wouldn't be good for [us]" (**42**). A Garth Brooks song speaks of seeing an old high school sweetheart

> **"Unanswered prayer" is God's gift to protect us from ourselves.**

later in life. He saw what kind of a person she really was and thanked God for not answering his youthful prayer that she would be his (Unanswered Prayer). We don't know the future and can't foresee the long-range effect of our requests. Frequently when we look back at our requests, we can thank God for His wisdom in overruling our foolishness.

REQUESTS NOT GRANTED THAT APPEAR TO BE IN GOD'S WILL

What about the cases where it is hard to see that the request would not be in God's will—healing from a horrible illness or stopping an instance of child abuse? We may never know why God did not prevent the accident that killed our loved one or why God did not heal a friend's terminal illness, even though fervent prayers were offered. Why didn't God heal the mother's leukemia when she had two children with cystic fibrosis and a younger son who needed total care because one part of his brain did not communicate with the other side?

We can't speak for God. He did not answer Job's exact requests. Requests for things that would be obviously good may not be granted. We do not know why God does not supernaturally intervene. In these cases we must trust in the wisdom and love of our heavenly Father.

Some persons may have a greater testimony to God's power through exhibiting grace and joy in their weakness and suffering than if they would have received miraculous physical healing. God grants them grace for each day but not physical healing. Paul told the Philippians that God would be glorified either through his release from prison or through his death for Christ (*Php 1:19-26*).

When I was dealing with my terminal lung disease, my friend since college, John Ransom, was one of the many who prayed for me. For a while, it looked as if I might die of the disease before I could get a transplant. At that time John was in good health. In the summer of 2005, John was diagnosed with inoperable pancreatic cancer. Soon after I learned of this, I visited my friend. We talked about the fact that I was the one who was facing the prospect of my death a few months before and he was praying for me. Now the tables were turned. He was facing his death and I was praying for his healing. I received new lungs and am doing well. He died of his disease in February, 2006.

Is this a clear instance of answered and unanswered prayer? In one case, healing was not granted. I believe God did answer prayers in *both* cases. God demonstrated His glory in both cases. In my case I was able to teach in Bible college two more years and continue my writing ministry. My recovered health has brought joy and inspiration to hundreds because they prayed faithfully for my health.

John and his wife have been towers of strength in their local congregation through some difficult times. John was greatly respected in both his local church and community. The way he prepared for and faced his death was an outstanding testimony to me and to a multitude of others. Even though it was not easy for his family, God was certainly glorified through John's sufferings and in the way he died.

C.S. Lewis said that the essence of a request "is that it may or may not be granted. And if an infinitely wise Being listens to the requests of finite and foolish creatures, of course He will sometimes grant and sometimes refuse them" (**Night, 4**).

Packer says, "Since our heavenly Father, who is wise as he is loving, answers his children's prayers in the best way, what he does or fails to do in our immediate situation may look and feel as if he is saying a flat no to us" (**Packer and Nystrom, 56**). When God does not grant a request that we feel is absolutely the best option, we must remember He is God and we do not have His eternal perspective and wisdom. When our prayers are foolish and selfish, God responds in ways to teach us patience, humility, and perseverance.

We oversimplify prayer when we view it as simply asking and receiving. Prayer is not merely request but is communication made possible because of our relationship with God. Prayer is talking with God, seeking to

> **When God does not grant a request, remember that we do not have His perspective and wisdom.**

know Him better and come into a fuller fellowship with Him. Every prayer must be offered seeking what is best from God's loving, all-knowing point of view.

TRUSTING GOD EVEN WHEN
WE DO NOT UNDERSTAND

This issue comes down to trusting God even when we don't understand. For reasons we do not understand, sometimes God heals a person in response to prayer. For reasons we do not understand, sometimes God chooses not to intervene. It may be impossible for a parent to fully explain to a child why a request is granted or not granted. Even when we do not understand, we can trust God to do what is best for His children in the big picture. This may not be clear to us with our limited view in the here and now.

> **When our Lord prayed to be spared the suffering of the cross, God did not grant this request.**

Jesus' experience in the Garden of Gethsemane may be the best commentary on the issue of ungranted prayer requests. Our Lord prayed to be spared the anticipated suffering. God in His wisdom did not grant this request, but did what was best. When our prayer requests are not granted, we need the same attitude as Christ's—*"Nevertheless, not as I will, but as you will"* (**Mt 26:39**).

We must be persistent in presenting our prayer requests to God. Much is accomplished on earth because of the prevailing prayers of godly believers. Don't quit praying because a particular request is not granted. Pray earnestly, passionately, persistently, seeking above all that God will be glorified and His will be done on earth as in heaven. We will grow in our fellowship and relationship with the Lord when His will is the supreme desire and request of our hearts.

Think about It

1. Do you believe Christians have unanswered prayers? Is that the best term?

2. What does it mean that Jesus' promises to grant our requests should be understood in their context?

3. In commenting on *Matthew 7:7-8* Bock says, "The passage is not simply a blank-check request, but a blank-check request for the necessities of the spiritual life." Explain.

4. What is the context of the promise *"If two of you agree on earth about anything they ask, it will be done for them"* (*Mt 18:19*)?

5. If prayer is not "a magic wand that allows us to get whatever we want" and is not "an engine by which we overcome the unwillingness of God," what is prayer?

6. What does it mean to pray "in Jesus' name"?

7. What three qualifications are found in *1 John 3:21-22* and *1 John 5:14-15* which modify the "whatever we ask we receive"?

8. Give biblical examples where healing was not granted.

9. How would it not be good for us if God granted our every request exactly as we asked?

10. Why is it not a cop-out to say we must trust God even when we do not understand?

CHAPTER TWELVE

HOW ARE CHRISTIANS TO HANDLE TRIALS?

(James 1:2-4,12)

Count it all joy, my brothers, when you meet trials of various kinds, for you know that the testing of your faith produces steadfastness.

James 1:2-3

A friend of mine, Darold, was the chairman of the board in a Christian church. He was very busy in his professional life. So Saturday night he was preparing his Sunday school lesson at the kitchen table. He received a phone call from a woman in the church upset over something the preacher had done. He tried to help her understand but to no avail. So after twenty minutes they hung up.

In a few minutes another lady in the church called and raked him over the coals about something the preacher had done. This went on for another twenty minutes or so. He tried to explain things to her but made no progress. By this time he was a little disgusted.

The same night another woman in the church called him and bawled him out for something the preacher was not doing right. He again tried to explain, but as before he made no progress. After more than twenty minutes again, they hung up. This time he was completely disgusted.

He threw up his hands and said, "I volunteer my time. It's not worth it!" Right away he knew he was wrong. He always told his Sunday school class that they should look to the Bible for answers to their questions and problems. Desperate for help he started reading in the Bible. He read several passages, nothing seemed to address his problem. But then he started reading in James. He read **James 1:2-4** in *The Living Bible*, *"Dear brothers, Is your life full of difficulties and temptations? Then be happy, for when the way is rough, your patience has a chance to grow. So let it grow and don't try to squirm out of your problems. For when your patience is finally in full bloom, then you will be ready for anything, strong in character, full and complete."* When he read that, he laughed out loud. His wife called in from the other room and asked "What's going on?"

My friend said that became his favorite passage. He also said being able to find joy in the middle of troubles is one of the most valuable lessons he has ever learned.

The genuineness of our faith will be tested by trials, but it is for our own good. We can grow to maturity through the experience of suffering. James teaches us that believers who handle trials with joy and faithful endurance will receive God's blessing (**Jas 1:2-4,12**).

THE COMMAND: REJOICE IN TRIALS

"Count it all joy, my brothers, when you meet trials of various kinds" (**Jas 1:2**).

James, with pastoral concern for his readers, addresses his fellow Christians who had suffered for their faith. Kent says, "James wastes no time in coming to an unpleasant subject and ordering a most difficult response" (36). To rejoice in trials seems as impossible as flying without wings.

> **To rejoice in trials seems as impossible as flying without wings.**

Jesus also says we are to rejoice in trials,

> Blessed are those who are persecuted for righteousness sake, for theirs is the kingdom of heaven. Blessed are you when others revile you and persecute you and utter all kinds of evil against you falsely on my account. Rejoice and be glad, for your reward is great in heaven, for so they persecuted the prophets who were before you. (**Mt 5:10-12**)

Paul and Peter agree, *"We rejoice in our sufferings, knowing that suffering produces endurance, and endurance produces character, and character produces hope"* (**Rom 5:2-4**). *"In this you rejoice, though now for a little while, as was necessary, you have been grieved by various trials"* (**1Pet 1:6**).

We observe this in the apostles, *"They left the presence of the council, rejoicing that they were counted worthy to suffer dishonor for the name"* (**Acts 5:41**). Paul exhibited the same attitude: *"Now I rejoice in my sufferings for your sake, and in my flesh I am filling up what is lacking in Christ's afflictions for the sake of his body, that is, the church"* (**Col 1:24**).

"Count it all joy" is a command requiring a definitive decision to adopt a joyful attitude. "What is remarkable about his command is that it applies to a situation in which a joyful reaction would be most unnatural: *when you meet various trials"* (**Kent, 36**). Most people are joyful when they avoid trials instead of rejoicing in the middle of trials.

> **We must decide to have a certain mental attitude toward trials.**

We need to make a definite decision in our minds and wills to have a certain mental attitude toward trials. *"Consider it pure joy"* (NIV). Literally, "all joy," meaning complete, wholehearted, genuine joy. We need to choose to have a consistent and pervasive attitude and outlook toward trials.

While "trials" can mean temptations to sin (**1Tm 6:9**) or external trials (**1Pet 4:12**), the context makes it clear that in **James 1:2** it means trials. Believers risk "falling into" these trials, which have the purpose of testing to produce endurance. Moo states, "With the qualification *various*, we should probably think both of the difficulties that are common to all people as well as the specific adversities that Christians must face as a result of their faith. . . . Whatever they be, trials are to be considered by the believer as an occasion for rejoicing" (**James, 59-60**).

Trials are the outward pressures, troubles, and circumstances of all kinds and varieties, such as sickness, loneliness, bereavement, financial reverses, social discrimination, that confront a person in everyday life.

> The trials to which James refers are the testing and refining situations in life, hard situations in which faith is sorely tried, such as persecution, a difficult moral choice, or a tragic experience. James does not gloss over the reality of the suffering involved—the tears, the pain, the sweat. Instead he points to a transformed perspective of those trials. If one looks at the difficult situation not merely from the perspective of the immediate problem but also from the perspective of the end

result God is producing, one can have a deep joy. This is not a surface happiness, but an anticipation of future reward in the end-times (eschatological joy). It is not only possible, but necessary (thus James commands it), for without it one may become so bogged down in present problems as to abandon the faith and give up the struggle altogether. Only with God's perspective, thus considering oneself already fortunate in anticipation of God's future reward, can the faith be maintained against the pressures of life. (**Davids, James, 26**)

Trials are sure to come; James says "whenever" not "if." They are unavoidable and can come at anytime. Not only minor irritations but major difficult experiences, including adversities of persecution. James does not have one kind of trial in mind, but all kinds of trials. One should grow strong through testing. We need to approach trials with the perspective of ultimate victory in Christ.

We Christians can expect to face sorrows, suffering, disappointments which will challenge our faith. "There will be the tests of the dangers, the sacrifices, the unpopularity which the Christian way must so often involve. But they are not meant to make us fall; they are meant to make us soar. They are not meant to make us weaker; they are meant to make us stronger. Therefore we should not bemoan them; we should rejoice in them" (**Barclay, James, 43**). Good athletes undergo strict hardship and training. It brings them joy when they are able to compete with excellence. I can't say that doing my exercise program at pulmonary rehab is fun. But I can say that each session I finish, I am glad for having exercised because of improved health.

> **Trials are not meant to make us fall, but to soar.**

Suppose your house burns down or your child dies or your spouse is diagnosed with terminal cancer. Should you as a Christian shout, "Praise the Lord!"? There is a proper response of sadness and grief, but supporting the grieving process is a deep joy in Christ. Through it all we must not give in to the natural response of grumbling, complaining, and bitterness. We must not become cynical and hopeless. Many try to escape their problems in alcohol, drugs, pleasure, work, and even suicide.

Our response to trials can determine whether God's overall purpose and plan will be derailed or fulfilled in our lives. James does not answer the question "Why do good people suffer?" He does make clear that even undeserved suffering as well as other trials are under the control of a God who wants the best for His people.

> ## We must not become cynical and hopeless.

James expects "a deliberate intelligent appraisal, not an emotional reaction. A Christian can look at the experience from God's perspective and recognize the trial not as a happy experience in itself but as the means of producing something most valuable. . . . The trial itself is not called a joy, but the encounter is" (**Kent, 36**).

Epp says, "To have joy does not necessarily mean we will be hilarious and laughing about the trials we are experiencing, but it means we will have a deep-seated confidence that God knows what He is doing and that the results will be for His glory and our good" (**Hiebert, *James*, 64**).[1]

> It is occasionally asserted that James asks his readers to *enjoy* their trials, but James did not say that. He was too realistic to make such a demand. He well knew that when such experiences strike, they are not joyous but grievous (***Heb. 12:11***). He did not say that they must *feel* it all joy or that trials *are* all joy. James was not inculcating a stoic resignation, which when engulfed by trials wears a forced smile and seeks to ignore the pain. Rather, James calls for a positive Christian attitude toward trials that he views as opportunities, under God's grace, for growth and development in the Christian life. Christian faith must apprehend that beneficial results are to be derived from such experiences and so accept them as occasions for rejoicing. (**ibid.**)

Trials are not to be courted or sought out or initiated. The joy is not detachment or indifference. James does not "suggest that Christians facing trials will have no response other than joy, as if we were commanded never to be saddened by difficulties. His point, rather, is that trials should be an occasion for genuine rejoicing" (**Moo, *Letter*, 53**). He explains why this is so in *verses 3-4*.

---

[1] Epp is quoted in Hiebert.

THE REASON: BECAUSE
THE TESTING OF TRIALS
PRODUCES ENDURANCE

"For you know that the testing of your faith produces steadfastness" (*Jas 1:3*).

James gives a reason for rejoicing when facing trials. We can have joy because we know that the testing of trials will produce endurance.

I have taught forty years in Bible college. I have had thousands of persons in my classes. But I could never tell if they were good students until after I had given them a few tests. It would save a lot of time and effort to eliminate testing, but it would not develop the students' abilities and potential, and it would not recognize their accomplishments.

Why can't we accept this surprising and unusual command to rejoice in trials? Trials can produce in us a deeper, stronger faith. These trials are a means of testing through which God strengthens our faith and produces endurance. "The difficulties of life are intended by God to refine our faith: heating it in the crucible of suffering so that impurities might be refined away and so that it might become pure and valuable before the Lord. The 'testing of faith' is not intended to determine whether a person has faith or not; it is intended to purify faith that already exists" (**ibid., 54-55**). James expects Christians to pass the test.

The reason for the trials is to produce "endurance" (NASB), "steadfastness" (ESV), "patient endurance" (RSV), "perseverance" (NIV).

> The picture is of a person successfully carrying a heavy load for a long time. The NT repeatedly emphasizes the need for Christians to cultivate this quality of perseverance or steadfastness when facing difficulty (see, e.g., *Luke 8:15; 2 Thess. 1:4; Rev. 2:2; 13:10*). But James suggests that trials can also produce this quality of endurance. Like a muscle that becomes strong when it faces resistance, so Christians learn to remain faithful to God over the long haul only when they face difficulty. (**ibid., 55**)

God wants us to remain firm and faithful to our commitment. This endurance is not gained apart from facing trials.

Someone, in a folksy way, has said, "There is know-ability, do-ability, and stick-ability, and the greatest of these is stick." Endurance is not a passive acceptance of whatever will be, will be. It is not resignation and/or stoicism. It is a strong decision of the will to be faithful to God regardless of what may come. "A person possessing such a virtue could be trusted to hold out, whatever the circumstances" (**Davids, James, 27**).

This steadfast endurance becomes stronger as it comes through testing. We see this steadfastness in Abraham as he passed the test concerning sacrificing Isaac. We see it in Job as he held on to his faith and commitment to God regardless of circumstances (*Jas 5:11*). Paul uses this word 16 times (e.g. *2Cor 6:4; 12:12; 1Th 1:3*). Revelation mentions it frequently (*1:9; 2:2; 13:10; 14:12*). It describes a battle-tested warrior or tempered metal.

"The believer experiences a testing in the sense of refining process. That is, his faith is being refined, much the same as gold is subjected to the smelter's fire (*Prov. 27:21*). As the goldsmith removes impurities that are foreign to the metal, so God purifies the believer's faith from sin" (**Kistemaker, 33**). The heat of the fire does not weaken the metal but rather makes it stronger.

> **Character development is a slow and painful process.**

Character is built through many decisions and actions. Character development is a slow and painful process of gaining strength through facing and enduring many trials (*Rom 5:2-4; 1Pet 1:6-7*).

James says that his readers know that this is the case. They have been taught to see God's hand in human history. They know this is a fallen world. They know they have been saved from sin but are still in a world of sin and difficulties. Motyer notes, "James comes to us as one facing, not concealing the facts. . . . his appeal is not for the adoption of a superficial gaiety but for a candid assessment of certain truth" (**Hiebert, 64**).

Believers have "the knowledge that enables them to evaluate their trials as occasions for rejoicing. The present tense participle indicates that his readers were not ignorant of the truth being set forth but had to continue to realize it in personal experience. The verb used (*ginosko*) suggests a 'knowledge grounded in personal experience.' As they adopt the attitude called for amid their trials, they will come to personal realization 'that the testing of your faith develops perseverance'" (**ibid., 64-65**).

"James assumes that faith is already present. The difficulties and problems we face in life, test our faith at the very core of who we are as spiritual beings. These trials strengthen our faith" (**ibid., 65**). He speaks of the personal acceptance and confidence in the gospel.

"The believer trusts in God for help, aid, strength, and comfort. He knows that God always responds to those with faith and provides the means to sustain the period of testing. The believer who possesses the virtue of steadfastness clings to God in faith, persists in doing God's will, and cannot be averted from his avowed purpose to serve his God" (**Kistemaker, 33-34**).

One of the things that amazed the pagans as they killed the early Christians was that they died singing. One Christian martyr was smiling as flames enveloped him. He was asked what he had to smile about. He responded, "I saw the glory of God and was glad." Those who keep their faith and integrity through trials are given strength to face even greater trials.

> **The pagans were amazed that the Christians died singing.**

Endurance is an essential attribute even though the means of achieving it is unpopular. God works in our lives by perfecting our character through suffering.

THE OUTCOME: THE DEVELOPMENT OF SPIRITUAL MATURITY

"And let steadfastness have its full effect, that you may be perfect and complete, lacking in nothing" (**Jas 1:4**).

Endurance or perseverance is not the final goal. It is the result of testing and leads to something even more important. Endurance must be allowed to complete its work. The ultimate goal of testing is the production of mature Christians. "The benefits of testing come only to believers who respond to them in the right way. Christians must *allow* endurance to do its intended work" (**Moo, Letter, 55**). The word "effect," ("result" [NASB], "work" [NIV]) summarizes the many dimensions of the ideal Christian character. The development of perseverance takes time. Be faithful through your trials so God can complete the work He began in you.

Davids says,

> **Perseverance**, however, is not a passive, teeth-gritting virtue, but a development in which the character is firmed up and

shaped around the central commitment to Christ. It does not happen overnight, for it is a process. The process needs to **finish its work**, or "have its complete effect," for it is the shaping of the whole person that is at issue. One must be careful not to short-circuit it: to pull the metal out of the fire too soon, to abort the developing child, to resist the schooling—to use three metaphors often used to describe the process. (*James, 27*)

It is not that one part of the personality is developed. "The goal is far more global. The person is formed, not just partly or simply morally, but totally, as a whole being, and is thus to be **mature and complete, not lacking anything**" (ibid., 28).[2]

"Perfect and complete" describes the state of one who faithfully endures trials. Spiritual wholeness requires a wholehearted, unreserved commitment to God and his will. This goal will be realized in salvation in the final end-times, but we continually strive to grow toward *"the measure of the stature of the fullness of Christ"* (**Eph 4:13**).

One who is not steadfast and does not endure trials lacks spiritual maturity. In this life we will not attain sinless perfection; but that should be our ultimate goal. "We should not 'lower the bar' on the expectation James sets for us. Nothing less than complete moral integrity will ultimately satisfy the God who is himself holy and righteous, completely set apart from sin" (**Moo, Letter, 56**).

Christian discipleship demands a commitment to total obedience to God in every part of our being and behavior. Character disciplined through trials prepares us to be the man or woman God intends us to be. Our response to every experience in life either contributes to or detracts from our spiritual growth. Our goal should be to honor Christ by our beliefs, character, and behavior.

> **Character disciplined through trials prepares us to be the man or woman God intends us to be.**

The word "complete" describes something whole, having all its parts, undamaged. "It adds to the thought that just as a person may be full grown but minus a leg or lame in some way, so a believer may be spiritually mature in other respects but not really complete if he

---

[2] Emphasis is in the original.

has no steadfastness in adversity" (**Kent, 38**). When we face trials, we often trust and depend more on God, thus we often grow in areas where we have been weak. Jesus was made perfect through suffering (**Heb 2:10**). He learned obedience through the things he suffered (**Heb 5:8**). "Complete" is the positive side and "lacking nothing" is the negative side. In Christ we have everything that really matters—deficient in nothing.

The testing of the trials of life, when faced with a confident joy and endurance, can promote growth of the whole spiritual person, producing a character that lacks no godly virtue. Paul calls this *"Christ is formed in you"* (**Gal 4:19**). Even when facing physical sickness, or financial or social setbacks or any other difficulty, it is spiritual wholeness and integrity that is of the supreme importance.

Adversity does not automatically produce maturity, we have to permit it to happen. Davids warns, "It is possible to short-circuit the process and thus not to develop properly and to live through the suffering in vain" (**James, 28**). God has equipped believers with all the spiritual resources necessary for us to endure whatever trials we face. Trusting God we can endure.

> **Adversity will not produce maturity unless we permit it to happen.**

Jesus says,

> "When a woman is giving birth, she has sorrow because her hour has come, but when she has delivered the baby, she no longer remembers the anguish, for joy that a human being has been born into the world. So also you have sorrow now, but I will see you again and your hearts will rejoice, and no one will take your joy from you" (**Jn 16:21-22**).

A proper perspective of seeing the big picture, of setting our sights on our eternal reward is essential if we can face trials with joy.

James tells us that if we handle trials in the right way, it will give endurance which will produce godly maturity and lead to our eternal reward. As hard as it may seem to rejoice in trials, James says it will help us. He suggests that if we lack wisdom, for example, about our trials, we should ask of God in faith. He will grant us generous help (**Jas 1:5**). This is just one area where we need wisdom, but we certainly need God's wisdom in order to handle trials with joy and perseverance. This wisdom comes through the Word of God and through Christ and the Holy Spirit living within us.

THE REWARD: RECEIVING
THE CROWN OF LIFE

"Blessed is the man who remains steadfast under trial, for when he has stood the test he will receive the crown of life, which God has promised to those who love him" (**Jas 1:12**).

Peter reaffirms, *"But if you should suffer for righteousness' sake, you will be blessed"* (**1Pet 3:14**). James says the one who endures under trials is truly blessed, really well off from God's point of view. It is not the one who is tested that is blessed but the one who endures testing.

> In **James 1:2-4** James has said that testing produces endurance; now he states that enduring creates true blessedness. Yet James is neither a masochist nor a stoic, neither claims that trials are fun nor that one should enjoy pain. Rather, he points out that the trials serve a purpose, the experiential proof of the reality of faith, and that should give one the perspective for deep joy. (**Davids, James, 34**)

When one stays faithful through trials, rewards will come. God welcomes the good and faithful servant. He promises a crown of life to those believers who love Him and faithfully finish the race.

In **James 1:2-4** James encourages believers to rejoice in trials with joy because such testing of their faith would produce perseverance. In **James 1:12**, he promises a reward for those who successfully endure trials by remaining firm in the midst of the testing. "Blessed" should not be translated happy. "A person who is 'blessed' may not be 'happy' at all. For our emotional state may and will vary with the circumstances of life. But we can be assured that, whatever those circumstances, if we endure them with faith and commitment to God, we will be the recipients of God's favor" (**Moo, Letter, 70**).

"Trial" refers to "any difficulty in life that may threaten our faithfulness to Christ: physical illness, financial reversal, the death of a loved one. James's wording suggests that he is not thinking of any particular trial, but of the nature or essence of 'trial'" (**ibid.**). Perseverance produces Christian character (**Jas 1:4**) and brings God's blessing (**Jas 1:12**).

The focus here is on the final blessing. "Crown" likely refers to a wreath of leaves worn by the victor in athletic contests. Athletes com-

A trial is any difficulty in life that threatens our faithfulness to Christ.

Chapter 12 — How Are Christians to Handle Trials?

205

pete to win a crown (*1Cor 9:25*). To those facing tribulation Jesus says, *"Be faithful unto death, and I will give you the crown of life"* (*Rev 2:10*). The reward is promised at the end of the age. *"And when the chief Shepherd appears, you will receive the unfading crown of glory"* (*1Pet 5:4*). The crown is our salvation. Those who endure in the race of life will receive eternal reward.

At the end of his life after enduring many trials, Paul affirms, *"I have fought the good fight, I have finished the race, I have kept the faith. Henceforth there is laid up for me the crown of righteousness, which the Lord, the righteous judge, will award to me on that Day, and not only to me but also to all who have loved his appearing"* (*2Tm 4:7-8*).

James's overall purpose is "to encourage believers to endure trials faithfully so that we might receive the reward that God has promised." Some Christians have trouble with serving Christ for rewards. "But the contemplation of heaven's rewards is found throughout the NT as a spur to our faithfulness in difficult circumstances here on earth. Keeping our eyes on the prize can help motivate us to maintain spiritual integrity when faced with the temptations and sufferings of earthly life. Moreover, as Mitton aptly observes, 'the rewards are of a kind that only a true Christian would be able to appreciate'" (**ibid., 70-71**).

"Looking to Jesus, the founder and perfecter of our faith, who for the joy that was set before him endured the cross, despising the shame, and is seated at the right hand of the throne of God" (*Heb 12:2*).

Think about It

1. What is your initial reaction to the command to rejoice in trials?

2. Describe the kind of joy we are to have when we experience trials?

3. What kind of trials is James talking about?

4. What should be the mind-set of a Christian approaching trials?

5. What reason does James give for the testing of trials?

6. Describe what James means by "steadfastness."

7. What does endurance produce?

8. What is the reward awaiting those who remain steadfast?

CHAPTER THIRTEEN

THE POWER AND PRESENCE OF GOD IN OUR LIVES

(Ephesians 3:14-21)

And behold, I am with you always, to the end of the age.
Matthew 28:20

Intense suffering leaves one helpless and weak. Medical science can only do so much for an illness. Often we are at the end of our available options. Tragic loss and the ensuing loneliness of grief can drain one of energy for life leaving one lonely and alienated. Assurance of the power and presence of God in our lives enables us to cope with and endure suffering.

Alfred was bright, fluent in five languages, and a chemist. He was known as "the mad scientist." In 1864, one of his chemical experiments exploded, killing his younger brother and four others. Alfred survived. Even though his government forbade him to rebuild his factory, he carried on his experiments with nitroglycerin on an old barge. He learned that the dangerous liquid could be stabilized by absorption into dry material. He patented his explosive invention in 1867. This invention made moving dirt and rock easy.

He called this explosive material by a word that suggested power, usefulness, and danger.

He chose a Greek word, *dynamis*, and called his invention dynamite. Alfred Nobel's name is well-known because he established and funded the Nobel Prize.

Kenny Boles states, "*Dynamis* power is not something to trifle with. The Greek

I. We Can Be Strengthened by the Spirit in Our Inner Being

II. Christ Can Dwell in Our Hearts through Faith

III. We Can Be Rooted and Grounded in Love

IV. We Can Have the Power to Understand Life and the World from God's Perspective

V. We Can Know the Love of Christ Which Passes Knowledge

VI. We Can Be Filled with the Fullness of God

version of the O.T. says that God dried up the Red Sea 'so that all the nations of the earth might know that the *dynamis* of the Lord is mighty, and that you might reverence the Lord your God forever' (*Josh 4:24*). The N.T. uses *dynamis* 118 times, especially in reference to the miracles of Jesus as an exhibition of divine power" (**Word Studies**).

In *Ephesians 3*, Paul prayed that we might know God's incomparably great *dynamis* which is at work in us who believe. This "dynamite" of God is available to work within us and is able to do immeasurably more than all we ask or imagine (*Eph 1:19; 3:21*).

Do you sense the power and presence of God in your life? When God comes into a life, He expects to do an extreme makeover, a total change and transformation. Are your attitudes, values, words, and actions any different from those of your non-Christian neighbors, coworkers, and class members? Do those who know and observe you see the power and presence of God in your life? Your coworkers, neighbors, classmates, family—what do they see in you?

In the midst of suffering, either as the sufferer or the caregiver, it is hard to feel powerful. In fact, observing or participating in suffering leaves one feeling helpless. The power promised to the Christian is an inner spiritual strength. Tragedy and suffering can wear one down. It can sap our spiritual vitality.

Is your spiritual life dry and empty? Has the fizz gone out of the Pepsi of your life? Has the new life in Christ gone downhill or even stagnated? Take inventory of your heart and spiritual health. When

Has the fizz gone out of the Pepsi of your life?

we feel a helplessness because of our situation, we can turn away from God feeling He is distant and not intervening in our lives. How much better if we would recognize our weakness, depending upon God more than ever for help.

The power and personal presence of God is available to each Christian. This promise is not limited to a few super Christians, but to every believer, regardless of one's circumstances. In *Ephesians 3:14-21* we overhear Paul's earnest prayer for the Ephesians. I'm sure it also expresses the Lord's desire for each believer.

> For this reason I bow my knees before the Father, from whom every family in heaven and on earth is named, that according to the riches of his glory he may grant you to be strengthened with power through his Spirit in you inner being, so that Christ may

dwell in your hearts through faith—that you, being rooted and grounded in love, may have strength to comprehend with all the saints what is the breadth and length and height and depth, and to know the love of Christ that surpasses knowledge, that you may be filled with all the fullness of God.

Now to him who is able to do far more abundantly than all that we ask or think, according to the power at work within us, to him be glory in the church and in Christ Jesus throughout all generations, forever and ever. Amen. (Eph 3:14-21)

God does not pour His power into us like we put gasoline into a car or the way an electrical source energizes a vacuum sweeper. His power is not a magic wand that will enable us to work a miracle on command. God's power comes into our lives when we allow Him to be personally present in our hearts and lives.

> **We are empowered by God when our hearts and lives become more Christlike.**

We are empowered by God when our hearts and lives, our attitudes and actions are becoming more Christlike.

"For this reason I bow my knees before the Father." What God has done in Christ moves Paul to pray in earnest submission and reverence to his heavenly Father, *"from whom every family in heaven and on earth is named"* (*Eph 3:14-15*). All human beings who have lived on this earth owe their origin to God. His image is stamped on each person. The very idea of fatherhood and family come from God.

The promised empowerment is *"according to the riches of his glory"* (*Eph 3:16a*). Because God is infinite His resources are unlimited. We have access to the abundance of God's glorious wealth and resources of wisdom, power, and love.

God's power is available to believers in any circumstance when we allow God to be present in every area of our life.

WE CAN BE STRENGTHENED BY THE SPIRIT IN OUR INNER BEING

"He may grant you to be strengthened with power through his Spirit in the inner being" (*Eph 3:16b*). The power of God's Spirit energizes the inner life of the believer. "Inner being" is the inner person, the real you: your mind, will, and spirit. The Holy Spirit lives in the believer's

eternal spirit. Paul frequently mentions power, strength, or might available from God (*2Cor 12:7-10; Eph 6:10; Php 4:13; Col 1:11; 1Tm 1:12; 2Tm 4:17*).

The Holy Spirit is given to those who obey.

How can we know we have the Holy Spirit living in us? Jesus said the Holy Spirit is given to those who ask (*Lk 11:13*). He promised us that the Holy Spirit would be like an artesian well of living water springing up within us (*Jn 7:38-39*). Peter told believers to repent and be baptized into Christ for remission of sins and they would receive the gift of the Holy Spirit (*Acts 2:38*). The Holy Spirit is given to those who obey God (*Acts 5:32*).

The Spirit does not occupy some part of our physical body, for example, inside our right shoulder. He lives in our spirit. How do we know? We are not given a warm fuzzy feeling and buzzing sound in some part of our body confirming that we have the Spirit. We know we have the Spirit the same way we know our sins are forgiven. We trust God's promises. If God says His Spirit dwells within us, we accept what He says. The fruit test is another indication we have the Spirit (*Gal 5:22-23*). If we manifest the fruit of the Spirit in our lives, then He truly dwells in us.

Our bodies are temples of the Holy Spirit through which we glorify God (*1Cor 6:19-20*).

> Anyone who does not have the Spirit of Christ does not belong to him. But if Christ is in you, although the body is dead because of sin, the Spirit is life because of righteousness. If the Spirit of him who raised Jesus from the dead dwells in you, he who raised Christ Jesus from the dead will also give life to your mortal bodies through his Spirit which dwells in you. (*Rom 8:9-11*)

We are not to live according to the flesh—that is, selfishly pleasing ourselves and ignoring God in our lives. *"For if you live according to the flesh you will die, but if by the Spirit you put to death the deeds of the body, you will live. For all who are led by the Spirit of God are sons of God"* (*Rom 8:13*). The Spirit will help us say no to temptation. The Spirit helps us in our weaknesses (*Rom 8:26*). We are led by the Spirit when we manifest the mind of Christ and say no to selfish, sinful attitudes and actions. When *Romans 8:14* and *Galatians 5:18* speak of being led by the Spirit, they are not talking about revelation of new information. They speak of a transformation of our character and conduct.

We must turn from the works of the flesh and produce the fruit of the Spirit (*Galatians 5*).

We are to *"Be filled with the Spirit."* (**Eph 5:18**) Years ago, an Illinois farm boy was showing a hog at the county fair. After leaving the pen, the pig got in a mud puddle before getting to the show ring. The young man had to wash the pig again. That evening he sat frustrated on the back steps of his farm house. He observed the cat cleaning and cleaning herself. He thought, "If I could only get the spirit of that cat into that pig." Our sin has caused our lives to be dirty. God offers to put His Spirit into our spirit to make us new persons.

God does not overrule our will. But if we want His help in resisting temptation and choosing the right path, we need to ask His help, seek His will, surrender and submit, trust and obey Him.

> **Our sin caused our lives to be dirty; God puts His Spirit into us to make us new persons.**

CHRIST CAN DWELL IN OUR HEARTS THROUGH FAITH

Paul prays *"that Christ may dwell in your hearts through faith"* (**Eph 3:17a**). "The ministry of the Spirit is devoted to making the presence and power of the risen Christ real to those whom he indwells; hence the experience of the indwelling Spirit and of the indwelling Christ is the same experience" (**Bruce, Colossians, 326**).

Why pray this? Isn't Christ already dwelling in the hearts of Christians? As we need to continually repent, so also we need to continually seek the rule of Christ in our hearts. The power and presence of Christ in our lives is limited only by our faith and trust in Him.

Jesus said, *"If anyone loves me, he will keep my word, and my Father will love him, and we will come to him and make our home with him"* (**Jn 14:23**). Paul adds, *"Christ in you, the hope of glory"* (**Col 1:27**). *"For we are the temple of the living God; as God said, 'I will make my dwelling among them and walk among them, and I will be their God, and they shall be my people'"* (**2Cor 6:16**). *"I have been crucified with Christ; it is no longer I who live, but Christ who lives in me; and the life I now live in the flesh I live by faith in the Son of God, who loved me and gave himself for me"* (**Gal 2:19-20**).

Christ does not force His way into our lives; He comes by our invitation. We have to genuinely seek Him. It is by our trust in Him that He lives in us. The word for "dwelling" does not mean inhabiting a place temporarily as a stranger. It designates a settling down permanently. Where the Lord dwells, He must rule. We are not our own, Christ owns the house. He wants to shape our lives.

Where the Lord dwells, He must rule. Paul says he was in travail until Christ was formed in the Galatians (*Gal 4:19*). It is easier to bring a person into Christ than it is to see Christ formed in the character and conduct of that person. It is Paul's desire that Christ be formed in each believer.

He wants us to have the mind in us that was also in Christ Jesus (*Php 2:5*). Get to know Christ personally. Read the Gospels. Learn His words and His works. Trust Him as your Lord. Absorb His attitude and values. Paul was ready to sacrifice everything for *"the surpassing worth of knowing Christ Jesus my Lord"* (*Php 3:8*).

Fill your minds with Christ and His teaching. Let Him be your constant companion and friend, your shepherd and teacher. Know Christ and let Him live in you. We need to pray the prayer of Richard of Chichester:

> Thanks be to thee, my Lord Jesus Christ,
> For all the benefits thou has won for me,
> For all the pains and insults thou has borne for me.
> O most merciful Redeemer, Friend and Brother,
> May I know thee more clearly,
> Love thee more dearly,
> And follow thee more nearly
> For ever and ever. (**Green, *New Life*, 57**)

We must not let suffering and hardships crowd Christ out of our lives. When we sense our need is an ideal time to get to know Christ better. Drawing strength from Him and identifying with His sufferings is a great source of strength. He understands and is sympathetic (*Heb 2:14-16; 4:15*).

WE CAN BE ROOTED AND GROUNDED IN LOVE

As Christian believers our lives have been *"rooted and grounded in love"* (*Eph 3:17b*). As plants need deep roots and buildings need good foundations, so we need to have a solid understanding of God's love for us. It is hard to have a meaningful relationship with God if you don't believe He loves you or if you do not love Him. Love is the basis of our stability in Christ. We find in God what love really is because God is love. When He redeems us, He begins creating a loving heart in us. Love is a fruit of the Spirit (*Gal 5:22*). The Spirit pours love into our hearts (*Rom 5:4*). When we feel nobody cares, He floods our hearts with love that is constant and abiding.

The two greatest commandments are love for God and love for others (*Mt 22:36-40*). Love is the identifying mark of the believer (*Jn 13:35*). Love is both the root and the fruit of the Christian life. God's love for us, especially as expressed on the cross, is the powerful magnet

> **Because God loves us, He acts in our best interest.**

that draws us to God (*Jn 3:14*). His kindness leads us to repentance. It is the love of Christ which constrains us to serve God and to serve others (*2Cor 5:14*). Knowing we are loved by God gives us confidence and trust. It is the basis for transformation of life. Regardless of our physical health or circumstances in life, God does in fact love us, and He has acted, is acting, and will act in our best interest.

WE CAN HAVE THE POWER TO UNDERSTAND LIFE AND THE WORLD FROM GOD'S PERSPECTIVE

Paul continues his petition that believers would *"have strength to comprehend with all the saints what is the breadth and length and height and depth"* (*Eph 3:18*). This comprehension is not for a favored few but is for all Christians to share. When we admit our human weakness, and our need of God, then we can find strength to understand life from God's viewpoint. This is not an inherited traditional belief but rather you understand what it means to trust Christ for yourself, comprehending with the mind and grasping the significance of the deep things of life.

When experiencing suffering, especially overwhelming tragedy and loss, life may not make sense. The disease, difficulty, or death may seen so senseless. The only way to regain our sense of balance is to see things as God sees them.

What are we to understand? Is it divine love? In the NIV translation of *Ephesians 3:18* the translators added *"the love of Christ"* which is not in the Greek text. Stott comments,

> Yet it seems to me legitimate to say that the love of Christ is "broad" enough to encompass all mankind (especially Jews and Gentiles, the theme of these chapters), "long" enough to last for eternity, "deep" enough to reach the most degraded sinner, and "high" enough to exalt him to heaven. Or, as Leslie Mitton expresses it, finding a parallel to *Romans 8:37-39*: "Whether you go forward or backward, up to the heights or down to the depths, nothing will separate us from the love of Christ." (*Ephesians*, 179)

Bruce sees it as grasping "God's revelation in its totality" (*Colossians*, 327). This was Paul's personal ambition. He did not claim to have attained, but he prayed that we might attain this ambition: to understand all things—God, human life, our life, the world, history, time, eternity, beauty—in a worldview that is true to God and His revelation. This demands a lifetime of growth in bringing every thought into captivity to obedience to Christ (*2Cor 10:5*).

Suffering can cloud one's understanding of the world and life. It forces us to think deeply about basic issues and questions. Instead of settling into despair and depression, we need to seek to understand the big picture from God's viewpoint.

When we were in England in 1993, I was visiting with a man who was new to the faith. He said, "I am the newest Christian in this church. Being a Christian has changed my perspective on everything." In Christ we are new creatures. Troubles in life can throw roadblocks, detours, and seeming dead ends in our way. If God made the world and created us, then what He says is more trustworthy than any human wisdom. Even though our human understanding is limited, we can seek to see everything in the light of God's truth. What a privilege to have the wisdom of God which helps us see the world and life as it actually is—as our loving God sees it.

> **"Being a Christian has changed my perspective on everything."**

WE CAN KNOW THE LOVE OF CHRIST WHICH PASSES KNOWLEDGE

Paul's desire and concern is that we *"know the love of Christ that surpasses knowledge"* (**Eph 3:18**). Such knowledge is gained by personal involvement and experience. Boles explains, "Not just intellectual knowledge concerning the details and dimensions of Christ's great love. He wants all Christians to really know that love through intimate, personal participation" (**Galatians, 259**).

The love of Christ is so deep that human beings will never have a complete or total understanding of it. With our finite minds we will never have total knowledge of God's loving plan of redemption. "There is always more to know; it is inexhaustible" (**Bruce, Colossians, 329**).

We can know and participate in His love. We can know experientially the love of Christ even though we

> **If you don't understand and accept the love of Christ, you don't yet understand Christianity.**

can't intellectually comprehend all that is involved in it. We need strength to love and wisdom to understand love. "Certainly the two cannot be separated, and it is partly by loving that we learn the meaning of his love" (**Stott, Ephesians, 137**).

Some struggle with the goodness of God. A former student of mine had trouble believing that God was really good and loving because of the atrocities he saw in Viet Nam. Another could not be convinced that God really loved him personally. If you don't understand and accept the love of Christ, you don't yet understand Christianity.

If you feel unloved by God, search your heart for the reason. You may have felt unloved by your parents or someone in this life. But don't project that on God. Make a study of the Scriptures on the love of God. Even more, you need to have an emotional response to the love of Christ expressed for you on the cross. Some people need to be loved by a gracious Christian friend before they can believe that God really loves them.

It is the love of Christ which can melt our selfish pride and arrogance. Daily we must personally accept the love of Christ in our lives.

WE CAN BE FILLED WITH
THE FULLNESS OF GOD

"That you may be filled with all the fullness of God" (**Eph 3:19b**) is an astounding prayer. To think that the infinite Creator, in all His vastness, could and would come and dwell in us individually and personally is an incredible thought. The fullness of deity dwelt in Christ (**Col 1:19; 2:9**) and *"you have come to fullness of life in him"* (**Col 2:10, RSV**). God *"works in you, both to will and to work for his good pleasure"* (**Php 2:13**).

God wants you to experience fully all His purpose for you in granting salvation and sonship. This fullness is present when *"Whatever you do, do all to the glory of God"* (**1Cor 10:31**). *"Whatever you do, in word or deed, do everything in the name of the Lord Jesus, giving thanks to God the Father through him"* (**Col 3:17**). May more and more of the true character of God be seen in our attitudes and actions, in our thoughts and our words, in every part of our lives.

> **We gain strength by knowing He is by our side.**

A sense of God's presence in our lives empowers us to live in His will. Our strength is renewed as we wait on the Lord (**Isa 40:30-31**). *"Fear not, for I am with you; be not dismayed, for I am your God; I will strengthen you, I will help you, I will uphold you with my righteous right hand"* (**Isa 41:10**; cf. **49:15**). We gain strength by knowing He is by our side.

All this sounds well and good. How can I experience more of the power and presence of God in my personal life? Growth in the Christian life is not automatic nor is it magic. But it is possible in your life and mine. The Spirit does not empower unwilling and indifferent persons. Do you want more of God's power and a greater awareness of His personal presence in your life? You cannot have it without serious seeking. Do you care enough to make the needed changes?

Paul appeals to us to not be conformed to the ideas and ways of the world but be transformed by the renewing of our minds (**Rom 12:2**). Here is a plan suggested by Dallas Willard, author of several books on spiritual disciplines (95-139).

1. *Make inventory of the ideas and images you hold.* Change must begin with your thoughts.

Identify your dominant ideas. What do you think about? The ideas you hold dear determine how you interpret life. What is most important to you? Financial success and security, popularity, acceptance, athletic success, health? Try to identify what ideas are most important to you. These influence your beliefs and behavior. What you think about results in your decisions about what you do and who you become.

Identify your dominant images. What image do you have of yourself? A good worker, a poor student, always honest, impatient person, life of the party, a shy person who doesn't meet people well, someone who is always messing up? "The image one has of oneself, for example, can override everything else and cause one to act in ways contrary to all reality and good sense" (100). What image do you have of God? Remote like an absentee landlord, too strict, wonderful beyond words, or uninterested in my problems? Identify how you really picture or think of God. A.W. Tozer says, "I believe there is scarcely an error in doctrine or a failure in Christian ethics that cannot be traced finally to imperfect and ignoble thoughts about God" (ibid.).

> **"There is scarcely . . . a failure in Christian ethics that cannot be traced to [faulty] thoughts about God."**

Our growth in Christ is often hindered by wrong ideas and images we hold in our minds about God and about ourselves. Suffering can distort our image of ourselves and of God. Growth in Christ is a process of replacing destructive ideas and images with the ideas and images that filled the mind of Jesus.

2. *Fill your mind with true information about God* and all reality as revealed in Scripture. "Without correct information, our ability to think has nothing to work on." Failure to know what God is really like and what He desires from us "destroys the soul, ruins society, and leaves people to eternal ruin" (104). Good thinking requires rejecting the false information about God and accepting that which is true about God and about yourself. "We must thoughtfully take the Word in, dwell upon it, ponder its meaning, explore its implications—especially as it relates to our own lives" (ibid.).

A family was in a devastating car accident, hit by two cars that were drag racing. Their daughter was killed. The other three children and the two parents have had to work through serious injuries. The

As we maintain daily communication with God we will know His enduring presence.

mother said the family had made a careful study of the book of Romans just before the accident happened. She said the teaching of Romans helped them cope with this tragedy. Their perspective on the tragedy was aided by their perspective on God.

Start by reading one of the Gospels and learn more about who Jesus is, what He did, and what He taught. Replace your ideas and images with His. Right thinking about Christ's words will help you experience more of the power and presence of God in your life. His last words assure us *"I am with you always, to the end of the age"* (**Mt 28:20**). Spend time in the Psalms to learn to know God better. As we maintain daily communication with God through His word and prayer we will know His enduring presence.

3. *Choose associations that encourage a closer relationship with Christ.* Friends can either support or tear down our walk with Christ. We need to be regular in our attendance in worship meetings with brothers and sisters in Christ. Jesus promised, *"For where two or three are gathered in my name, there am I among them"* (**Mt 18:20**).

I was in the hospital in St Louis in June 2004, recovering from my double lung transplant. A few days into my recovery I hit a significant bump in the road. Due to a small leak in one of my new lungs, air was pumped under my skin. Subcutaneous emphysema, they called it. My arms, chest, neck, and face were puffed up so I could barely see out of my squinty eyes. I was discouraged, uncomfortable, and afraid. I felt as if the swelling would shut off my ability to breathe. My pain was stronger than the pain pills. What help the pain pills provided was gone long before I could have the next pills. It was my darkest time in the whole process.

I waited in an observation unit anticipating having a surgical procedure the next morning to correct the problem. About four o'clock in the morning my wife, Barbara, came into the room. She was an angel of encouragement to me helping me handle my discouragement. She kept telling me it was going to be okay. She assured me that God would take care of me and I just needed to trust that He would. Her presence helped me settle down so I could deal with the situation.

Paul's prayer assures us that we have divine help. We have the encouragement and assistance of the Holy Spirit, Christ, and God the Father to live in us personally and give us the power we need to meet any situation in this life.

Plan for Renovating the Heart

1. Make an inventory of the ideas and images you hold.
2. Fill your mind with true information about God and all reality as revealed in Scripture.
3. Choose associations that encourage a closer relationship with Christ.

Dallas Willard, *Renovation of the Heart:*
Putting on the Character of Christ.

Paul concludes his prayer *"Now to him who is able to do far more abundantly than all we ask or think, according to the power at work within us, to him be glory in the church and in Christ Jesus throughout all generations, for ever and ever. Amen"* (**Eph 3:20-21**).

The word for "more abundantly" is made up of parts of words meaning "above, out of, and around." When you are tempted to say, "God can't do that with me," remember God is able to do far more than we can ask or imagine *"according to the power at work within us."* The same power of God that resurrected Christ from the dead (**Eph 1:19-20**) is available to us. The Spirit strengthens our inner being. Christ dwells in our hearts through faith. God works in our lives.

God gives us power. Glory must be given to Him. What a privilege offered to us that we can live in such a way that God is glorified because of us. This glory will go on forever and ever, now and in eternity. Paul's amen means "So let it be" in your life and mine.

> **The same power of God that resurrected Christ is available to us.**

In times of suffering we either are overwhelmed by God's absence or we are drawn to experience His presence and power in a real and personal way. It is up to us to let Paul's prayer be fulfilled in our lives.

Under His wings I am safely abiding;
Though the night deepens and tempests are wild,
Still I can trust Him:
I know He will keep me;
He has redeemed me and I am His child.

Under His wings, what a refuge in sorrow!
How the heart yearningly turns to His rest!
Often when earth has no balm for my healing,
There I find comfort, and there I am blest. (**Cushing, 279**)

Think about It

1. In what ways does suffering make us feel helpless and lonely?

2. What kind of power from God is offered to the believer?

3. How can we be assured that the Holy Spirit is living in us?

4. Contrast living by the flesh and living by the Spirit.

5. In what ways does Christ dwell in our lives?

6. Why is it important to the sufferer to know that God loves him or her.

7. How does it help us when we see all reality from God's point of view?

8. What are the three steps in Willard's plan for renovating the heart?

9. What connection do you see in sensing God's daily presence in our lives and experiencing the power of God in our lives?

CHAPTER FOURTEEN

OUR LIVING HOPE

(*1 Peter 1:3-9*)

According to his great mercy, he has caused us to be born again to a living hope through the resurrection of Jesus Christ from the dead.
1 Peter 1:3

A uthor C.S. Lewis observed that we have longings that this world cannot satisfy. The actual reality of travel or relationships does not measure up to the promise of our first anticipations. Creatures are born with desires that have a means of fulfillment, for example food for hunger. Lewis states,

> If I find in myself a desire which no experience in this world can satisfy, the most probable explanation is that I was made for another world. If none of my earthly pleasures satisfy it, that does not prove that the universe is a fraud. Probably earthly pleasures were never meant to satisfy it, but only to arouse it, to suggest the real thing. . . . I must keep alive in myself the desire for my true country, which I shall never find till after death; I must never let it get snowed under or turned aside; I must make it the main object of life to press on to that other country and to help others do the same. (***Christianity***, **118**)

Alister McGrath in *The Unknown God* says that after people satisfy their physical hunger, they long for something that will really satisfy.

> The great certainty of our time seems to be that satisfaction is nowhere to be found. We roam around, searching without finding, yearning without being satisfied. . . . Part of the cruel irony of human existence seems to be that the things we thought would make us happy fail to do so. . . . our anticipation of what we will find

I. Grounded in the Resurrection of Christ
II. Guarded through Faith
III. Hope versus Hopelessness

221

proves vastly preferable to what we actually find on our arrival. (8-9)

Suppose our longing for fulfillment points to something we have yet to discover—something that really has the ability to satisfy us? What if our yearning is a clue to the meaning of the universe? What if our sense of emptiness is like a signpost, pointing us in a certain direction? What if we were to explore what that direction might be, and what might await us? (11)

What if we are *meant* to want to relate to God? Might our sense of emptiness and lack of fulfillment be intended to point us to something or someone who could fulfill it? (25)

Our deepest longings can find fulfillment only in Christ. Our deepest longings can find fulfillment only in Christ. As Christians we have been given a living hope through the resurrection of Christ and our hope is guarded by faith until our final salvation.

GROUNDED IN THE RESURRECTION OF CHRIST

Peter states, *"Blessed be the God and Father of our Lord Jesus Christ! According to his great mercy, he has caused us to be born again to a living hope through the resurrection of Jesus Christ from the dead, to an inheritance that is imperishable, undefiled, and unfading, kept in heaven for you"* (*1Pet 1:3-4*).

God is praised because He is the Father of Jesus Christ and has *"caused us to be born again to a living hope."* This life-changing experience is a total reorientation to life with values, priorities, basic beliefs, and priorities changed. While it is not deserved, God, who is *"rich in mercy"* (*Eph 2:4*) makes it possible.

Our living hope is an eager expectation and hope of life beyond this life. This personal and active hope grows and increases as we continue our walk with Christ. Christ's resurrection assures us that because He lives even after death we too shall live again after death. Without the resurrection we would have no new birth and our hope would be meaningless.

Atheist Jean-Paul Sartre, in 1980 in his journal described his despair fearing a third world war on this wretched planet that he felt had no purpose or goal for mankind.

One cannot think such things. They tempt you incessantly, especially if you are old and think, "Oh well, I'll be dead in five years at the most." In fact, I think ten, but it might be five. In any case the world seems ugly, bad, and without hope. There, that's the cry of despair of an old man who will die in despair. But that's exactly what I resist. I know I shall die in hope. But that hope needs a foundation. (**McGrath,** *Unknown*, **103**)

Within a month he was dead. Without God one is without hope (*Eph 2:12*).

"If a man dies, will he live again?" Is death extinction or is it a doorway to a future life? Jesus Christ conquered death and returned to assure us of victory over death (*1Cor 15:54-57; Heb 2:14-15*). C.S. Lewis says Jesus "forced open a door that had been locked since the death of the first man. He has met, fought, and beaten the king of death. Everything is different because he has done so. This is the beginning of the new creation: a new chapter in cosmic history has opened" (*Miracles*, **173**). On that resurrection morning our longings and hopes were verified. Because Christ lives, we too shall live. His resurrection gives us a solid ground for hope.

> # Is death extinction or is it a doorway to a future life?

Rollo May, a therapist, was in Greece recovering from a nervous breakdown. He visited a Greek Orthodox church at Easter. Although he was not a believer, he wrote, "I was seized then by a moment of spiritual reality: what would it mean for our world if He had truly risen?" (**Yancey,** *Where*, **248**) The all-important question must be answered: Did Jesus actually rise from the dead? If He did not, then Christianity is nonsense. If He did, we can have new life now and a certain hope of eternal life in a world beyond this one. Konrad Adenauer, one-time chancellor of Germany, said, "If Jesus Christ is not alive, I see no hope for the human race." Paul says that if Christ was not risen then our faith is empty; his preaching was false; we're still in our sins; and we have no hope (*1Cor 15:12-21*).

Michael Green tells of visiting a man in a London hospital dying of leukemia. He had been a specialist in the disease. He was angry, not because of the disease itself, but because he was in his forties and the church leaders he had heard had not affirmed the resurrection of Christ. He had been an agnostic for years, but while lying in bed he had read two books which brought him a strong and joyful faith in the resurrected Christ. He asked, "Why have I not had the evidence clearly put to me before?" (*Death*, 17)

Those seeking to know about life after death should investigate the evidence for the resurrection of Christ.[1] If Christ is risen from the dead, then we have found the answer. Only here do we find a God who cares enough to die for us and rise again to assure us that we can have eternal life with Him. Christians need to tell the world what death looks like to the only one who conquered death and returned to life. Christ offers the only true victory over death.

Our hope is grounded in the resurrection of Jesus. Our faith must affirm the risen Christ. *"If you confess with your mouth that Jesus is Lord and believe in your heart that God raised him from the dead, you will be saved"* (*Rom 10:9*). Repentance from sin is imperative because judgment before Christ is assured by the resurrection (*Acts 17:30-31*). Paul says that repentant believers who are baptized into Christ *"were buried therefore with him by baptism into death, in order that, just as Christ was raised from the dead by the glory of the Father, we too might walk in newness of life. For if we have been united with him in a death like his, we shall certainly be united with him in a resurrection like his"* (*Rom 6:4-5*). *"Having been buried with him in baptism, in which you were also raised with him through faith in the powerful working of God, who raised him from the dead"* (*Col 2:12*). Peter refers to those saved from the flood, and then he says, *"Baptism, which corresponds to this, now saves you, not as a removal of dirt from the body but as an appeal to God for a good conscience, through the resurrection of Jesus Christ"* (*1Pet 3:21*; cf. *Jn 3:5,7*; *Tts 3:5*).

As physical birth is a beginning that is expected to lead to growth to maturity, so new birth into Christ leads to a living hope. Peter communicates this hope to those who are suffering. Davids comments,

> Pastorally this future orientation is important for our author, for a suffering people who may see only more pain and deprivation ahead need to be able to pierce the dark clouds and fasten on a vision of hope if they are to stay on track.
>
> This hope is not a desperate holding-on to a faded dream, a dead hope, but a living one, founded on reality, for it is grounded in "the resurrection of Jesus Christ from the dead." As Paul had argued, because Jesus really did shatter the gates of death and exists now as our living Lord, those who have

[1] For further study of the evidence for the resurrection: Lee Strobel, *The Case for Christ* (Grand Rapids: Zondervan, 2000), and Gary R. Habermas and Michael R. Licona, *The Case for the Resurrection of Jesus* (Grand Rapids: Kregel, 2004).

committed themselves to him share in his new life and can expect to participate fully in it in the future (*Rom. 6:4-5; 1 Cor.15*). It is this reality which will enable the readers to face even death without fear, for death is not an end for the Christian, but a beginning. (*Peter*, 52)

Unlike earthly inheritances which are temporary, believers have an eternal investment. We are promised the final and ultimate victory over sin and all its destructive effects. In the NT, inheritance refers to the salvation believers receive when they depart from this earthly life and are received into eternal glory. Davids says, "The point is that while Christians may suffer in this age and so have no future here, there is waiting for the faithful a reward as sure and as real as that of Abraham, a reward far better than an earthly land and far more lasting" (**ibid., 52-53**).

An authentic and realistic hope enables suffering persons, even those who are dying, to deal with reality. A cancer patient said, "I do not consider myself dying of cancer, but living despite it. I do not look upon each day as another day closer to death, but as another day of life, to be appreciated and enjoyed" (**Yancey, *Where*, 211**).

Our living hope is not a groundless optimism. God does not heal every believer who prays for healing. God does not avert every tragedy. But whether we recover from an illness or whether we die, we have a hope that lives right on into eternal life. A survivor of Hitler's death camp affirms this, "It is a well-known fact of the concentration camps that those who had strong religious and moral convictions managed life there much better than the rest. Their beliefs, including belief in an afterlife, gave them a strength to endure which was far above that of most others" (**ibid., 213**).

> **Whether we recover or die, we have a hope that lives right on into eternal life.**

Our inheritance has been and is kept in heaven (*1Pet 1:4*). God has already reserved our inheritance and this gives us assurance in the present. Our inheritance will not *perish*—cannot be destroyed or grow old with time. This stands in stark contrast with earthly possessions which do decay and will be destroyed. Our inheritance will not *spoil*—cannot be corrupted or polluted—but is kept without blemish. It is not tarnished with sin and contains nothing unworthy of God's approval. Our inheritance will not *fade*—is not subject to variation or change. Its beauty and glory will never diminish. Our living hope in no way will disappoint those trusting in Christ.

Paul said,

The beauty and glory of our inheritance will never diminish.

For the Lord himself will descend from heaven with a cry of command, with the voice of an archangel, and with the sound of the trumpet of God. And the dead in Christ will rise first. Then we who are alive, who are left, will be caught up together with them in the clouds to meet the Lord in the air; and so we will always be with the Lord. (1Th 4:16-18)

In the late Middle Ages men speculated about the possibility of a sea route to India. Could one navigate around the south tip of Africa? No one knew for sure. All attempts to round the cape had failed. This treacherous headland where the Atlantic and Indian oceans met was called the Cape of Storms. It was the scene of many wrecks. At last in 1498 one sailor, Vasco da Gama, successfully rounded the cape and reached the East. That treacherous cape was renamed The Cape of Good Hope.

Michael Green draws this comparison:

> The enigma of life after death is rather like that. Up to the time when Jesus died and rose again, death was like that Cape of Storms, littered with wrecks. Until his successful rounding of that Cape and return, men had nothing to go on but speculation about the after life. His resurrection has turned it into the Cape of Good Hope. He has opened up for his people a way to a new and rich land which he has shown exists. And because he has satisfactorily rounded that perilous Cape, he is well equipped to act as pilot to others. (**Death, 62-63**)

Our hope is grounded on the resurrection of Jesus from the grave.

Dietrich Bonhoeffer, a German theologian, was imprisoned by Hitler in World War II, and executed on April 8, 1945. Before his death, he led a service for his fellow prisoners at their request. His text was *1 Peter 1:3*. As the guards marched him to his death his last message was "This is the end—but for me the beginning of life" (**ibid., 64**).

On October 11, 1999, our 34-year-old son, Mark, was killed in a truck accident. The first class I taught at Ozark Christian College a week later was on the subject of the resurrection of Jesus. It was a great and timely topic for me. We feel an overwhelming loss in our lives but we have a living hope based on the resurrection of our Lord and Savior Jesus Christ.

GUARDED BY FAITH

By God's power, believers are *"guarded through faith for a salvation ready to be revealed in the last time"* (**1Pet 1:5**). We live in a hostile world, but our living hope and our salvation in Christ is kept secure through our faith. We are saved by faith. We are protected through faith. God's power and human responsibility are joined together in faith. God's power is available to us as we trust Him.

Peter's word "guarded" is a military term, meaning carefully watched and kept safe. *"You are continually being guarded"* affirms that God's power is available to us to protect us from danger if we continue to trust Him. *"In all circumstances take up the shield of faith, with which you can extinguish all the flaming darts of the evil one"* (**Eph 6:16**).

Our final salvation is the ultimate goal of such protection. The fullness of our salvation will be realized when in God's appointed time Jesus returns to earth to wrap up human history. We joyfully look forward to that Day. In contrast with the insecurity of earthly investments, our inheritance in heaven is secure and certain because it is guaranteed by God.

Peter said,

> In this you rejoice, though now for a little while, as was necessary, you have been grieved by various trials, so that the tested genuineness of your faith—more precious than gold that perishes though it is tested by fire—may be found to result in praise and glory and honor at the revelation of Jesus Christ. Though you do not now see him, you believe in him and rejoice with joy that is inexpressible and filled with glory, obtaining the outcome of your faith, the salvation of your souls. (*1Pet 1:6-9*).

Our living hope and our anticipated ultimate salvation give cause for great joy. This is not a shallow rejoicing but a deep spiritual joy. However the Christian life is not nonstop joy. Our spiritual joy does not remove the fact that while we live in this fallen world we often have to face many kinds of trials which bring suffering and grief.

Christians are not exempt from trials. We get terminal illnesses, have babies with

The Christian life is not nonstop joy.

Down's syndrome, lose jobs, live in poverty, lose loved ones, and 100% die. When we face a situation that challenges the foundations of our faith, we must hold on to our faith regardless of the darkness and seeming silence of God. We need a faith that enables us to face whatever trial may come.

Philip Yancey states, "Hope gives us the power to look beyond circumstances that otherwise appear hopeless. Hope keeps hostages alive when they have no rational proof that anyone cares about their plight; it entices farmers to plant seeds in spring after three straight years of drought" (*Invisible*, 95).

> The Bible models both simple faith and hang-on-against-all-odds fidelity. Job, Abraham, Habakkuk and his fellow prophets, as well as many of the heroes of faith mentioned in Hebrews 11, endured long droughts when miracles did not happen, when urgent prayers dropped back to earth unanswered, when God seemed not just invisible but wholly absent. We who follow in their path today may sometimes experience times of unusual closeness when God seems responsive to our every need; we may also experience times when God stays silent and all the Bible promises seem glaringly false. (**ibid., 53**)

True faith is trust based on good evidence, but we proceed without complete knowledge. Faith requires obedience without knowing everything. As finite human beings we cannot know everything, but we can humbly trust the wise God who loves us and invests

Faith keeps trusting even when we cannot see.

us with worth and value. Faith keeps trusting God even when we cannot see any purpose or reason for the trials.

We must not blame God when bad things happen to good people. Yancey observes,

> Jesus grieved over many things that happen on this planet, a sure sign that God regrets them far more than we do. Not once did Jesus counsel someone to accept suffering as God's will; rather he went about healing illness and disability. The Bible supplies no systematic answers to the "Why?" questions and often avoids them entirely. . . . no time-bound human, living on a rebellious planet, blind to the realities of the unseen world, has the ability to comprehend such questions. (**ibid., 57**)

> Mature faith . . . reassembles all the events of life around trust in a loving God. When good things happen, I accept them as gifts from God, worthy of thanksgiving. When bad things happen, I do not take them as necessarily sent by God—I see evidence in the Bible to the contrary—and I find in them no reason to divorce God. Rather, I trust that God can use even those bad things for my benefit. (**ibid., 65**)

Because of the great and precious promises (*2Pet 1:4*), we believers have changed values that enable us to rejoice in our great salvation even though we face trials in this life. In the perspective of eternal salvation our trials and suffering become insignificant and are for only a little while. *"For this slight momentary affliction is preparing for us an eternal weight of glory beyond all comparison, as we look not to the things that are seen but to the things that are unseen. For the things that are seen are transient, but the things that are unseen are eternal"* (*2Cor 4:17*).

God, in His wisdom, has given human beings free will and set up the world as it is. He allows bad things to happen to believers, but we should not blame Him for the bad things. If we face these trials with faith, they can develop steadfastness so that we may be *"perfect and complete, lacking in nothing"* (*Jas 1:4*). *"Suffering produces endurance, and endurance produces character, and character produces hope, and hope does not disappoint us"* (*Rom 5:3-5, RSV*).

We can continually have a deep spiritual joy because of our salvation, even though from time to time we will be suffering in various trials. A normal Christian life will include both suffering and joy. We encounter many difficulties living in this fallen world, but in faith and hope we look to the unseen reality beyond this present brief life and rejoice.

Davids says,

> Hope should lead to joy. The "rejoice" is not a continual feeling of hilarity nor a denial of the reality of pain and suffering, but an anticipatory joy experienced even now, despite the outward circumstances, because that believers know that their sufferings are only "for a little while" and that Christ has come (*Luke 10:21; John 8:56; Acts 2:26*), that God has revealed his saving grace to them (*Acts 16:24*), and that they will take part in the consummated joy of God's glory and salvation at the approaching end of the age (*Jude 24; Rev. 19:7*). Such joy was already present in the celebration of the Lord's Supper (*Acts 2:47*), which was itself an anticipation of the messianic

banquet in heaven. Peter is not giving a command here, but expressing the experience of the early church resulting from their conversion. (*Peter, 55*)

As a German teenager Jurgen Moltmann was drafted and sent to the front lines during World War II. He was captured by the Allies, and spent the next three years in prison camps. When Hitler's regime fell, many Germans gave up all hope. Moltmann said, "What kept me from it was a rebirth to a new life."

He had taken only two books into battle: Goethe's poems and the complete works of Nietzsche, neither books of hope. But a chaplain gave him a NT with Psalms included. As he read, he became convinced that God "was present even behind the barbed wire—no, most of all behind the barbed wire." When he was released from prison, he gave up his plan to study quantum physics and instead founded a new movement in theology, the theology of hope (**Yancey, *Invisible*, 77-78**).

Our hope is rooted in God's faithfulness in past history and supremely in the resurrection of Jesus. We do not understand all the

God does not approve the evil in the world. | suffering and chaos in this fallen world today, but it does not mean that God is not all-good nor all-powerful. God does not approve the evil in the world, but a day is coming when God will administer perfect justice.

Gold is made more valuable by fire burning away any impurities. Faith is more important than this seemingly indestructible precious metal. Gold will eventually perish. When we experience trials, if we keep trusting in God, our faith becomes more genuine and pure. The result of this testing will show the genuineness of one's faith (*1Pet 1:7*). James says *"the testing of your faith produces steadfastness"* (*Jas 1:3*). Trials strip away any shallowness and insincerity in our faith. This purified, genuine faith is much more precious than gold or any earthly possession. The believer knows that God will supply what we really need (*Php 4:19*).

When our Lord returns, the faithful followers of Christ will hear that *"Well done, good and faithful servant"* (*Mt 25:21*). Those faithful unto death will receive the crown of life (*Rev 2:10*). We shall share in heavenly glory and honor when we enter His eternal presence.

Understanding and trusting in this hope helps us accept and endure trials. Even when we can see no reason for a trial, we trust God because He is God and is worthy of our trust. "It is in times when the reason for hardship cannot be seen that trust in God alone seems to become most pure and precious in his sight" (**Grudem, 65**).

Jeremiah writes of a bush that puts its roots in the desert soil. When it receives rain, it flourishes, but in times of drought, it shrivels and dies. Jeremiah draws a contrast with this plant and the person who lives by faith.

> *Blessed is the man who trusts in the LORD,*
> *whose trust is the LORD.*
> *He is like a tree planted by water,*
> *that sends out its roots by the stream,*
> *and does not fear when heat comes,*
> *for its leaves remain green,*
> *and is not anxious in the year of drought,*
> *for it does not cease to bear fruit. (**Jer 17:7-8**)*

The Bible does not promise a life where everything is rosy. Rather it emphasizes a life of faith which prepares us for the tough times.

Believers have a deep continuing personal love for Jesus even though we have never seen Him physically in person with our physical eyes. Yet His spiritual presence is just as real as if He were present in body with

> **The Bible does not promise a life where all is rosy, but one which prepares us for the tough times.**

us today. Jesus said, *"Blessed are those who have not seen and yet have believed"* (**Jn 20:29**). *"We walk by faith, not by sight"* (**2Cor 5:7**). Faith involves a continuing trust, confidence, and dependence upon God.

Knowing and loving Jesus enables us to continually rejoice with a glorious and deep joy and peace that defies verbal expression. It is the joy of heaven before we get to heaven because of our spiritual fellowship with the living Christ.

Rejoicing is possible because we know in the end we will receive the final salvation of our souls when we are delivered from this fallen world into the eternal presence of our Lord. Our living hope assures us of salvation today. We will realize it in its fullness in the final Day of the Lord.

HOPE VERSUS
HOPELESSNESS

As young men, Charles Templeton and Billy Graham were friends who alternated in the pulpit in preaching rallies. Both were effective evangelists. Templeton became an agnostic because he felt a loving God could not exist when terrible things happened to innocent people. Before Graham began his Los Angeles crusade in 1949, he had some questions about trusting the Bible. Templeton tried to convince him that one could no longer believe all the Bible. Graham made his choice to trust the Bible as the Word of God.

Templeton was in his 80s when he died of Alzheimer's in 2001. He had spent his last fifty years as an opponent of Christianity. He expressed his bitter and hopeless agnosticism in his latest book, *Farewell to God: My Reasons for Rejecting the Christian Faith*. Graham is in his 80s suffering with Parkinson's disease. He has spent the last fifty years preaching a message of faith and hope. Graham has a living hope. Templeton died without hope.

We must build our hope on the risen Christ and guard our hope by faith. What does the future hold for us? The choices we are making today will decide.

> **What does the future hold for us? The choices we are making today will decide.**

Think about It

1. What point do Lewis and McGrath make about our yearning for something this world cannot provide?

2. What is the basis or foundation of our living hope?

3. How are the new birth and the resurrection of Jesus related?

4. Why is the resurrection of Jesus important?

5. How does Peter describe our hope?

6. How does the resurrection change one's view of death?

7. Peter says our hope is guarded through what?

8. How does hope influence how people deal with suffering?

9. What effect do trials have on the life of a believer?

10. What is the key difference in regard to hope in Charles Templeton and Billy Graham?

CHAPTER FIFTEEN

"TO LIVE IS CHRIST, TO DIE IS GAIN"

(*Philippians 1:21*)

I came that they may have life and have it abundantly.
John 10:10

Suffering forces us to think about the meaning of life and death. Gerald Sittser was devastated when his vehicle was hit by a drunk driver killing his mother, wife, and daughter. He says that for months he tried to reorder in his mind the events of the day to avoid the accident. He describes some of the thoughts that tormented him,

> I blamed myself for being a selfish husband, an inattentive father, or an aloof son. I wondered if my family had been cursed. I entertained the idea that the accident was a demonic attack. I looked with cynicism on the absurdity of life. Maybe, I thought, there really is no God and no meaning to life. . . . I could not discover any explanation that made sense of the tragedy. An answer to the "Why?" question eluded me. (*Grace*, 97)

His brother-in-law helped him realize that in wanting to change events so he could alter the future, he was wanting to be God. He told Sittser that since that option was closed to him, he should brace himself for accidents and live in hope. Sittser says he worked through his thoughts realizing, "Somehow we manage to live reasonably well, expecting the best and, when the time comes to face the worst, accepting it as part of the bargain of living in a fallen world. . . . We love again, work again, and hope again. We think it is worth the risk and trouble to live in the world, though terrors surely await us, and we take our chances that, all things considered, life is still worth living." He affirms, "Life is indeed worth living to me, though it took me a long while to come to that conclusion" (**ibid., 100**).

When Paul was in prison in Rome, he, too, reflected on the meaning of life,

> For I know that through your prayers and the help of the Spirit of Jesus Christ this will turn out for my deliverance, as it is my eager expectation and hope that I will not be at all ashamed, but that with full courage now as always Christ will be honored in my body, whether by life or by death. For to me to live is Christ, and to die is gain. If I am to live in the flesh, that means fruitful labor for me. Yet which I shall choose I cannot tell. I am hard pressed between the two. My desire is to depart and be with Christ, for this is far better. But to remain in the flesh is more necessary on your account. Convinced of this, I know that I will remain and continue with you all, for your progress and joy in the faith, so that in me you may have ample cause to glory in Christ Jesus, because of my coming to you again. (**Php 1:19-26**)

In this chapter we are going to focus on one of the clearest and most powerful statements that the apostle Paul wrote. It is the purpose statement for his life, *"For to me to live is Christ, and to die is gain"* (*Php 1:21*).

TO LIVE IS CHRIST

The words *"to live, Christ"* and *"to die, gain"* have a poetic force in the Greek language: "to live, Christ /*Christos*/; to die, gain /*kerdos*/." This statement sums up Paul's life—his priorities, his commitment, his ministry, his motivation, his confidence, and his estimate of death.

After Paul's conversion, Jesus Christ was the center of his life. Everything he said and did revolved around Christ. He did not live for self or for personal goals. He did not live for wealth, pleasure, or fame. Christ was the single purpose that unified his life. Living for Christ was a passion that motivated, energized, and transformed his life. The goal of pleasing Christ guided his activities, interests, and pursuits.

> **After Paul's conversion, Jesus Christ was the center of his life.**

In no way did Paul want to bring shame on the name of Christ, either in life or death. Honoring Christ overshadowed the issue of whether he would be executed or whether he would continue living. He wanted Christ "to be glorified even if the verdict were to go against him. . . . he vows that since Christ is the singular passion of his life, he wins in either case, whether released or executed" (**Fee, 70**).

Gordon Fee says,

> Thus if Paul is released as he expects, he will continue (*now as always*) in full pursuit of knowing Christ and making him known. Likewise, if he is executed, the goal of living has thus been reached: he will finally have gained Christ. . . . This expressed not a death wish, not dissatisfaction with life, nor desire to be done with troubles and trials; it is the forthright assessment of one whose immediate future is somewhat uncertain but whose ultimate future is both certain and to be desired. . . . Such a statement, of course, has meaning only for one to whom the first clause is a vibrant, living reality. Otherwise death is a loss, or "gain" only in the sense of escape. (**70-71**)

Paul knew he could be executed any day. He says if he is granted more life, that means service to Christ; but if he is put to death, it still means being with Christ in a greater degree.

"What is life?" is one of the most basic questions we can ask. The sad fact is that many go through their existence never honestly thinking about the meaning of life. What a waste to take this precious gift of life for granted without thinking seriously what it means.

I remember when I took college courses in biology and zoology, *life* was not defined. Rather *life* was described by how living organisms behaved. Some of the most basic terms, such as *life* and *time*, are the most difficult words to define. Paul simply affirms that living is Christ.

WHAT LIFE IS NOT

Jesus explains, *"One's life does not consist in the abundance of his possessions"* (**Lk 12:15**). *"For whoever would save his life will lose it, but whoever loses his life for my sake and the gospel's will save it. For what does it profit a man to gain the whole world and forfeit his life?"* (**Mk 8:35-37**). He warns us not to equate life with caring for the needs of our body, *"Do not be anxious about your life, what you will eat, or what you will drink; nor about your body, what you will put on. Is not life more than food, and the body more than clothing?"* (**Mt 6:25**).

The *hedonist*, who views life as pleasure, is wrong; "Eat, drink, and be merry, for tomorrow we die" expresses a shallow view of life. Life

> **"Eat, drink, and be merry" expresses a shallow view of life.**

is not having one pleasure after another. that leaves one unsatisfied and empty (*Ecc 2:1*). Paul says that a woman *"who lives for pleasure is dead even while she lives"* (*1Tm 5:6, NIV*).

On the other hand, the *pessimist* is wrong, viewing life as a senseless situation that must be endured. Life is considered meaningless so we must "Grin and bear it." Shakespeare in *Macbeth* states the cynic's view of life:

> Out, out brief candle!
> Life's but a walking shadow; a poor player
> That struts and frets his hour upon the stage,
> And then is heard no more; it is a tale
> Told by an idiot, full of sound and fury,
> Signifying nothing. (*Macbeth*, V,v,17)

The *ascetic* wrongly blames all of life's problems on the fact that we live in a body. He or she retreats from the world believing that real living means mortifying the body, denying oneself any and all pleasure. Gautama Buddha, when he saw the ravages of old age, disease, and death, wanted answers to life's questions. In his search, he abandoned his wife, home, and material comforts. He concluded that suffering is caused by human desire, so desire should be extinguished (**Zacharias, *Man*, 50**). When we define life by the bad things we do not do, we live in the shadows but the real substance belongs to Christ (*Col 2:17*).

The *humanist* sees life as self-achievement and accomplishment. Do-gooders think that the way to the good life is by improving the world. Stephen Gould, evolutionary humanist, admitted that the facts of nature do not give meaning to life. "We must construct these answers ourselves—from our own wisdom and ethical sense. There is no other way" (**ibid., 55**). However, for those who reject God, the questions about life and death remain unanswered. If God is real, then meaning can be found in both life and death.

When confronted with unmitigated hatred, W.H. Auden had difficulty in defining evil, given his humanistic presuppositions. This struggle led to his conversion to Christianity which explained human depravity and gave the answer for its cure (**ibid., 49**).

Fame and fortune do not give meaning to life. Jack Higgins, author, at the high point of his career stated, "When you get to the top, there's nothing there." Lee Iacocca confessed, "Here I am in the twilight years of my life, still wondering what it's all about. . . . I can tell you this, fame and fortune is for the birds" (**ibid., 56, 58**).

Education and scholarship can become an end in itself. Intellectualism is the worship of one's mind. Use your mind in loving God. But all intellectuals need to remember, *"If anyone imagines that he knows something, he does not yet know as he ought to know"* (*1Cor 8:2*). Information is merely "stuff" without wisdom.

> **Information is merely "stuff" without wisdom.**

The *atheist* defines life in mechanistic terms—mere matter in random chemical reactions. Meaning and virtue are lost. "The noblest is reduced to the lowest, and love is merely glandular" (**ibid., 86**). Life becomes empty and meaningless. H.L. Mencken gives his sour opinion, "The problem with life is not its tragedy, but that it's a bore" (**ibid., 88**).

Ravi Zacharias asks, "Can man live without God? Of course he can, in a physical sense. Can he live without God in a reasonable way? The answer to that is No! because such a person is compelled to deny a moral law, to abandon hope, to forfeit meaning, and to risk no recovery if he is wrong" (**ibid., 61**).

Many Christians would have to admit that our families, our work, our activities are the most important things in our lives. Our loved ones are precious indeed, but love for Christ must have priority over family. If family is first, "when they are taken from us, our life, our world, collapses and we have nothing left" (**Lloyd-Jones, *Joy*, 90**).

Performing religious duties can become an end instead of a means of serving Christ. Martyn Lloyd-Jones warned, "One of the greatest dangers facing preachers is the danger that they will live on their own activity: speaking, preaching, being engaged in church, being very active about their religion. There is a danger of living on all this until suddenly, when the activity is gone, one is left empty-handed" (**ibid., 91**). Doing religious things must not be a substitute for living for Christ.

Apart from Christ, there is no true life. After he found Christ, Paul considered his former accomplishments and life as worthless waste.

But whatever gain I had, I counted as loss for the sake of Christ. Indeed, I count everything as loss because of the surpassing worth of knowing Christ Jesus my Lord. For his sake I have suffered the loss of all things and count them as rubbish, in order that I may gain Christ and be found in him, not having a righteousness of my own that comes from the law, but that which comes through faith in Christ, the righteousness from God that depends on faith—that I may know him and the power of his resurrection, and may share his sufferings, becoming like him in his death, that by any means possible I may attain the resurrection from the dead. (**Php 3:7-11**)

Zacharias says that in

Jesus Christ, the hungers of the mind and heart find their fulfillment. For in Christ we find coherence and consolation as He reveals to us, in the most verifiable terms of truth and experience, the nature of man, the nature of reality, the nature of history, the nature of our destiny, and the nature of suffering. (**Man, 179**)

The hedonist lives for now; the utopian lives for the future, traditionalists live for the past. The Christian lives for Christ.

WHAT TRUE LIFE IS

Happiness and fulfillment in life does not depend upon circumstances but upon personal relationships. We find joy in personal relationships—love between a man and a woman, devotion between parents and children, and friendship between those who share common values and vision. But if life is to be lived to the full, we must have a personal relationship with God our Father and the Lord Jesus Christ.

John says of Jesus, *"In him was life, and the life was the light of men"* (**Jn 1:14**). Jesus said, *"I came that they may have life, and have it abundantly"* (**Jn 10:10**). *"I am the way, the truth, and the life"* (**Jn 14:6**). In his first letter, John says *"In this the love of God was made manifest among us, that God sent his only Son into the world, so that we might live through him. . . . Whoever has the Son has life; whoever does not have the Son of God does not have life"* (**1Jn 4:9; 5:12**). Peter states, *"His divine power has granted to us all things that pertain to life and godliness, through the knowledge of him who called us to his own glory and excellence"* (**1Pet 1:3**).

Those who find Christ, find meaning, purpose, and value in life. Christ not only has the answers to life's deepest questions, but *He is the answer.* Malcolm Muggeridge lived for years away from Christ before finding a personal relationship with the Lord. He evaluated the fame, financial success, and influence he had achieved. He comment-

| **Christ not only has the answers; He is the answer.**

ed, "Multiply these tiny triumphs by millions, add them all up together, and they are nothing, less than nothing. . . . measured against one drop of that living water Christ offers to the spiritually thirsty, irrespective of who or what they are" (**Zacharias,** *Man*, **77**).[1]

We find truth and love in Christ. We can sing with George Matheson,

> O Love that will not let me go,
> I rest my weary soul in Thee,
> I give Thee back the life I owe
> That in life's ocean depths its flow
> May richer, fuller be.[2]

Paul's love for Christ dominated and controlled the whole of his life—what he thought, felt, and did. *"To live is Christ."* Here Paul is not talking about eating and drinking, sleeping and rising, working and playing. He is talking about what really matters and makes life worthwhile. His supreme desire was to know Christ better and love Him more.

In Christ, he found the highest wisdom. He found his deepest desires for peace, joy, and freedom fulfilled. In Christ he found all that really matters. The Moravian leader, Count Zinzendorf's motto was "I have one passion, it is he and he alone" (**Lloyd-Jones,** *Joy*, **95**). Lloyd-Jones encourages us, "Let us dwell upon him; let us meditate upon him . . . . let us do all we can to get to know him better, for to know him is to love him" (**ibid.**). Can we say with Paul that living means Christ? The Christians who can truly say this are the ones who have made a difference in the world.

The truth and beauty of life in Christ shines brightly in contrast with the devaluation of human life in the Greco-Roman world evident in these practices: infanticide, which included the killing of unwanted babies (outlawed in the mid 4th century), abandoning

---

[1] Quoted from Malcolm Muggeridge, *Jesus Rediscovered* (Garden City, NY: Doubleday, 1969).
[2] "O Love That Will Not Let Me Go," Public domain.

unwanted babies on the garbage dump without guilt or remorse, and aborting unwanted babies; the brutal slaughter of multitudes of human beings in the gladiatorial games for public entertainment (finally outlawed by the beginning of the 5th century); the advocacy and practice of suicide. Life was cheap in the Roman empire. It was Christ living in His followers that challenged these practices (**Schmidt, 49-78**). As many in our country follow human values instead of God's, we see a growing devaluation of life.

What is most important in your life? Take an inventory of your life judging by how you spend your time, by how you spend your money, by what you think and dream about, by what you talk about and by what you most want to do.

C.S. Lewis describes how Christ wants to be our life. Christ says,

> Give me All. I don't want so much of your time and so much of your money and so much of your work: I want You. I have not come to torment your natural self, but to kill it. No half-measures are any good. I don't want to cut off a branch here and a branch there, I want to have the whole tree down. I don't want to drill the tooth, or crown it, or stop it, but to have it out. Hand over the whole natural self, all the desires which you think innocent as well as the ones you think wicked—the whole outfit. I will give you a new self instead. In fact, I will give you Myself: my own will shall become yours. (*Christianity*, 167)

The terrible thing, the almost impossible thing, is to hand over your whole self—all your wishes and precautions—to Christ. But it is far easier than what we are all trying to do instead. For what we are trying to do is to retain what we call "ourselves," to keep personal happiness as our great aim in life, and yet at the same time be "good." We are all trying to let our mind and heart go their own way—centered on money or pleasure or ambition—and hoping, in spite of this, to behave honestly and chastely and humbly. And that is exactly what Christ warned us you could not do. As He said, a thistle cannot produce figs. If I am a field that contains nothing but grass-seed, I cannot produce wheat. Cutting the grass may keep it short: but I shall still produce grass and no wheat. If I want to produce wheat, the change must go deeper than the surface. I must be ploughed up and re-sown. (**ibid., 168**)

Giving Christ everything is easier than what we are trying to do instead.

"Human will becomes truly creative and truly our own when it is wholly God's, and this is one of the many senses in which he that loses his soul shall find it" (**Lewis**, *Pain*, **101**).

"So whether you eat or drink, or whatever you do, do all to the glory of God" (*1Cor 10:31*). *"And whatever you do, in word or deed, do everything in the name of the Lord Jesus, giving thanks to God the Father through him"* (*Col 3:17*). *"If then you have been raised with Christ, seek the things that are above, where Christ is, seated at the right hand of God. Set your minds on things that are above, not on things that are on earth. For you have died, and your life is hidden with Christ in God"* (*Col 3:1-3*).

Michael Green said,

> "The Christian is free to live life to the full, as he was intended to, sharing his experiences every day and hour with his Maker, Redeemer and Indweller. If there is any answer to the deepest enigmas of life which is more radical, more exciting, more adventurous than that, I should like to hear of it" (*Runaway*, **111**).

When I was in college, I remember coming to the conclusion that maturity was finding the true answers to these questions: Who am I? Why am I here? Where am I going? I decided on a purpose statement for my life that has guided me throughout my adult life—*My purpose in life is to teach and practice the word of God*. Look at your life. State in one sentence the essential purpose of your life.

TO DIE IS GAIN

We live in a culture that refuses to think realistically about death. Most avoid the subject of death and dislike it, regarding it as an unhealthy subject. We are often shielded from face-to-face confrontation with death, and we postpone it as long as possible. On the other hand, death seen frequently on TV news and in movies and in novels, seems so far away, so unreal, not something that will be for us personally.

Wealth and power can give a false sense of invincibility. Mohammed Ali, a heavyweight boxer, was known for his boast "I am the greatest." Ali was on a flight experiencing turbulence. The passengers were instructed to fasten their seat belts. Ali did not. The flight attendant told him to observe the captain's

We are all terminal.

orders. He said, "Superman don't need no seatbelt." The flight attendant answered, "Superman don't need no airplane, either" (**Zacharias, Man, 7**). None of us is invincible. It is appointed that we all will die (**Heb 9:27**). We are all terminal.

Can we identify with Paul in saying *"to die is gain"*? How do we view own deaths? Many are terrified at the thought of death, as the Hebrews writer speaks of those who *"through fear of death were subject to lifelong slavery"* (**Heb 2:15**). Some have a stoic resignation about their inevitable end. Others have a defiant attitude, unwisely thinking it is not for them.

For Paul, death was not a faraway fiction but a real up-close-and-personal possibility. He knew he could be executed any day or he could be freed thus delaying his death.

His eager and intense expectation is that Christ be exalted whether through his life or through his death (**Php 1:18-20**). His deep desire and confident expectation was that Christ would be honored either *"by life or by death."* Whether he receives a death sentence or is released and allowed to continue in ministry, his ultimate goal is his final salvation.

He realistically faces his options. "Paul genuinely considers his choice to live rather than to die to be the more difficult and sacrificial choice. . . . Christ is more important than life itself to him, and the joy and progress of his fellow Christians more important than departing to be with Christ" (**Thielman, 83**).

He describes death as departing and being with Christ. The idea of the word "depart" is breaking camp, taking down your tent and moving on in your journey. Paul says our earthly home will be destroyed (**2Cor 5:1**). While we are in this earthly "tent," we long for our dwelling in heaven, so

> that what is mortal may be swallowed up by life. . . . So we are always of good courage. We know that while we are at home in the body we are away from the Lord, for we walk by faith, not by sight. Yes we are of good courage, and we would rather be away from the body and at home with the Lord. So whether we are at home or away, we make it our aim to please him. (*2Cor 5:4,6-9*)

James defines death as *"the body apart from the spirit"* (**Jas 2:26**). Peter describes death as putting off the tent of his body (**2Pet 1:13-14**). "The idea was that this is a temporary world where you live in tents; there are no permanent buildings here. Death means breaking up the camp, striking the tent, moving on to the permanent residence which is awaiting you. That is how Paul views the act of death—just a moving from this world to the next" (**Lloyd-Jones, *Joy*, 104-105**).

The physical event of death can be very traumatic and painful, as probably Paul's death was. Death is gain in the sense that it is the gateway through which one enters into the next world. When Christians die, we gain entrance into the eternal blessed state.

James Boice states,

> Death for the Christian is never pictured in the Bible as a gain over the worst in this life. *It is portrayed as an improvement on the best.* Certainly it is in this sense that Paul intends his words to the Philippians. We might imagine that Paul was suffering in prison and was anxious for a speedy release, even by the portal of death. But this is just the opposite of what Paul experienced. Paul's life was full. He had been enriched with fellowship with Christ. (**94**)

As Christians we have a fulfilling life in this world, but death will usher us into a fuller and more satisfying fellowship with Christ. Paul says Christ brought life and immortality to light (***2Tm 1:10***). Because of His resurrection he defeated death, defanging this enemy. (***Heb 2:14-15; 1Cor 15:50-58***). Jesus assures us, *"I am the resurrection and the life. Whoever believes in me, though he die, yet shall he live"* (***Jn 11:25***). *"Because I live, you also will live"* (***Jn 14:19***; cf. ***Jn 5:26,28-29***).

After death we will no longer have to wrestle with *"the body of this death"* with its selfish and sinful desires. We will be free from the power, practice, and pollution of sin. Disease, pain, and accidents will no longer disrupt our existence.

Here we are exiles and strangers; there we will have arrived in our heavenly homeland. Here we have a temporary and transient tent; there we will have a permanent dwelling in *"the city that has foundations, whose designer and builder is God"* (***Heb 11:10***, cf. ***vv. 14-16***). Heaven is the final home for the believer after his or her earthly sojourn. Death is the gate we pass through on our way home. *"Our citizenship is in heaven, and from it we await a Savior, the Lord Jesus Christ, who will transform our lowly body to be like his glorious body, by the power that enables him even to subject all things to himself"* (***Php 3:20-21***).

Death is the gate we pass through on our way home.

Instead of seeing through a glass darkly we shall see *"face to face."* Martyn Lloyd-Jones said, "We shall see things clearly then, the whole sweep of the great plan of salvation. Oh, to see God and the wonder and the glory of it, to know and to understand without limit or hindrance!" (*Joy*, **106-107**) We will have uninterrupted fellowship with Christ forever. Here we live for Christ but at times the fellowship is disrupted. The real reason to want to go to heaven is to be with Christ.

> The only one who can confidently say, "to die is gain", is the man who has said, "to me to live is Christ". . . . That is what enabled Paul to say it. Christ was the consuming passion of his life: to know him, to dwell with him, that is the thing, said Paul, that is my life, and therefore to die must be gain; to go home, to be with Christ, is very far better. (**ibid., 108**)

In the 1800s, John G. Paton was planning to go as a missionary to the South Sea Islands. An older gentleman warned him, "You will be eaten by Cannibals!"

Paton replied, "Mr. Dickson, you are advanced in years now, and your own prospect is soon to be laid in the grave, there to be eaten by worms; I confess to you, that if I can but live and die serving and honouring the Lord Jesus, it will make no difference to me whether I am eaten by Cannibals or by worms; and in the Great Day my resurrection body will arise as fair as yours in the likeness of our risen Redeemer" (**Carson**, *Basics*, **31**).

Leo Tolstoy, the great Russian novelist of the 19th century, as a young man abandoned the church and Christian belief. He described his ungodly lifestyle: "I put men to death in war, I fought duels to slay others, I lost at cards, wasted my substance wrung from the sweat of peasants, punished the latter cruelly, rioted with loose women, and deceived men. Lying, robbery, adultery of all kinds, drunkenness, violence, murder. . . . There was not one crime which I did not commit" (**Tolstoi, 5**).

Unhappy with his life he searched for meaning in life. He felt that both science and philosophy left him without hope or meaning in life. He studied Islam, Buddhism, and Christianity. He was repulsed by the religious leaders of his day because they professed Christian faith but lived no differently than pagans. The faith of the peasants, who truly lived their faith, found meaning in life, and could face death with a quiet confidence, impressed him. He returned to his trust in God. He realized that the only time his life had meaning was when he believed and sought to serve God.

If you were told you had only so long to live, what would you do? In 2000 that became a very personal question for me. Being diagnosed with a terminal disease caused me to think seriously about the issues of life and death. I decided that whether I had one day, one year, or ten years, I would live for Christ by teaching and practicing the Word of God. Facing death brings life's purpose into focus. In fact, it is death that forces us to think of the meaning of life. Whatever your circumstance in life, making a lifelong commitment to Christ will bring fulfillment and meaning to your life and victory when you enter the gateway of death.

Just before Fred Fish, a faithful Christian minister, died, having lost a battle with cancer, he said, "I will live until I die. And then I will

> **Facing death brings life's purpose into focus.**

really begin to live." That catches the spirit of *Philippians 1:21*, *"For to me, to live is Christ and to die is gain."*

Think about It

1. What is Paul's dominant desire while he is in prison in Rome?

2. What are the consequences resulting from our answer to the question "What is life?"

3. Identify several things that life is not.

4. What value did Paul place on his earthly accomplishments?

5. Cite Scriptures showing that Christ is the source of true life.

6. State what you believe really matters in life.

7. Summarize what C.S. Lewis said Christ wants to do with our life.

8. How would you answer those who say the Christian life is boring and unexciting.

9. Do you think that our culture faces death realistically? Why?

10. Give New Testament pictures or definitions of death.

11 State in one sentence your purpose in life.

Part 3

The Problem of Evil and Suffering

CHAPTER SIXTEEN

HOW SUFFERERS RESPOND TO GOD

My soul is in anguish,
How long, O LORD, how long?
Psalm 6:3

uffering prompts thoughts about God. Anger, bitterness, and a clenched fist toward God are common responses to suffering. Many believers question and doubt God as they struggle with suffering. Others reject the God of the Bible and create in their minds a god acceptable to them. Still others reject the idea of a god completely. Some respond by trusting God and knowing His grace is sufficient. How people respond to suffering and evil is directly related to their response to God.

American Christians have been accused of having a weak theology on suffering. How should we view suffering? How do terrible tragedies and horrendous evils affect our view of God? We need to seriously face these questions as a preparation for coping with any suffering that comes our way. We also need to gain the best understanding of this issue so we can minister effectively to those around us who are suffering.

A Christian mother was in her home having her quiet time with God. Her five-year-old son accidentally hung himself in a tree in the yard. This tragedy did not occur because of sin or punishment. Such a horrible reality does not fit comfortably in the "God will give you all your wishes" theology. This mother had to deal with the very personal question of why her God would allow this unspeakable evil to happen to them.

We can't escape the serious issue of reconciling suffering with the idea of a good God, especially *our* suffering with our relationship with our personal God.

I. Trust God
II. Question God
III. Blame God
IV. Reject God

TRUST GOD

Many believers trust God and accept suffering. Not everyone who experiences great tragedy and suffering is angry with God and questions Him. Because of a deep relationship with God and understanding that we live in a fallen world, some do not blame God for their suffering.

Dr. Ben Carson, head of pediatric neurosurgery at Johns Hopkins University Hospital, was interviewed by Charlie Rose on Public Broadcasting Television. Carson had undergone surgery for an aggressive form of prostate cancer. Rose said he knew Carson was a believer, and he wondered if he was angry with God because of his cancer. Carson responded, "Oh, no. God doesn't make mistakes." He explained that because of what God had done in his life, he would not question His wisdom.[1]

Throughout the whole ordeal Carson was confident in God; he states:

> Even in the bleakest moments—thinking that I may have had metastatic disease to the spine—my faith was strong. As I've said before, I believe God never makes mistakes. This gives me great confidence. Even if I die, it will be for a reason, and God will make the best of it. To my dying breath, I will have confidence in God, and be sure that He will take care of everything. By the same token I didn't think God would let me die, even if I did have metastatic disease to the spine—He could solve the problem and cure me. It wasn't going to happen.[2]

Trusting God does not make the suffering a light matter nor take away the real pain and hardship. Tragic circumstances can draw us closer to God and make us depend upon Him for strength and help.

Trusting God can help one keep things in perspective.

Trusting God can help one keep things in perspective. Several other examples help illustrate the results suffering can have.

Several years ago, Nelson King gave a devotion at a campfire at an Indiana Christian Service Camp. He held up both hands. He had only stubs. His fingers were gone. He told of being in a plane in World War II. He said a friend was having trouble with his oxygen.

[1] The Charlie Rose Show, Public Broadcasting System, October 16, 2002.
[2] http://news.adventist.org/data/2002/07/1029857890/index.html.en.

Nelson took off his gloves to help. His fingers froze and he lost them. In the hospital recuperating he read a Bible and found Christ. Holding up his hands, with deep emotion he said, "Don't feel sorry for these stubs. It was because of them that I found Christ."[3]

Sometimes suffering solidifies faith and clarifies life. One woman's routine surgery revealed a malignant tumor. The surgeon explained to the patient what he found and what it meant. He explained what damage had already been done to her vital organs and what the chemotherapy would involve. He said she had six months to a year to live. She responded, "It's all right. I'm ready for what God has in store for me." R.C. Sproul said of her, "My friend lived for two years, surprising everyone, including the doctors. She remained productive. She visited Israel. She got her house in order. She cared for her family. She died with grace and dignity." She was a Christian who trusted God as she prepared herself mentally and spiritually for death (11-12).

James Dobson told of a TV documentary of three people and their response to their medical diagnoses and treatments. Two of the people, who apparently had no faith, reacted with anger and bitterness and seemed at odds with others.

Though Dobson never met the third person, he made a strong impression on Dobson. The man was a black pastor of a small inner-city Baptist church. He was in his late 60s when the doctor told him and his wife that he had only a few months to live. Trusting the Lord, he simply came to terms with his illness and its apparent outcome.

The cameras recorded his final sermon before he died. Dobson summarized the message:

> Some of you have asked me if I'm mad at God for this disease that has taken over my body. I'll tell you honestly that I have nothing but love in my heart for my Lord. He didn't do this to me. We live in a sinful world where sickness and death are the curse man has brought upon himself. And I'm going to a better place where there will be no more tears, no suffering and no heartache. So don't feel bad for me.
>
> Besides, our Lord suffered and died for our sins. Why should I not share in His suffering?
>
> Then he began to sing, without accompaniment, in an old broken voice:

[3] Reported to me personally by Gordon Clymer who was present on that occasion.

Must Jesus bear the cross alone,
And all the world go free?
No, there's a cross for everyone,
And there's a cross for me.

How happy are the saints above,
Who once went sorr'wing here;
But now they taste unmingled love,
And joy without a tear.

The consecrated cross I'll bear,
Till death shall set me free,
And then go home my crown to wear,
For there's a crown for me.[4]

Trusting God does not mean all one's questions are answered. In suffering we can trust God even when we do not understand.

QUESTION GOD

In a Peanuts cartoon, Snoopy has a big bandage on his foot. He muses, "Having a broken foot makes you want to ask questions." In the next frame, he sits up and cries out, "Like, why me?" Often suffering prompts believers to question God, asking, "Why?" Job certainly did not have all his questions answered. But when calamity fell on him, he held onto his faith in God, even when he was upset with God and seemingly angry as he questioned God at times. The text informs us, *"in all this Job did not sin or charge God with wrong"* (**Job 1:22**).

Facing tragedy, personal calamity, overwhelming grief leads some to throw up their hands, questioning why God is doing this to them. After being married three years, John Mark Hicks' wife died with a blood clot after a routine surgery. Hicks compared himself to C.S. Lewis, "Like C.S. Lewis, after the death of his wife of three years, I was not 'in much danger of ceasing to believe in God' as much as 'coming to believe such dreadful things about Him'" (***Trust***, **17**). Lewis in *A Grief Observed* asks, "Where is God?" He continues,

> When you are happy, so happy that you have no sense of needing Him . . . you will be—or so it feels—welcomed with open arms. But go to Him when your need is desperate, when all other help is vain, and what do you find? A door slammed in your face, and a sound of bolting and double bolting on the inside. (**5-6**)

[4] James Dobson, "Why Did God Let This Happen to Me?" http://www.family.org/docstudy/excerpts/A0011942.html.

Christians may be shaken to their foundations by the death of a loved one, the diagnosis of a terminal illness, or some other horrible evil. They haven't rejected God, but they are emotionally upset with Him and they begin to doubt His love for them or His power. Their minds and hearts are confused and in a pit of darkness.

Many believers who have written of their grief experience have described a dark period when their relationship with God was deeply strained. In many cases this is an emotional struggle with honest doubt, and not a matter of settled intellectual unbelief.

In situations of tragedy, unanswered prayers, and hard times in life, believers at times are moved to honest doubt and even unbelief. Whether one is dealing with honest doubt or intellectual unbelief, it is important to find one who can help you think through these issues. It is best to carefully think through the problem of suffering and evil before troublesome times come into your life.

BLAME GOD

Many blame God for the horrible evils that happen in our world. Alister McGrath states, "Instead of acknowledging that there seems to be something wrong with human nature causing people to inflict suffering on others, they have taken the easy way out, blaming God for all the ills of the world. . . . Trying to pin the blame on God is a crude evasion of human responsibility; it is as unfair as it is unrealistic" (*Suffering*, 18-19).

> "Trying to pin the blame on God is a crude evasion of human responsibility."

Many blame God even for their own evil behavior. A boxer who had killed his opponent in the ring said, "Sometimes I wonder why God does the things He does." A woman, who became pregnant by her boyfriend, asked God, "Why have You allowed this to happen to me?" The South Carolina mother, who pushed her two sons into a lake to drown, said she screamed, "Oh God! Oh God, no! What have I done? Why did you let this happen?" Philip Yancey asks "Did God arrange these incidents?" He answers, "To the contrary, I see them as spectacular demonstrations of human freedom exercised on a fallen planet" (**Yancey**, *Invisible*, 56-57).

Yancey asks, "Is God somehow responsible for the suffering in this world?" He answers that in an indirect way He is. "But giving a child a pair of ice skates, knowing that he may fall, is a very different matter from knocking him down on the ice" (*Where*, **65-66**). Yancey observes:

> Any discussion of the unfairness of suffering must begin with the fact that God is not pleased with the condition of the planet either. . . . To judge God solely by the present would be a tragic mistake. . . . The Bible communicates no message with more certainty than God's *displeasure* with the state of creation and the state of humanity. (**ibid., 67**)

Some argue that if God is in sovereign control of the universe and history, then everything that happens is His will. However, we must distinguish between the directive and permissive will of God. We see God's directive will in what He commands and directs. These things will come to pass because He is the supreme authority in the universe. Yet in God's permissive will He has chosen to permit humans to make free choices which may go against His desires for them.

God's directive will states that salvation is found only in Christ. His desire is that all come to repentance and be saved. In His permissive will He allows those who refuse Him to be lost eternally. It is not true that everything that happens is God's directive will, but it is true that everything that happens is allowed by His permissive will.

Sin brought devastation, disease, and death into the world, but God set in motion His plan of redemption to rescue fallen, alienated sinners and restore them to loving fellowship with Himself. Understanding the creation and the fall helps us have a basis for trusting in a loving, all-powerful God.

> **In God's permissive will He allows those who refuse Him to be lost eternally.**

REJECT GOD

Unbelievers reject God. Most atheists use the argument of suffering and evil against Christian theism. Some cling to a god of their own making. They reject or modify the God of the Bible, specifically His goodness, power, and/or knowledge. Of course all religions and atheists still have to deal with the hard reality of evil and suffering.

In the light of the horrors of the Holocaust, some affirmed atheism. Richard Rubenstein, a radical Jewish theologian, said, "Of one thing I am convinced: more than the bodies of my people went up in smoke at Auschwitz. The God of the covenant died there" (**718**).

Elie Wiesel was taken to Auschwitz at age 15. His mother, father, and younger sister were murdered by the Nazis. He survived, but his faith in God suffered. He describes in graphic detail hangings and burning of bodies. "Never shall I forget those flames which consumed my faith forever. . . . Never shall I forget those moments which murdered my God and my soul and turned my dreams to dust" (**44**). His later writings show that he did believe in God even when he expressed anger and protest against God.

During the 1970s Reeve Robert Brenner surveyed 1,000 Holocaust survivors. How had the Holocaust affected their belief in God? Almost one-half said it had in no way affected their belief in God. Eleven percent said they had rejected all belief in God as a result of their experience and they had not regained their faith. Brenner observed that their atheism was more an emotional reaction of anger and hurt against God for abandoning them. Five percent changed from atheism to belief in God because of the Holocaust (**Yancey, Where**, 152).

The tragic loss of three thousand lives in the Twin Towers in New York City on September 11, 2001, brought forth many cries against God. A program on Public Broadcasting System quoted several.[5]

Ann Ulanov, professor of psychiatry and religion at Union Theological Seminary in New York City, said, "September 11 is so horrible—and horrible for years and years to come—that it can just smash any image of God who has a providential plan for me, those I love, my group, my nation, this world." She continued, "The all-good God can be smashed, and yet even the non-God image can be smashed, because the outpouring of kindness, simple acts of kindness, challenged a lot of people who thought you can't really believe in anything."

An orthodox Rabbi Brad Hirschfield says he wanted to believe in a "very personal, very nurturing, very caring" God. He says he knows it is ridiculous "to believe in that God, because if that God exists, that God was dethroned a long time ago" through all of human history.

Manhattan Episcopal priest, Joseph Griesedieck, in the days after September 11, said he sensed a contrast between sanitized worship and the horror at Ground Zero. He stated,

Prior to September 11, the face of God for me was one that was strong, secure, consistent. A face that, while at times seemed distant, can more or less be counted on to be there. Who kept things in order; the sun would come up, the sun would go down. Who would provide, could be counted on. And after September 11, the face of God was a blank slate for me. God couldn't be counted on in the way that I thought God could be counted on. That's what I felt as I stood on Ground Zero. God seemed absent. It was frightening, because the attributes that I had depended upon in the past, when thinking about the face of God, had all been stripped away, and I was left with nothing but that thing we call faith. But faith in what? I wasn't sure.

Atheist Ian McEwan, said he "felt, more than ever, confirmed in my unbelief. What God, what loving God, could possibly allow this to happen?" He sees prayer to be "almost infantile, this appeal to an entity who could intervene—who clearly hasn't intervened." He rejects belief in God as "an offense to reason."

An XTC song, entitled "Dear God," complained to God for letting humans down, bringing wars, drowning babies, suggesting that God is "just someone's unholy hoax." The song ends by denying belief in "you—dear God."[6] Isn't it interesting that those who profess not to believe in God still complain to God?

At the heart of how people respond to suffering is how they respond to God. Common responses are trust and acceptance, questioning and doubt, blame and accusation, or rejection and denial.

> **Isn't it interesting that those who profess not to believe in God still complain to God?**

Philip Yancey identifies two issues relating to suffering: the cause and our response. He says we may never understand why we are experiencing a specific suffering. However, we can control our response. He concludes, "The most important issue facing Christians who suffer is not 'Is God responsible?' but 'How should I react now that this terrible thing has happened?'" (*Where*, 106)

A basic understanding of God's role in human suffering is an essential first step in developing a Christian approach to the problem of suffering. Parts One and Two of this book dealt with God's teach-

[6] Quoted in http://www.dare-connexions.org/suffer.html.

ing concerning suffering and how His role in suffering helps us properly control our response to suffering and evil. This part will discuss the problem of evil and suffering more in detail. How we should understand and respond to the problem of suffering and evil will be addressed. A concluding chapter will identify wrong solutions to this problem.

Think about It

1. Give two examples of Christians faced with suffering who did not become angry with God but trusted the future to God.

2. Give examples of genuine believers who got angry with God when faced with great suffering.

3. Is God responsible for the suffering in the world? Explain.

4. How does the distinction between the permissive and directive will of God relate to the common tendency to blame God for suffering?

5. Give examples of horrendous evils that have occasioned some to reject the God of Christianity.

6. List the four responses of people to God when confronted with great suffering.

7. What point did Yancey make about cause and response to suffering?

CHAPTER SEVENTEEN

RESPONDING TO THE PROBLEM OF EVIL AND SUFFERING

Always being prepared to make a defense to anyone who asks you for a reason for the hope that is in you; yet do it with gentleness and respect.
1 Peter 3:15-16

The problem of evil and suffering is the most common objection to belief in a loving, personal God. We find questions about God and suffering being asked in the Old Testament Scriptures, as well as by Greek, Roman, and Oriental thinkers centuries before Christ. In the thirteenth century, Thomas Aquinas said he found only two serious objections to the existence of God—the problem of evil and suffering and the view that natural and human science could adequately account for all we experience without God (Q,2,a.3). He responded by presenting five lines of evidence defending the existence of God.

This subject of evil and suffering has been of great interest to philosophers and theologians. It has found expression in literary works, e.g., Fyodor Dostoyevsky and Voltaire. The discussions continue today. Between 1960 and 1990, more than 4,200 publications in English addressed the problem of evil (**Whitney**).

The heart of the problem is: How can an absolutely good God who is all-knowing and all-powerful be compatible with the world He created since it contains evil and suffering?

The attempt to justify or vindicate belief in God in the face of evil is called *theodicy*. We will never completely understand the complex issue of why God permits evil and suffering in His world. We can show that it is not logically inconsistent to believe in a loving and powerful God and the existence of evil. Biblical teaching helps us endure suffering, putting it in proper context in God's world. We also can learn how to better minister to those who are suffering.

What is evil? Some have held that matter is evil and spirit is good. According to the Bible, God did not use preexisting evil matter to create the universe. Rather He created the world from nothing. Evil is not a substance; but as Augustine maintained, it is a lack or a misuse of the good. *Moral evil* may be defined as suffering and harm caused by a human agent, e.g., murder, rape, and hate. By far the majority of evil and suffering in the world is caused by the actions of people. *Natural evil* may be defined as suffering or harm not caused by a human agent, e.g., hurricanes, droughts, and floods. Human agency is not completely absent in these events because people make choices that put themselves in potential harm's way. When a house built in a regularly flooded area is destroyed by a flood, the natural evil is mixed with human choice. Some dictatorial governments have made political decisions which resulted in famine and starvation.

Some horrendous evils have made it hard for naturalists to excuse evil as ignorance or social maladjustment. Such events would include the Nazi Holocaust, the thirty to fifty million killed in the Russian revolution, the 800,000 Tutsis killed by the Hutus in less than three months in Rwanda in the 1990s. In America, the killing of 3,000 in the attacks on the Twin Towers in New York, September 11, 2001, made it hard for relativists to say that it should be tolerated as personal choice. It borders on insanity not to call these events evil.

Os Guinness observes,

> The right to believe anything does not mean that anything anyone believes is right. The former is freedom of conscience and must always be respected unconditionally; the latter idea is nonsense and must often be opposed, but it can be a license for evil itself. Many an evil would have done none of its terrible damage downstream if it had been challenged upstream at its source. (14)

Blatant evil and horrible suffering do in fact exist in our world. Wisdom dictates that we take it seriously. How do wickedness, pain, and suffering fit into the Christian's thinking about God and the world? Pain and suffering include physical, bodily pain from disease, disorders, and injuries, as well as psychological and mental suffering, such as depression and grief over tragic loss.

Every thinking believer has to deal with this issue sooner or later. It is important to our personal relationship and trust in God There is great value in studying this issue before personal tragedy strikes in one's life.

First, we will discuss the problem of evil under two general headings. Next, will be a statement and response to the intellectual problem of evil and suffering, and then consideration will be given to the emotional problem of evil and suffering. The chapter will conclude with some guidelines for responding to those who are troubled with this problem. Chapter 18 will critique some wrong solutions to the problem of evil and suffering.

PROBLEMS OF EVIL AND SUFFERING

Both believers and unbelievers deal with the problem of evil and suffering. Questions about wickedness and suffering are commonly spoken of as the problem of evil. The various expressions of this challenge to Christian theism may be identified under two general headings: the intellectual problem and the emotional problem. One form of the intellectual problem of evil holds that a contradiction exists between the existence of evil and the existence of God. Another expression of intellectual problem is the argument that horrendous nature and huge amounts of evil constitute negative evidence against belief in God. The intellectual problem is also designated as the philosophical problem of evil.

The emotional problem of evil usually relates to a particular experience of suffering. It may involve hurt feelings that a loving, all-powerful God would allow such evil and suffering to happen to them or to those they love. This encounter with evil leads many to be angry or upset with God. This type of problem often plagues believers who experience tragic loss or some horrendous evil. This may also be called the religious problem of evil.

As we seek to understand this challenge to faith, we must distinguish between the intellectual problem and

We must distinguish between the intellectual problem and the emotional problem.

the emotional problem. Identifying the nature of the problem guides one in deciding how to respond to the questioner.

A world of difference exists between discussing the problem theoretically in a classroom and the practical emotions felt when you have just been notified that your child has been killed in an accident. Ronald Nash wisely observes, "When someone is troubled by aspects of the theoretical or philosophical problem of evil, the assistance of a good philosopher or apologist may help. But when we are confronted by the personal problem of evil, what we may need is a wise and caring friend, pastor or counselor" (208).

C.S. Lewis dealt with the intellectual problem in *The Problem of Pain* as he sought to reconcile the reality of evil with the belief in an all-powerful, all-loving, personal God. After observing his wife suffer and die with cancer, he wrote *A Grief Observed*. Here Lewis deals with the problem on an emotional level, seeking to answer the question in his heart asking how his God could allow the death of his wife with the accompanying suffering that directly attacked their lives.

John Feinberg, a seminary professor, wrote his masters thesis and his doctoral dissertation on the intellectual problem of evil. His book *The Many Faces of Evil* surveys several approaches to the problem of evil. In middle age, his wife was diagnosed with Huntington's Disease, a genetically transmitted disease. After onset in midlife, this disease results in mental and physical deterioration and premature death. Each of their three children has a 50% chance of having this disease. His book *Where Is God?* describes his struggles with the emotional or religious problem of evil and suffering.

Peter Kreeft describes the two sides of the problem:

> The gut-level problem of evil moves us to rebellion rather than to philosophy. It springs from concrete, individual cases of suffering, like dying children—as concrete as a blow to the gut. But the second level of the problem, the thought level, is important too, for it threatens faith, our lifeline to God. The first, personal form of the problem asks, How can I trust a God who lets my child die? The second, philosophical form of the problem asks, Why doesn't the evidence of evil prove that God is not running this show? The personal form feels, the philosophical form thinks. Both are important because both are essential aspects of our humanity.(*Sense*, 28)

Those who disbelieve in God do not have the theoretical problem that believers have with the problem of evil. Since they deny God that

God exists, there can be no contradiction between God and evil. However, unbelievers still have to deal with the harsh realities of evil and suffering in this world. Believers are more likely to wrestle with the emotional problem, because they may have trouble understanding why their God would allow horrible evils and suffering to happen to them and those they love.

Our approach to the problem of evil and suffering is influenced by several factors, including our view of the nature of God and the nature of human beings, and our understanding of the world and of evil. The purpose of this chapter is to show that neither the intellectual nor the emotional problem of evil and suffering refutes the reality of an all-good, all-powerful, and all-wise God.

> **Neither problem refutes the reality of an all-good, all-powerful, and all-wise God.**

The Intellectual and Emotional Problems of Evil and Suffering Contrasted

The Intellectual Problem	The Emotional Problem
Philosophical thinking	Religious feelings
Theoretical	Personal
Most often expressed by atheists and other unbelievers	Most often expressed by believers
Calls for rational explanation	Calls for comfort and reassurance
Assistance can be given by a philosopher, an apologist, and mature Christian thinkers	Assistance can be given by caring friends, ministers, and counselors

---

THE INTELLECTUAL PROBLEM OF EVIL AND SUFFERING

Philosophers have long wrestled with the problem of evil on an intellectual level. The Roman philosopher Boethius (c. AD 480–524) asked, "If there be a God, from whence proceed so many evils?" (**1.pr 4**) David Hume, an eighteenth-century Scottish skeptic, in *Dialogues*

Concerning Natural Religion, has Philo say to Demea, "Epicurus's old questions are yet unanswered. Is he [the deity] willing to prevent evil, but not able? then is he impotent. Is he able, but not willing? then is he malevolent. Is he both able and willing? whence then is evil?" (**pt 10**) Does evil disprove God?

THE LOGICAL ARGUMENT: THE EXISTENCE OF EVIL

According to this argument, if God is all-powerful and doesn't stop suffering, then He is not loving. If He is loving and doesn't stop pain, then He is not all-powerful. Therefore, the existence of evil and suffering rules out the existence of an all-loving and all-powerful deity. This is called the logical problem because it sees a contradiction between the existence of both God and evil.

Antony Flew writes, "The issue is whether to assert at the same time that there is an infinitely good God, second that he is an all-powerful Creator, and third that there are evils in his universe, is to contradict yourself" (**48**). He believed this argument established atheism.[1]

In an article in 1955, atheist John Mackie contends that theism is irrational.

> In its simplest form the problem is this: God is omnipotent; God is wholly good; yet evil exists. There seems to be some contradiction between these three propositions, so that if any two of them were true the third would be false. But at the same time all three are essential parts of most theological positions; the theologian, it seems, at once *must* adhere and *cannot consistently* adhere to all three. (**Evil, 92-93**)

Mackie continues:

> However the contradiction does not arise immediately; to show it we need some additional premises, or perhaps some quasi-logical rules connecting the terms "good" and "evil" and "omnipotent." These additional principles are that good is opposed to evil, in such a way that a good thing always eliminates evil as far as it can, and that there are no limits to what an omnipotent thing can do. From these it follows that a good omnipotent thing eliminates evil completely, and then the propositions that a good omnipotent thing exists, and that evil exists, are incompatible. (**ibid., 93**)

[1] Recently Flew has come to believe in a deist type of God.

Mackie sees a logical contradiction between the statements: "God is omnipotent," "God is wholly good," and "yet evil exists." The theist, he alleges, believes what cannot be proved and is actually disproved by other beliefs he holds.

The Logical Argument from Evil

1) If God is all-powerful, He can and should eliminate evil.
2) If God is absolutely morally good, He should want to eliminate evil.
3) Evil exists.
4) Therefore, an all-powerful, absolutely morally good God does not exist.

A Christian response to this statement of the intellectual problem of evil needs to show that the belief in an all-good and all-powerful God is not incompatible with the existence of evil. *Atheistic philosophers have been unable to prove that belief in God involves a logical contradiction.*

Alvin Plantinga is a Christian philosopher who deserves much credit for the resurgence of Christian philosophy in the last 25 years. One of his significant contributions has been to provide a method by which believers can demonstrate the consistency of their set of beliefs on the problem of evil.

It was not possible to create a world of free creatures that always did what was right.

Plantinga argues that it is logically possible that the only way God could create a world that contains persons with free will is by creating a world in which it is possible that persons can make morally wrong choices. At least one creature may choose to do wrong at least once. If so, it was not possible to create a world of free creatures that always did what was right. Free creatures could misuse their freedom. It was not possible to create a world having free creatures but no evil. He concludes that it is possible that an all-powerful and absolutely good God could create a world which contains some evil. Therefore the existence of evil is not logically incompatible with belief in the existence of God (*Freedom*, 12-24).

In giving a free-will defense Plantinga shows that it is possible that God has good reasons why He allows evil. He calls this a defense, not a theodicy. He does not claim to prove the reason for evil, but he describes a state of affairs, that, if actual, would explain the presence of evil. See Chapter 2 for further discussion of the free-will defense.

Contemporary non-Christian philosophers generally now admit that the problem of evil does not present a logical contradiction for belief in God. Mackie, later admitted that his earlier position "does not, after all, show that the central doctrines of theism are logically inconsistent with one another" (*Miracle,* **154**). William Rowe, an atheist, admitted that no one had proved that the existence of evil is logically inconsistent with the existence of a theistic God. He continues, "Indeed, there is a fairly compelling argument for the view that the existence of evil is logically consistent with the theistic God" (**Atheism, 10 fn.**). He cites Plantinga's *God, Freedom, and Evil* as an example.

God can be morally justified in permitting evil that He could prevent. We may not know the reason, but that does not prove no such reason exists.

THE EVIDENTIAL ARGUMENT:
THE NATURE AND AMOUNT OF EVIL

Atheistic philosophers have not given up. They restated the problem into an inductive version. Instead of saying that the existence of evil makes the belief in God *necessarily* false, some philosophers are now saying that the evidence of evil makes the belief in God *probably* false. Sometimes this is called the probabilistic argument. They have shifted their attention to the nature and amount of evil and suffering. Emphasis is made that the world contains senseless and meaningless evil. They argue that the amount of pointless, gratuitous, horrendous evil in the world makes the existence of God unlikely.

The most common form of this argument holds that senseless or gratuitous (unwarranted or unjustified) evil makes the existence of God improbable. It is argued that no possible greater good can reasonably justify why God would permit horrendous evil and suffering.

Perhaps one would have to be omniscient to know whether or not there is senseless evil in the world. The Christian view holds that there is a reason why evil exists in the world as we saw in Chapter 2.

Responses to this inductive argument hold that God permits evil to make possible a greater good or avoid a greater evil.

Ronald Nash says,

> Any sensitive and observant person must admit that many evils in the world appear to be gratuitous: accidents that strike people down in the prime of life, diseases that result in long periods of horrible suffering, birth defects, natural disasters that can suddenly kill hundreds of people and destroy the lives of survivors. But given the limitations of human knowledge, it is hard to see how any human being could actually *know* that some particular evil is totally senseless and purposeless. It seems, then, that the most any human can know is that some evils appear gratuitous. But of course such a claim . . . would not entail the conclusion that God does not exist. (**218**)

The case of Joseph being sold into slavery by his brothers is an example of good being brought out of evil. Joseph suffered because of this decision, but blessing came to his family and his people in the end. He affirmed, *"You meant evil against me, but God meant it for good, to bring it about that many people should be kept alive, as they are today"* (**Gen 50:20**). In this instance we can see God had a morally sufficient reason for allowing the evil.

The Logical and Evidential Problems of Evil Contrasted

Logical Argument of Evil	Evidential Argument of Evil
The existence of evil refutes the existence of God	The existence of evil provides evidence against belief in God
Deductive	Inductive
More aggressive	More modest
Holds belief in God to be logically impossible	Holds belief in God is implausible
Charges theism with internal contradiction	Holds theism is irrational because of negative external evidence

---

The biblical teaching concerning eternal punishment in hell presents a stumbling block to many. Atheists

Can hell be harmonized with a loving God?

have called this teaching barbaric. Liberal theology did not accept eternal torment. Some evangelical leaders also question the doctrine. Some churches have generally ignored teaching about hell for fear of offending outsiders. Others have adopted the view of annihilation of the wicked dead after a limited period of suffering. Can hell be harmonized with a loving God?

Regardless of one's opinion of the teaching of hell, Scripture teaches it, especially our Lord Jesus Himself; it is the traditional teaching of the church through the centuries; and it accords with reason.

Figurative language is used to speak of hell. This does not imply unreality, but figurative expressions are necessary when speaking of realities outside our physical universe. These expressions are not fictions but they point to a spiritual reality outside our physical world where *"flesh and blood cannot inherit"* (*1Cor 15:50*).

Biblical Descriptions of Hell

"fiery furnace" (*Mt 13:42,50*)
"destroy body and soul" (*Mt 10:28*)
"lake of fire and sulfur" (*Rev 20:10,14,15*)
"tormented with fire and sulfur" (*Rev 14:10*)
"the second death" (*Rev 10:14*)
"worm does not die" and "fire is not quenched" (*Mk 9:48*)
"smoke of their torment goes up forever and ever"
(*Rev 14:11;* cf. *Rev 19:3*)
"outer darkness" and "weeping and gnashing of teeth"
(*Mt 8:12; 22:13; 25:30*)
"eternal punishment" (*Mt 25:46*)
"wrath and fury" and "tribulation and distress" (*Rom 2:8-9*)
exclusion from God's presence
(*Mt 22:1-14; 25:1-13,46; Lk 16:19-31; 2Th 1:7-9*)

These biblical images and expressions are used to describe a reality which is beyond our world of time and space. Since we are dealing with figurative language, we need to avoid being overly literal. Everything the Bible affirms is true, but figurative statements are not true literally. We do not know the exact nature of hell as described. However, the sobering truth is that these statements of Scripture do speak of a very real place of suffering.

> **The Bible does not picture God as a gleeful eternal torturer.**

The Bible does not picture God as a gleeful eternal torturer as is sometimes mistakenly presented. Hell was not intended for human beings but for the devil and his angels (*Mt 25:41*). God's heartfelt desire is that no one would have to enter hell (*2Pet 3:9*). God in His abundant mercy became a man and died a horrible death to save us from being eternally separated from Him.

Salvation requires self-surrender. Some will never surrender their self-rule. Would heaven be heaven if it included those who will not submit to God's rule? Can God accept an evil person who misuses and abuses others for his or her self-interest and never repents? Lewis says we must not confuse forgiving with condoning. "To condone an evil is simply to ignore it, to treat it as if it were good. But forgiveness needs to be accepted as well as offered if it is to be complete: and a man who admits no guilt can accept no forgiveness" (*Problem*, 124).

In hell one can be utterly self-absorbed. C.S. Lewis says, "I willingly believe that the dammed are, in one sense, successful, rebels to the end; that the doors of hell are locked on the *inside*" (**ibid., 130**). Those there have the freedom they demanded and are self-enslaved. God allows them to be separated from Him.

Lewis continues:

> In the long run the answer to all those who object to the doctrine of hell, is itself a question: "What are you asking God to do?" To wipe out their past sins and, at all costs, to give them a fresh start, smoothing every difficulty and offering every miraculous help? But He has done so, on Calvary. To forgive them? They will not be forgiven. To leave them alone? Alas, I am afraid that is what He does. (**ibid.**)

> There are only two kinds of people in the end: those who say to God, "Thy will be done," and those to whom God says, in the end, "*Thy* will be done." All that are in Hell, choose it. Without that self-choice there could be no Hell. No soul that seriously and constantly desires joy will ever miss it. Those who seek find. To those who knock it is opened. (***Divorce***, 72-73)

THE EMOTIONAL PROBLEM
OF EVIL AND SUFFERING

On the level of lived experience almost everyone has been pained by the presence of evil and suffering in the world especially when we experience it directly. This personal experience of the reality of evil differs considerably from philosophical speculation about the problem of evil. No one in the midst of a tragic experience is merely an objective observer. Since we are all involved in the world of suffering this is not merely an academic discussion.

It is helpful to study the challenge presented by the intellectual arguments from evil before you experience a tragic event of some kind. Seek to resolve the intellectual arguments from evil and suffering. When suffering does come into your life, you'll have to deal primarily with the emotional problem instead of having to wrestle with both aspects of the problem.

> **It is helpful to study the challenge before you experience a tragic event of some kind.**

Alvin Plantinga responds to the intellectual problem of evil in *God, Freedom, and Evil*. He then identifies the problem faced by believers:

> In the presence of his own suffering or that of someone near to him he may find it difficult to maintain what he takes to be the proper attitude towards God. Faced with great personal suffering or misfortune, he may be tempted to rebel against God, to shake his fist in God's face, or even to give up belief in God altogether. But this is a problem of a different dimension. Such a problem calls, not for philosophical enlightenment, but for pastoral care. **(64-65)**

John Feinberg, after having taught and written extensively on the problem of evil, shares his experience, "For many years, I thought the intellectual answers I had constructed would be sufficient for someone in the midst of trials and afflictions. All of that changed for me in 1987 when my wife was diagnosed with Huntington's Disease" (**Still Believe, 249-250**).

Feinberg describes the emotional problem of evil and suffering:

> When news of this disease came, a host of emotions came with it: bewilderment, a sense of hopelessness and helplessness, a feeling of abandonment, and anger. As a Christian, I knew we aren't promised exception from problems and trials,

but I never expected something like this. With one diagnosis, a dark cloud had formed above my family that would not dissipate for the rest of our lives. At that point, the problem of evil moved from an intellectual problem that I could calmly reflect on in the solitude of my study to a real-life trauma that has to be confronted every day of my life. (**ibid., 250**)

In our teaching in churches and in Christian colleges we need to help believers realize the difference between the intellectual and emotional problems of evil and suffering. Even though Feinberg was well prepared to deal with the intellectual problem, he found that inadequate for dealing with the emotional problem.

Feinberg comments:

> But during this time of emotional and spiritual turmoil, none of the intellectual answers proved to be even the least comforting. As I thought about that, I came to an important realization. The religious problem of evil, the crisis of faith precipitated by suffering, at rock bottom is not primarily an intellectual question but an emotional problem. There are, of course, intellectual questions that the sufferer asks, and at an appropriate point in the grieving process when the afflicted is ready to hear the answers, it is appropriate to offer them. However, that point rarely comes during the shock of the terrible news. At that point, the sufferer needs comfort and care, not a dissertation on the logical consistency of God's existence and evil. (**ibid.**)

Every thinking person has to deal with questions such as, Why does a good God allow so much suffering? Why do good people and the innocent have to suffer? You may have developed a workable intellectual approach to dealing with the problem of evil. However, when intense suffering or personal tragedy crowds into our lives, we are forced to deal with the issue of suffering on an emotional and personal level. You do not think logically when your heart is broken.

When personal tragedy crowds into our lives, we must deal on an emotional and personal level.

It is common for Christians who suffer to have some frustrations and even questions for God. Some are especially troubled to the extent that it creates a crisis in their relationship with God. In ministering to those who are struggling with the emotional problem of evil and suffering, seek to respond to their personal needs. Chapters 19, 20, and 21 in this book offer suggestions for understanding and helping those who are hurting. You do not have to be an intellectual to help those dealing with emotional doubt and questions. You do need to be a sympathetic listener and a caring friend.

Moreland and Craig help us put the emotional problem of evil in proper perspective:

> When God asks us to undergo suffering that seems unmerited, pointless and unnecessary, meditation on the cross of Christ can help to give us the moral strength and courage needed to bear the cross that we're asked to carry. So, paradoxically, even though the problem of evil is the greatest objection to the existence of God, at the end of the day God is the only solution to the problem of evil. If God does not exist, then we are locked without hope in a world filled with gratuitous and unredeemed suffering. God is the final answer to the problem of evil, for he redeems us from evil and takes us into the everlasting joy of an incommensurable good, fellowship with himself. **(552)**

Guidelines for Responding to Persons Troubled by the Problem of Evil and Suffering

Listen carefully so that you know what question the person is actually asking. Respect for others requires that we learn from them what their question is rather than assuming we know. Seek to respond to the person's real question. Don't answer what they are not asking.

Determine if they have an intellectual problem with evil or if they have an emotional problem because of some specific instance of evil.

If they are troubled by the intellectual problem of evil, they should be given a solid defense of the faith. If they are dealing with the emotional problem of evil, they need pastoral and personal support and love.

Recognize the sufferer's pain and loss. Regardless of your opinion of their situation or point of view, empathize with their hurt.

Avoid pat answers which oversimplify. This complex issue is difficult and multifaceted having no simple solution. Be willing to admit it when you don't have an answer.

Don't minimize their question nor downplay or rationalize the evil in question. This is a serious matter with far-reaching consequences. Francis Schaeffer frequently said, "Every honest question deserves an honest answer."

Be perceptive in determining if the person asking "why" questions is really ready to receive an intellectual answer. Avoid giving intellectual explanations prematurely. Often that may come later after you have listened and shown loving support. In many cases that is not what the person really needs, at least at first.

Think about It

1. Do you know of a person who has wrestled with the problem of evil and suffering? Briefly explain.

2. Why is it important to recognize and identify the two kinds of the problem of evil and suffering?

3. Briefly contrast the two kinds of problems of evil and suffering.

4. What is the logical problem of evil and what is the current status of this argument among philosophers?

5. State the evidential problem of evil.

6. In the light of the logical argument being a deductive argument and the evidential argument being an inductive argument, what is the degree of certainty of each of these two arguments?

7. What response can be given to the evidential problem of evil?

8. Describe the emotional problem of evil? How does it differ from the intellectual problem of evil?

9. Summarize Feinberg's experience with the emotional problem of evil and suffering.

10. Which of the guidelines listed for responding to someone troubled with the problem of evil and suffering were most helpful to you?

CHAPTER EIGHTEEN

INADEQUATE APPROACHES TO THE PROBLEM OF EVIL AND SUFFERING

We destroy arguments and every lofty opinion raised against the knowledge of God, and take every thought captive to obey Christ.
2 Corinthians 10:5

A worldview is one's beliefs about the basic questions dealing with the world and life. What we think about issues, such as reality, truth, God, humanity, the world, morality, and history make up our worldview. All worldviews must address the problem of evil. Even those who deny God have to account for evil. How we view God, human beings, morality, and the world is at the heart of how we approach this problem.

As generally stated, the problem of evil arises because theists affirm that: 1) an eternal, personal God exists; 2) God is loving and wholly good; 3) God is sovereign and all-powerful; 4) God is all-knowing, all-wise; and 5) evil exists. Many see an inconsistency in affirming all five of these statements. Is the best solution to this problem just to reject one of these beliefs?

Many proposed solutions to the problem of evil either deny or modify the Christian view of God. Unsatisfactory solutions seek to resolve the problem by denying at least one of these: the reality of God, the goodness of God, the power of God, the omniscience and foreknowledge of God, or the reality of evil. Since Christian theists affirm all of these statements, they reject as wrong any approach that denies any of these five affirmations.

This chapter will state and seek to show the inadequacy of five unbiblical approaches that attempt to solve the problem of evil.

I. God Does Not Exist
II. God Is Not All Good
III. God Is Not All-Powerful
IV. God Is Not All-Knowing
V. Evil Does Not Exist

GOD DOES NOT EXIST

In their denial of the existence of God, atheists often reason, "Evil exists; therefore God does not exist." This appears to be the simplest

The atheist's argument is easy to state but impossible to establish.

solution to the problem of evil and suffering. But as we saw in the last chapter, it is not a reasonable solution. The atheist's argument is easy to state, but it is impossible to establish.

It is common today for atheistic philosophers to prefer to talk of the evidential argument from evil rather the logical argument from evil. They hold that it is not a problem except for those who believe in God. They insist that the existence of evil in the world is negative evidence against believing that a personal, loving, all-powerful God does exist. Yet even the atheist cannot explain why some things are horribly evil because his view cannot account for moral evil.

Peter Kreeft says,

> Spiritual evil could not evolve from mindless matter. Moral evil can come only from moral agents, souls. And where did they come from? From something less than themselves, blind matter? Less can't make more; there can't be more in an effect than in its causes. If you admit the existence of moral evil, you must trace it back to moral agents or souls, and souls to God, not to molecules. (*Sense*, 31)

C.S. Lewis, when he objected to the existence God on the basis of evil, realized he derived his concept of justice from God, thus assuming God in order to deny Him.

> My argument against God was that the universe seemed so cruel and unjust. But how had I got this idea of *just* and *unjust*? A man does not call a line crooked unless he has some idea of a straight line. What was I comparing this universe with when I called it unjust? If the whole show was bad and senseless from A to Z, so to speak, why did I, who was supposed to be part of the show, find myself in such violent reaction against it? . . . Of course I could have given up my idea of justice by saying it was nothing but a private idea of my own. But if I did that, then my argument against God collapsed too—for the argument depended on saying that the world was really unjust, not simply that it did not happen to please my private fancies. Thus in the very act of trying to prove that God did not exist—in other words, that the whole of reality

was senseless—I found I was forced to assume that one part of reality—namely my idea of justice—was full of sense. Consequently atheism turns out to be too simple. If the whole universe has no meaning, we should never have found out that it has no meaning: just as, if there were no light in the universe and therefore no creatures with eyes, we should never know it was dark. *Dark* would be without meaning. (*Christianity*, 31)

If no God exists, then how did human beings come up with a standard of goodness by which we judge something as evil? Lewis asks, "If the universe is so bad . . . how on earth did human beings ever come to attribute it to the activity of a wise and good Creator?" When the atheist denies an Ultimate Good, he or she lacks any basis for defining evil.

To call something evil, is to acknowledge the existence of a moral standard, which must come from a Moral Lawgiver. All human beings have some kind of morality, some sense of "ought" and "ought

> **When the atheist denies an Ultimate Good, he or she lacks any basis for defining evil.**

not." These moral judgments cannot be explained by environment and physical experiences. Lewis concludes, "Attempts to resolve the moral experience into something else always presuppose the very thing they are trying to prove" (*Problem*, 10).

Ravi Zacharias was lecturing at the University of Nottingham, England, when a skeptic stated, "There cannot possibly be a God with all the evil and suffering that exists in the world."

Zacharias asked, "When you say there is such a thing as evil, are you not assuming that there is such a thing as good?"

"Of course," the questioner replied.

"But when you assume there is such a thing as good, are you not also assuming that there is such a thing as a moral law on the basis of which to distinguish between good and evil?"

"I suppose so," came the hesitant and much softer reply.

Zacharias then reminded him of a debate between Copleston, a believer, and Russell, an unbeliever. Copleston asked Russell if he believed in good and bad. Russell said he did. Copleston asked how he distinguished between the two. Russell said he did as he distinguished between colors. Copleston said that he distinguished between colors by seeing, so how did he distinguish between good and bad? Russell's sharp reply was "On the basis of feeling, what else?"

Zacharias said that someone should have told him in some cultures people loved their neighbors and in others they ate their neighbors. Were both of these actions based on feelings? Whose feelings? Zacharias drove home his point, "In other words, there must be a moral law, a standard by which to determine good and bad. How else can one make the determination? My questioner finally granted that assumption without hesitation."

Zacharias continued, "If, then, there is a moral law, you must posit a moral lawgiver. But that is who you are trying to disprove and not prove. If there is no moral lawgiver, there is no moral law. If there is no moral law, there is no good. If there is no good, there is no evil. I am not sure what your question is" (*Cries*, **66-67**).

Atheism involves a contradiction. It assumes evil but has no objective basis to define evil. If this universe, including human beings, exists by accident, on what basis can one determine right from wrong? The naturalist must explain why horrible tragedies and atrocities are not just products of the blind forces of nature.

Alvin Plantinga says:

> What is genuinely appalling is not suffering as much as human wickedness. But can there be any such thing as horrifying wickedness if naturalism is true? I don't see how. There can be such a thing only if there is a way rational creatures are supposed to live, obliged to live, and the force of normativity is such that appalling and horrifying nature of genuine wickedness is its inverse. Naturalism can perhaps handle foolishness and irrationality, acting contrary to what are your own interests. It can't accommodate appalling wickedness. (**Christian Life,** 73)

The reality of evil counts as much against atheism as it does against theism. We must not say that the reality of evil proves either atheism or theism. Which position gives the most reasonable explanation of the existence of moral evil in the universe? Christian theism gives a better explanation of evil as we have discussed in earlier chapters. Atheism fails to define moral evil because a moral God must exist who created moral beings

The reality of evil counts as much against atheism as it does against theism.

and is Himself the standard of morality. If we had no concept of God, from whom we derive our concept of good, how would we know something is evil?

Atheism robs both life and death of meaning. Kreeft says,

> When the atheist meets God face-to-face where he expected to meet nothingness, when the atheist finds that God rather than death is the ultimate reality, he will see that his philosophy was the cheapest answer ever invented—cheap because it refused the only thing that is infinitely not cheap, the God who is infinite value, infinite goodness. (*Sense*, 32)

GOD IS NOT MORALLY GOOD

Another wrong answer to the problem of evil denies the absolute moral goodness of God. This view finds many different expressions.

Pantheism holds that all that exists is God, therefore all that exists is essentially good. Evil is included within the nature of God. Hinduism is basically pantheistic in holding that no personal God exists whose goodness could be questioned and no redemption is possible. What we call good and evil make up the same reality. Since all that exists is God, all that exists is good. No effective standard exists by which we can distinguish between good and evil.

Zacharias, who was born and raised in India says of Hinduism, "By declaring everything in the physical world to be nonreal, illusory, changing, transitory, it ends up with philosophical problems beyond measure." One asks, "What has brought on this 'illusion' of evil, if everything is part and parcel of the divine reality?" (*Jesus*, 115)

> There is a classic passage in the *Bhagavad-Gita* in which Krishna counsels young Arjuna, who is on the battlefield, facing the possibility of killing his own half-brothers. He struggles and cannot bring himself to do this. Krishna, who comes as his chariot-driver, talks to him about his duty. This was his duty, to fulfill his caste's responsibility as a warrior. This is the way life moves on. But he told Arjuna not to fear to do his duty, for all good and evil are fused in the one ultimate reality, Brahman. In Brahman, says Krishna, the distinction breaks down. That which appears evil is only the lesser reality. In the end, all life, all good, all evil, flow from God and back to Him or it. "Go to war and do your job." This convergence of everything into one absolute reality forms the hub of the answer to the question behind the question. One can see how a sense of

fatalism dominates when all reality is inexorably and inevitably unfolding. (**ibid., 115**)

Hinduism says the perception of evil is a result of ignorance. But the absolute is ultimately responsible for this ignorance. Reincarnation is central to their view of evil. Karma is the principle or rule that you reap in a reincarnation what you have sown in a previous life. "Hinduism here conveys an inherited sense of wrong, which is lived out in the next life, in vegetable, animal, or human form. This doctrine is nonnegotiable in Hindu philosophy" (**ibid., 117**).

Belief in reincarnation is counter-compassionate.

Belief in reincarnation is counter-compassionate. If you help the suffering and starving, you work against karma. Removing their suffering will only mean they have to come back for more suffering to work off their debt. The thrust of social humanitarian work in India is due to Christian influence, not Hindu. Hinduism does not provide a valid or practical solution to the problem of evil.

Buddhism was founded in the sixth century BC by Siddhartha Gautama, the Buddha (Enlightened One). This revision of Hinduism also holds to karma and reincarnation. Buddhism includes atheistic and pantheistic elements. They prefer not to use the term "God" in referring to Absolute Reality. "The opening lines of the Buddhist scriptures say that every individual is the sum total of what he or she thought in his or her past life." Suffering is the result of sins in one's past life (**ibid., 117**).

Buddhists emphasize four noble truths:
1) Life is suffering.
2) Suffering is caused by desire.
3) Suffering can be eliminated by eliminating desire.
4) Desire can be eliminated by right action and right belief.

According to Buddhism we have desires because we think things are permanent. Nothing is permanent, not even the self, so we should stop all desiring. The goal of Buddhism in the state of enlightenment is to extinguish the self and all desire, hence ending all evil and suffering.

This is escapism, rather than realistically dealing with the problem of evil. With no distinction between God and the world, Buddhism is without a valid basis for distinguishing good from evil. All physical things, including people, are illusions. The worth of the individual is lost in eastern pantheistic mysticism. Motivation to address the evils in this world is lost. Buddhism is found wanting in its view of God and evil and suffering.

The New Age Movement accepts a pantheistic worldview. God is everything and we are gods. The Star Wars movies popularized the concept of God as impersonal Force. The distinction between good and evil is blurred. The New Age spirituality offers no practical help for dealing with the issues of sin, suffering, and death. "The Force" is certainly not the God of the Bible. New Age thinking and other pantheistic views suffer from the same inadequacies of Hinduism and Buddhism.

Making God equal to the world is a view attractive to many because it removes death and hell. An im-

> **"The Force" is certainly not the God of the Bible.**

personal God cannot give worth and value to the individual person. This view of God is unlivable because any standard of right and wrong is lost. A God who is not good and loving is a God who cannot be loved, worshiped, or trusted. Such a God is not able to save us or give us hope.

Those who are animistic (nature is full of spirits) and who practice forms of paganism hold that bad things that happen to a person are punishment for wrongdoing. Various rituals are performed to appease their gods. Those who practice paganism do not believe in a personal God who is wholly good and loving.

Some throw up their hands at the evil and suffering in the world and conclude that whatever will be, will be. This view says no answer can be given to the problem of evil and suffering. They acknowledge God's power at the expense of His goodness. This fatalism results in depression and hopelessness. While the God of the Bible has sovereign power, He also is good and loving.

When bad things happen, some have decided to deny God's goodness and love. When confronted with the horrendous evils in the world, they angrily accuse God of being unloving and indifferent to hurting people. As stated in Chapter 16, some felt they could no longer believe in a good and loving God in the light of the Jewish Holocaust or the destruction of the Twin Towers in New York on September 11, 2001.

The Bible in no way supports the denial of God's goodness. No-where does it suggest the idea that God could or would do something wrong or evil. The passages that say God "repented" (*Gen 6:6; Ex 32:14*) do not affirm that God changed but rather that the circum-stances changed.

The Bible affirms God's power and His goodness. God created man for fellowship with Himself. Sin broke that relationship. God set in process a plan of redeeming lost human beings back to fellowship with Him. God patiently and lovingly worked with the Hebrew peo-ple who were often rebellious and disobedient to prepare for the cen-terpiece of human history—God becoming man in Jesus of Naza-reth. He came to be the Savior for all who would trust Him as Savior and Lord.

> ## God created man for fellowship with Himself. Sin broke that relationship.

God made the world and human beings good, but sin ruined that. The sin of our first parents resulted in the loss of goodness and hap-piness. A wise and loving God allowed that sin and its terrible conse-quences, but He implemented a plan to overcome the evil in human hearts and lives through His plan of salvation.

Peter Kreeft tells of his four- or five-year-old daughter trying to thread a needle. She kept trying and hit her finger and made it bleed a couple of times. He was watching her but she did not see him.

> My first instinct was to go and do it for her, since I saw a drop of blood. But wisely I held back, because I said to myself, "She can do it." After about five minutes, she finally did it. I came out of hiding and she said, "Daddy, daddy—look what I did! Look at what I did!" She was so proud she had threaded the needle that she had forgotten all about the pain.
>
> That time the pain was a good thing for her. I was wise enough to have foreseen it was good for her. Now, certainly God is much wiser than I was with my daughter. So it's at least possible that God is wise enough to foresee that we need some pain for rea-sons which we may not understand but which he foresees as being necessary to some eventual good. There, he's not being evil by allowing that pain to exist. (**Strobel, *Faith*, 41**)

GOD IS NOT ALL-POWERFUL

Believing God is all-powerful does not mean he can do anything, including absolutely impossible and self-contradictory things, such as make a square circle. However, the God of the Bible is able to do anything logically possible that He chooses to do. Why hasn't He chosen to eliminate pain and suffering?

Some limit God's power in their effort to solve the problem of evil. Wenham states,

Some limit God's power in their effort to solve the problem of evil.

In their well-meaning attempt to avoid implicating God in evil they have deprived him of his control of the world; this applies to happenings both great and small. Take, for instance, the Nazi persecution of the Jews. However perplexing it may be, it is an inescapable fact that God did not step in as the millions were driven into the gas chambers. God's inactivity creates a tremendous problem to those who believe that he is in control, but at least they are convinced that his justice and wisdom and love will be finally vindicated. But to those who do not believe that he is in control, his passivity suggests the appalling possibility that God did not intervene, not because he did not want to, but because he could not do so. If this is so with the big things, it is so with the little crises of our individual lives. It profoundly affects everyday Christian living, for it means that we cannot turn to him confident of his power to intervene if he wishes to do so; we cannot *entrust* anything to him. If God wishes to control evil, but cannot do so, we are reduced to Dualism, with a god of good waging inconclusive war against a god of evil. In such circumstances the would-be Christian, deprived of the ability to trust, cannot be expected to put up much of a fight. "Faith" without trust becomes a shadowy thing, no longer a power to overcome the world. (**44**)[1]

Dualism is that view that good and evil are eternal, opposite realities involved in a never-ending conflict with each other. Spirit and matter are both ultimate substances, equally powerful. God, the good spirit, is in conflict with the evil spirit who is responsible for matter and the physical world.

Gnosticism, a mixture of Greek dualism and Christian ideas, presented a challenge to the early church. Spirit was viewed as good and matter as evil. A demiurge, an offshoot of God, is responsible for creating the present material world full of evil. This view derives evil ulti-

[1] See C.S. Lewis, *Mere Christianity*, 33.

mately from God; consequently the good spirit cannot overcome the evil. Evil is outside God's control. It is eternally there and God has to work with it. This view offers no victory or hope.

Finitism limits the power of God, holding that God is finite or limited in power. In this view a loving God exists, but He is not all-powerful. God lacks the power to adequately deal with evil.

Process theology views God as the soul of the universe. God evolves and changes even as the universe evolves. James Taylor describes this view, "We have a God who is limited by that part of him (the universe) that is imperfect and changing. Given this, the laws of nature are the laws of God's nature. Therefore, God cannot prevent evil from occurring by suspending the laws of nature (because God cannot change his nature)" (145).

Rabbi Kushner, in his bestseller *When Bad Things Happen to Good People*, popularized the view of a God who is good but lacks power. He explains how he coped with tragedy in his own life. His only son, Aaron, had a disease causing premature aging. Aaron died in his teens. The rabbi describes his dilemma,

> I believed that I was following God's ways and doing his work. How could this be happening to my family? If God existed, if he was minimally fair, let alone loving and forgiving, how could he do this to me? And even if I could persuade myself that I deserved this punishment for some sin of neglect or pride that I was not aware of, on what grounds did Aaron have to suffer? (2)

Kushner concludes that suffering exists on the planet because God is a God of justice, but not a God of power. The world gets out of control. God is outraged at pain and evil, but He lacks the power to do anything about it. "God would like people to get what they deserve in life, but He cannot always arrange it" (43). Kushner chooses to believe in a good God who is not totally powerful instead of a powerful God who is not totally good. His God is not all-powerful and not all-knowing. He cannot overcome all evil even though He tries His best. In affirming God's love at the expense of His power Kushner ends up with a naturalistic God.

In affirming God's love at the expense of His power Kushner ends up with a naturalistic God.

Peter Kreeft concludes, "Kushner's God fails the crucial test, the death test. A naturalistic God cannot solve the problem of death. Death is nature's trump card. It takes the supernatural to trump death" (*Sense*, 37). Kushner's God is not the all-powerful Creator of the Bible, but is a limited being who does not have supernatural power over nature. With Kushner's God, we are left uncertain about ultimate meaning, living with the real possibility that evil may triumph in the end.

If God cannot check the forces of evil, how can we expect man to do so? Norman Geisler states,

> Finitism does not offer satisfactory answers to the question of God and evil. It does not answer why God brought the world into existence if He knew it would be evil. It fails to explain why evil does not appear to be destroyed nor does this view even guarantee that it will. . . . How can God be finite when every finite thing must be caused? . . . How can a finite God guarantee the overthrow of evil and the final triumph of good? Only an infinite God who is in sovereign control of the universe can really guarantee the defeat of evil. (*Roots*, 28-29)

Views that deny that God is all-powerful must be rejected because the Bible pictures God as sovereign over nature and history.

GOD IS NOT ALL-KNOWING

Open theism is a view that holds that God does not know what will happen in the future because, if He had complete foreknowledge, we would not be truly free. Those holding this position believe that God does not know in advance the future free decisions of His creatures. The future is open, and God learns what will happen as it occurs. God cannot prevent tragic events from happening, but He feels the pain of those who suffer. God may repent of His past actions, knowing that He may have inadvertently contributed to human suffering. Even though our tragedies are unforeseen by God, according to the open theists, He stands ready to help us rebuild our lives through His counsel. In this view God does not know what future free decisions will be made that would frustrate His efforts to work things for good.[2]

---

[2] Advocates of open theism include: John Sanders, *The God Who Risks: A Theology of Providence* (Downers Grove, IL: InterVarsity, 1998), and Gregory A. Boyd, *God of the Possible: A Biblical Introduction to the Open View of God* (Grand Rapids: Baker Books, 2000). Responses to open theism include Bruce A. Ware,

Boyd, in his *Is God to Blame: Beyond Pat Answers to the Problem of Suffering*, reacts to what he calls the blueprint worldview. He says this view holds that a divine reason exists for everything that happens. Everything that happens is what God wants to occur. I would agree with Boyd in rejecting this view.

I cannot accept his defense of a limited God. He gives two variables that affect what God can and can't do.

> The first is that the world in which agents relate must be regular, predictable and orderly. Thus God can't suspend the laws of nature whenever they might work against us. The second is that agents must possess irrevocable freedom. God simply can't override free wills whenever they might conflict with his will. Because God decided to create this kind of world, he can't ensure that his will is carried out in every situation. He must tolerate and wisely work around the irrevocable freedom of human and spirit agents. **(125)**

The Bible contains too many instances where God suspends the laws of nature for His purposes and where He does override human choices for one to accept the position of open theists.

Those who thus limit God's knowledge of the future seek to comfort those suffering by saying God could not have known what was going to happen and therefore it was out of His hands. This approach to the problem of evil and suffering ends up diminishing God.

If God does not know the future, how did He predict so many things with unerring accuracy through His prophets? For example, Cyrus is named and called God's anointed and shepherd over one hundred years before Cyrus was born (*Isa 44:28–45:6*). If God does not know the future, what benefit is our hope and confidence in our prayers? Is human suffering pointless, catching God with surprise?

The open theism approach to the problem ends up diminishing God.

The Scriptures teach that God does have exhaustive knowledge of the past, the present, and the future. The Bible teaches the omniscience of God, meaning His knowledge is total and infinite. It is with-

God's Lesser Glory: The Diminished God of Open Theism (Wheaton, IL: Crossway, 2000), and Millard J. Erickson, *What Does God Know and When Does He Know It? The Current Controversy over Divine Foreknowledge* (Grand Rapids: Zondervan, 2003).

out limits. God *"knows everything"* (**1Jn 3:20**). *"His understanding is infinite"* (**Ps 147:5, NASB**). God declares, *"I am God, and there is no other; I am God, and there is no one like Me, declaring the end from the beginning, and from ancient times things which have not been done"* (**Isa 46:9-10, NASB**).

Jack Cottrell states, God has "complete *foreknowledge* of the entire future history of his creation, including the free-will decisions of human beings. . . . The infinite God is not limited by time in that his consciousness transcends the now-moment and embraces the totality of history—past, present, and future—in a single act of knowing" (**85-86**). God's foreknowledge of all events does not mean that He predestines all events.

> **God's foreknowledge does not mean that He predestines all events; His omnipotence does not mean everything happens as He wants.**

God's omnipotence does not mean everything that happens is what God wants to happen. According to the Bible, God permits evil, but He is sovereign and in control over all things. Evil and human suffering occur with God's knowledge and permission. Wenham reasons, "God's omnipotence would seem to be a necessary outcome of the fact of his Creatorhood. To think of God creating out of nothing all the minute particles of our vast universe (to say nothing of its non-material wonders) and then not having perfect knowledge and control of them seems absurd" (**42-43**). God knows the number of hairs on your head and the number of stars. Not one sparrow falls to the ground without His knowledge (**Mt 10:30; Ps 147:4; Mt 10:29; Eph 1:11**).

God can work through suffering to accomplish His purposes which are good. The songwriter stated:

> God is too wise to be mistaken; God is too good to be unkind,
> So when you don't understand, when you can't see his plan;
> When you can't trace his hand, trust his heart.[3]

³ Quoted in **Ware, 213**. "Trust His Heart," written by Eddie Carswell and Babbie Mason, 1989, May Sun Music, Causing Change Music, Word Music and Dayspring Music.

Chapter 18
Inadequate Approaches

EVIL DOES NOT EXIST

Illusionism seeks to resolve the problem of evil by denying the existence of evil. Hinduism, a version of illusionism, is a monism which believes that all reality is ultimately one and is good. Things in the world that appear to be diverse are only illusions just as evil is only an illusion. Brahman or God is the only reality. The physical world including suffering only appears to be real.

The Christian Science religion holds this philosophy. Founder Mary Baker Eddy taught that evil is only an illusion. Evil, sickness, and death are not real. We can ask what is the cause of the illusion? "If evil is only an illusion, why does it *seem* so real?" Edward Lear wrote:

> A certain faith-healer of Deal
> Asserted: "Pain is not real."
> "Then pray tell me why,"
> Came the patient's reply.
> "When I sit on a pin
> And puncture my skin,
> Do I hate what I fancy I feel?" (**Geisler, *Roots*, 17**)

Does it make any practical difference whether or not I call pain and evil an illusion or consider it a reality? "Those who believe that evil and the world are illusions do not actually function as if this were so" (**ibid., 18**).

The only valid approach to the problem of evil and suffering is the biblical view of a personal God—who is all-good, all-powerful, all-knowing—and a real world where evil exists. The Christian worldview reveals why evil exists and gives strength for coping with suffering. While this view does not answer every question, it is the most satisfactory explanation of evil and suffering. The Christian approach to suffering affirms: 1) God exists; 2) God is all-good and loving; 3) God is all-powerful; 4) God knows all things about the future; 5) evil exists.

The Christian worldview reveals why evil exists.

Only one God exists who can help us endure suffering and minister to those who are suffering—the God who created the universe and human beings (*Genesis 1–2*). God revealed Himself in His power and wisdom to Job (*Job 38–39*). This sovereign Lord came in human form in Jesus Christ, suffering with us, dying on the cross, and rising victorious over death. Trust Him. Only He can give you the ultimate victory.

Think about It

1. What is a worldview?

2. List the five affirmations Christian theists make concerning the problem of evil.

3. What convinced C.S. Lewis that his defense of atheism based on evil was not reasonable?

4. When something is called evil, one is assuming what?

5. Plantinga says naturalism cannot explain what?

6. What does pantheism say about good and evil?

7. What is lost if God is impersonal?

8. What illustration does Peter Kreeft give to point out that God is not evil because he allows pain to exist?

9. How does dualism differ from Christianity?

10. Describe Kushner's God.

11. What do open theists believe about God's limited knowledge?

12. What groups teach that evil does not exist?

Part 4

Helping
the
Hurting

CHAPTER NINETEEN

MINISTRY TO THE HURTING

Comfort one another.
2 Corinthians 13:11

G od cares for sufferers and suffers with them. Believers who have the mind of Christ will seek to minister to those suffering. Ministry to the hurting is an essential part of the Christian life. Paul reminds us, *"If one member suffers, all suffer together"* (***1Cor 12:26a***). *"Weep with those who weep"* (***Rom 12:15b***). The *"God of all comfort . . . comforts us in all our affliction, so that we may be able to comfort those who are in any affliction, with the comfort with which we ourselves are comforted by God"* (***2Cor 1:3b,4***).

THE GRACE OF GRIEVING

Paul wants us to understand the promises concerning Christians who have died *"that you may not grieve as others do who have no hope"* (***1Th 4:13***). He states that the believer's hope for resurrection to a new life with the Lord is grounded in the fact that Jesus rose from the grave. He concludes, *"Therefore encourage one another with these words"* (***1Th 4:18***).

It is a mistake to assume Christians do not need to grieve because we have hope of life beyond the grave. Our faith and hope may be solid and strong, but the loss of a loved one brings great pain and an indescribable sense of sadness and loss.

God designed the grieving process as a way of coping with the loss of loved ones and other tragic losses. It is insensitive, unrealistic, and unbiblical to suggest that Christians do not need to grieve. It is unhealthy for Christians to pretend that they

> **It is unhealthy for Christians to pretend that they do not need to grieve.**

do not need to grieve. Alan Wolfelt, a grief care specialist, writes, *"You can not heal without mourning or expressing your grief outwardly.* Denying your grief, running from it, or minimizing it only seems to make it more confusing and overwhelming" (3).

Grief is the mental, emotional, and spiritual pain and sorrow we feel when we lose someone or something we love. It may be the loss of a child, a spouse, a relative, a job, a pet, a home, one's health, or something else we hold dear. Grief may be mild or deep and intense depending on the intensity of our love for the person or thing that is lost. The makeup of our personality also affects how we grieve. Bereavement—the loss by death of a loved one—brings the most disorientating kind of grief. In prolonged illnesses leading to death, grieving begins long before death occurs. In cases where the death of the loved one is unanticipated, grief hits like a hammer and the initial stages are harder to handle. In divorce the hurt is permanent, but it lacks the closure and finality of death because conflicted consequences continue.

When a tragic loss occurs, grief is more all-consuming and devastating than we ever thought it could be. Words are inadequate to express what we feel. Shock leaves you half-numb, making it difficult to comprehend what others say or to formulate your own thoughts in coherent sentences.

Grieving is a process of adjusting to the death of a loved one or some serious loss of health or great tragedy. In grief we deal with the challenges that bereavement and loss bring. Grief is not a problem to be solved or something to get over and then all will be well. Grieving the death of a loved one involves a process of adjustment in which we have to relearn the world as we transition from loving the person in their presence to loving them in their absence.

Freud and those he influenced counseled survivors to detach themselves from memories of their dead loved one. Mourning was considered immature. Current Christian counselors who stress emotional attachment in personal relationships say "The grieving process is a natural, innate, God-given means for humans to accept, adjust to, and live on in the light of the death of loved ones" (**May, 365**). It helps the family restructure a new life in light of the death of a loved one.

In contrast to Freudian counselors, counselors stressing attachment view "loss and its resultant grief not as something primarily to 'get over' but as a natural part of life that requires adjustment to a new reality" (**ibid., 363**). Sharon Hart May says, "Studies show that the ability for children and adults to alter and then continue their relationship with their deceased loved one was both comforting and productive. The assurance of the continued bond allowed the bereaved to cope with the loss and make necessary changes in light of it" (**ibid.**).

One does not soon get over and forget the amputation of a leg. It is a situation that requires daily coping with the new realities presented. In the same way, in the days and years after a loved one dies you face situations that are different because the person is now absent instead of present. After his wife died, C.S. Lewis said, "The act of living is different all through. Her absence is like the sky, spread over everything" (*Grief*, 11). Even years later something will happen that triggers a flashback bringing a strong emotional sense of loss. The process of grieving involves adjusting to and coping with new realities. It is more of a journey than a destination.

> **The process of grieving is more of a journey than a destination.**

Sharon Hart May says, "The entire grief process normally takes from 1 to 3 years to resolve, and must be respected as part of living." She reported on a study that followed 1200 adult mourners for two years after the death of their loved ones. The study found that "the phase of shock and numbness peaks during the first two weeks after the death of a loved one. Mourners also reported experiencing a sense of disbelief again after one year" (**366-367**).

Norman Wright, grief and crisis counselor, in *Will My Life Ever Be the Same?* describes "being ambushed by grief" after a significant loss. "It's an ongoing onslaught of grief that hits you suddenly when you least expect it. You may choke up or cry, your chest may feel constricted, and a wave of sadness may overwhelm you. This is a normal response, but when it happens you need to stop everything else and deal with your feelings" (**93**).

As one begins to come to grips with the reality of death, he or she may experience pain, sorrow, anger, and guilt. Often one is unable to concentrate, relax, and sleep. Mourners may suppress their emotions fearing they will burden family or embarrass themselves socially.

Sharon Hart May describes some grieving experiences:

> Anger arises that is often directed toward the deceased, the comforters, and those who may be remotely responsible for the death of the loved one. When this anger is turned inward the bereaved experiences a sense of guilt, blaming him or herself for not having done more, having done the wrong thing, or having done too little. Many, especially children, fear that their indifference, angry feelings, or wishful prayers played a part in the death. It is important for the family system to allow the expression and experience of grief by each family member. Mourners need to express their guilt in a safe and supportive environment to sort out what they realistically are, and are not, responsible for. . . .
>
> Between the 5th and 9th month after the death of a loved one, the bereaved may find oneself disorientated, though it is still not until one year that the pain of grief tends to peak. . . . This season is also marked by depression, guilt, fluctuation of weight, and an awareness of the reality of the death. There is a loss of joy and meaning in life, and getting through the day requires much effort. (**367-368**)

When trying to reassess life, the bereaved person is often frustrated by memory lapses and a sense of confusion. He or she may experience physical problems, fearing a serious illness. In ministering to those grieving who have such experiences, we have to help them realize they are not crazy but are dealing with some things common to the grieving process.

In *How We Grieve*, death educator and counselor, Thomas Attig describes ". . . grieving as a process of relearning the world that requires that we relearn physical surroundings and find a new place including fellow survivors, the deceased, and (for some of us) God, and relearn ourselves, that is, our ways of being who we are." (**ix**). When we grieve we must "relearn our selves as we adjust our daily life patterns, redirect the stories of our lives, and establish new patterns of connection with the world" (**ibid.**)

Norman Wright explains some of the adjustments encountered in bereavement,

One of the tasks of grief is learning how to function without this person in your life. You won't have the interactions and validation you were used to experiencing with that person. The loss of their physical presence in your life means that your needs, hopes, dreams, expectations, feelings, and thoughts will change. Slowly, over time, the reality of separation begins to sink in and you realize, "For now, I exist without this person as a part of my life. (*Life,* **93**)

But death only ends your physical relationship with the person.

Thomas Attig in *The Heart of Grief: Death and the Search for Lasting Love* describes grieving as a transition from loving the lost loved one in their presence to adjusting to loving that person in separation or absence. Love does not quit loving (*1Cor 13:8*). Grieving does not mean a forgetting or a complete letting go of the person who has died. Grieving helps one transition to a lasting love that acknowledges and appreciates the one who has died. Attig says, "Many have told me of places in their hearts where they hold and love those who have died. I have learned how cherishing memories and continuing to care about some of what they cared about has enriched survivors' practical, soulful, and spiritual lives. . . . And I have witnessed how the hope for lasting love can motivate us to grieve in ways that bring consolation and restore our wholeness" (**xiv**).

"Sometimes our holding on to the past of those who have died is obsessive, preoccupying, or excessive" (**ibid., xvi**). Such a response makes it so one cannot carry on the daily functions of life. While this is unhealthy and should be avoided, that

> **Through the process of grieving we relearn and reshape our lives in a new reality.**

is no reason to let go of the good in our relationship with our loved one. "We can constructively hold on to the good in lives now ended and sustain rewarding connection to the past" (**ibid.**). When one is gone, everything changes in our relationships with our family and others in our communities. Through the process of grieving we have to relearn and reshape our lives in a new reality without the lost loved one.

The depth and intensity of grief is affected by several things, including: the depth of love for the lost person, the amount and kind of interaction and dependence upon the person, the years and kinds of investment you have made in the person, what is missed in regard to lost future associations with the person, and the recent accumulation of other traumatic events.

Our relationships with others often include both constructive and destructive aspects. "Typically, we continue to love others while they live because what we love about them or about sharing life with them matters more to us than what disappoints or bothers us. We struggle to hold on to and cultivate the good and to let go of the rest. We continue this struggle when they die" (**ibid., xvii**). Hold on to the good and let go of the rest.

"If our journeys in grief are to lead us to lasting love, we must reshape our feelings, desires, motivations, habits, dispositions, expectations and hopes" (**ibid., xviii**). This process may be painful. But one can move beyond hurt and anxieties and cherish the good memories of the past. "Our journey in grief can bring us to lasting love that honors those who have died, enriches our lives in survival, and takes a place alongside our other relationships with fellow survivors and new people who enter our lives" (**ibid., xix**). We need to give thanks to God for His grace in giving us the grieving process so we can relearn the world and live productive lives after our loss.

> **Give thanks to God for His grace in giving us the grieving process.**

THE MINISTRY OF COMFORTING

Those who have passed through the valley of suffering can have a genuine ministry in helping others who are suffering. Suffering does not make us expert counselors but it can help us learn to be sympathetic and caring for those who are hurting. When our son died, some people who had also lost a child explained to us how we would feel and what to expect. This was little help. Others who had lost a child did not feel that this made them authorities on the subject. They said very little but they quietly showed with their caring presence a genuine love. Their help was invaluable.

We must be willing to accept comfort and help from others. Especially in the early stages of grief we need to rely on wise counsel of trusted friends. Because of shock and confusion, we may say things we do not mean and make bad and regrettable decisions. A trusted and wise friend can help one navigate through the jumbled maze we call grief. Professional counseling may be needed. Receiving and accepting comfort may be preparation for being able to comfort others later.

Someone has said, "There is a stewardship of grief." Experience with suffering and being comforted should prepare us to comfort others who are afflicted (*2Cor 1:3-4*). When a loved one dies, there is a sense of loss, emptiness, and loneliness. It is love for the hurting and recognition and empathy for their loss that will enable us to be effective comforters. You do not need to be a professional counselor to comfort the grieving and hurting, but love for the person *is* a requirement.

> **Receiving and accepting comfort may be preparation for being able to comfort others later.**

If you have not experienced grief, it is important to listen to the experiences of persons who have experienced grief to gain an understanding to help you support and comfort those who grieve. In ministering to those who are grieving we need to realize that a "respect for individuals as they grieve requires both that we not interfere in their grieving or exacerbate their vulnerability and that we facilitate their return to flourishing and full community with fellow survivors" (**Attig, *Relearning*, ix**). Losses disrupt and change our lives. In seeking to minister to the grieving, Attig advises, "You must learn the details of the story each survivor has to tell about how the loss has changed profoundly his or her experience of the world and has limited what is possible in the next chapters of each biography. You must learn the different ways the death disrupts the flow of each survivor's life story. You must learn how each survivor faces distinct challenges and struggles to go on in the next chapters of life" (**ibid., 7**).

THE MINISTRY OF UNDERSTANDING

If we want to help the hurting, we need to learn to recognize pain intensifiers. Dr. Paul Brand identified five intensifiers—fear, anger, guilt, loneliness, and helplessness—that heighten the perception of pain within the conscious mind and disrupt the healing that can come through the grieving process.

FEAR

Fear increases pain. "When an injured person is afraid, muscles tense and contract, increasing the pressure on damaged nerves and causing even more pain" (**Brand and Yancey, 263**). Many times the fear a person feels contributes as much or more to the pain felt as the actual cause. Dr. Brand says, "The gentle and honest wisdom of health practitioners and the loving support of friends and relatives are the best remedies. I have found that the time I spend 'disarming' fear for my patients has a major impact on their attitude toward recovery, and especially their attitude toward pain" (**ibid., 264**).

Abused children, battered women, terrorized neighborhoods, and people in many other similar types of circumstances experience fears and suffering. A child who has lost a parent often fears losing the other parent. Children of divorce can fear they were responsible for the family breakup. Stability and structure can help build assurance and confidence in the child. Grandparents and close friends can help provide a network of security.

> **Help the person not let the fear get out of proportion to the actual danger.**

One may be helped by talking about his or her fears with a caregiver or a friend. What is important is to try to help the person not let the fear get out of proportion to the actual danger. When we master our fears, we are on our way to mastering the pain. Building confidence in a loving all-powerful God helps one deal with fears.

ANGER

Anger and bitterness actually contribute to the pain and suffering that people experience and often prevent timely healing. Dr. Brand states, "Too often I have seen the physiological effect on people who became angry with their employer, or the driver of the other car, or the previous surgeon, or a spouse who lacked sympathy, or God. The anger must be dealt with, of course; it does not go away on its own. But if it is not dealt with, if it is allowed to fester in the mind and soul, the anger may release its poison in the body, affecting pain and healing" (**ibid., 270**).

Being a listening ear for a friend who is working through anger is an unpleasant task but at times is a necessary step in helping them overcome this hindrance to their healing. Finding forgiveness from God and being forgiving toward others can free one to progress in dealing with pain and suffering.

GUILT

"Counselors at chronic pain centers, too, report that their most challenging, 'pain-prone' patients have deep-rooted feelings of guilt and may well interpret their pain as a form of punishment. . . . Hundreds of patients I have treated—Muslim, Hindu, Jewish, and Christian—have tormented themselves with questions of guilt and punishment. What have I done wrong? Why me? What is God trying to tell me? Why do I deserve this fate?" (ibid., 271-272)

As a committed Christian, Dr. Brand observed,

> If God is using human suffering as a form of punishment, he certainly has picked an obscure way to communicate his displeasure. The most basic fact about punishment is that it only works if the person knows the reason for it. It does absolute harm, not good, to punish a child unless the child understands why he or she is being punished. Yet most patients I have treated feel mainly confused, not chastened, by suffering. (ibid., 272-273)

The biblical record includes several specific cases where the suffering experienced by people was a punishment by God—for example the Babylonian captivity. Dr. Brand states,

> These biblical examples have little in common with the pain and suffering most people undergo today. Millions of babies are born with birth defects every year. Whom is God punishing, and why? . . . I see no close parallel between the suffering most of us experience today and the punishment presented in the Bible, which follows repeated warnings against specific behavior. . . . Indeed, it seems safe to say that the vast majority of sicknesses and disasters have nothing to do with punishment. (ibid., 273-274)

LONELINESS

Pain and suffering separates and isolates one from others. It is easy to feel alone and forsaken. Having the presence of a caring person can contribute greatly to one's ability to cope with pain and grief. One does not have to be a professional counselor to minister to the loneliness of a suffering person. Dr. Brand said that when he asked his patients, "Who helped you most?" they usually describe "a quiet, unassuming person: someone who was there whenever needed, who listened more than talked, who didn't keep glancing down at a watch, who hugged and touched, and cried" (**ibid., 277**) *Their love for the person overcomes any fear of the person's grief.*

The world is cold and lonely when one feels alienated from God. Help the sufferer find reassurance in the presence of a caring God. The presence of a caring believer can help the sufferer begin to regain a sense of God's personal presence in his or her life.

HELPLESSNESS

A clear relationship exists between a sense of control and the level of perceived pain. Dr. Brand says,

> I have treated patients with acute arthritis who have the same degree of degeneration but respond in opposite ways to the pain it produces. One woman stays in bed all day, clutching the affected hand in genuine agony, and will not even attempt to pick up a pencil. The other says to me, "Yes, my hand hurts. But I'd go crazy just lying around. I've got to work as best I can. After a while, I forget about the pain." Behind those two responses lies a great difference in personality, belief system, confidence, and expectations about health. The "pain-prone" person sees herself as a victim, unfairly cursed. The disorder defines her identity. The second sees herself as a regular human being somewhat slowed down by pain. I have had some arthritis patients who strike me as genuinely heroic about pain. In the morning they slowly force their stiff hands open; it hurts, yes, but the fact that they feel *in charge* gives them a measure of control that keeps pain from dominating. (**280**)

It is important for a health professional or care giver to help the sufferer regain control over his or her body. Medical treatments can only do so much; much of the healing process comes from within the patient. Encourage the sufferers to do whatever they can do for themselves.

Seek a balance of helping where needed but not overdoing it. Overzealous helpers who won't let the sufferer do anything for himself or herself actually hinder the recovery process. Even terminal patients should be allowed to do what they are capable of doing.

They don't want to feel completely useless. Our goal should be to empower the sufferer rather than contribute to their sense of helplessness.

Norman Cousins was a man who had a crippling disease of the connective tissue of the spine. In the hospital he experienced all of these pain intensifiers—fear, anger, guilt, helplessness, and loneliness.

> **Our goal should be to empower the sufferer rather than contribute to a sense of helplessness.**

Dr. Siegel said the patients most likely to get well are those who do not meekly submit but seek second opinions and question procedures. Cousins was one of those patients who fought against the pain intensifiers. "Cousins's entire approach was based on his belief that, since negative emotions demonstrably produce chemical changes in the body, then positive emotions—hope, faith, love, joy, will to live, creativity, playfulness—should counteract them and help drive out the intensifiers of pain" (**ibid., 286**).

We may not be able to deal with the cause of a person's pain and suffering but we can often contribute to the mental health and well-being of the sufferer. Recognizing and dealing with these pain intensifiers can help us be more effective comforters.

THE MINISTRY OF CARING

The key to helping the hurting is not only knowledge or skill but especially a genuine love for others. It is a spirit of caring for the best interest of the other person. Next to the greatest commandment of loving God is *"You shall love your neighbor as yourself"* (**Mt 22:39**). The Golden Rule should guide us as we seek to comfort the afflicted and help the weak. *"So whatever you wish that others would do to you, do also to them, for this is the Law and the Prophets"* (**Mt 7:12**).

Our words of comfort and deeds of helpfulness should not be motivated from guilt or pity or from a desire to meet an external requirement of charity. Comforting others must not be motivated by a desire to make ourselves appear gracious and pious. Genuine caring should motivate the believer who wants to be a helper.

In America when a terminal illness hits one mate, frequently the other spouse splits. This results when the marriage is one of convenience and useful only as long as it meets one's selfish needs. Marriage is meant to be based on a lifelong commitment of unselfish love for each other. We see this kind of love in *A Promise Kept: The Story of an Unforgettable Love* by Robertson McQuilkin who cared over twenty years for his wife during her battle with Alzheimer's disease. Another inspiring story is Edwin V. Hayden's *Beloved Sufferer: How One Man Copes with His Wife's Disabling Illness*. Mrs. Hayden suffered with Parkinson's disease. These stories highlight the difference a caring relationship can make in helping one who is suffering.

Paul writes, *"And we urge you, brothers, admonish the idle, encourage the fainthearted, help the weak, be patient with them all"* (**1Th 5:14**). The Hebrews writer recognizes that we need daily encouragement from other believers (**Heb 3:13**).

> Let us hold fast the confession of our hope without wavering, for he who promised is faithful. And let us consider how to stir up one another to love and good works, not neglecting to meet together, as is the habit of some, but encouraging one another, and all the more as you see the Day drawing near. (**Heb 10:23-25**)

Jesus designed the church to be a family-type fellowship and community where individuals with different abilities and responsibilities work together to help one another as together we seek to serve our Lord Jesus Christ. Every Christian is called upon to love one another, to encourage and to help others. Leaders need to model the ministry of caring and encouragement. They also need to provide instruction and training in this regard as well.

Leaders need to provide instruction and training in the ministry of caring and encouragement.

Caring comes from the heart, but it finds expression in words and actions. The Proverbs highlight the importance and power of words. *"Anxiety in a man's heart weighs him down, but a good word makes him glad"* (**Prov 12:25**). *"Gracious words are like a honeycomb, sweetness to the soul and health to the body"* (**Prov 16:24**). *"Death and life are in the power of the tongue"* (**Prov 18:21**). *"A word fitly spoken is like apples of gold in a setting of silver"* (**Prov 25:11**). James speaks of the great influence of the tongue for good or bad (**Jas 3:2-10**). Paul counsels, *"Let no corrupting talk come out of your mouths, but only such as is good for building up, as fits the occasion, that it may give grace to those who hear"* (**Eph 5:29**).

Care givers need to watch their words so that they treat others as persons not as a means to their selfish ends. Good conversational skills, such as maintaining eye contact and listening carefully so we understand what was said, communicate genuine caring. We like being around people who really care about us instead of those who are only interested in their own agendas or self-promotion. *"In humility count others more significant then yourselves. Let each of you look not only to his own interests, but also to the interests of others"* (**Php 2:3b-4**). We need to be like Timothy of whom Paul writes, *"For I have no one like him, who will be genuinely concerned for your welfare. They all seek their own interests, not those of Jesus Christ"* (**Php 2:20-21**).

Think about It

1. Since Christians believe in life in heaven beyond death, why do believers grieve the loss of a loved one?

2. How does the Christian grieve differently from the non-Christian (**1Th 4:13**)?

3. Explain the idea of loving a lost loved one in their absence after having loved them in their presence.

4. Why do we have to relearn life after a loved one dies?

5. What is meant by a "stewardship of grief"?

6. What are the five pain intensifiers listed by Dr. Paul Brand?

7. How will recognizing and understanding the role these intensifiers play in increasing pain help us to be better comforters to the afflicted?

8. How does the suffering experienced today differ from the cases in the Bible where suffering was clearly God's punishment for wrongdoing?

9. How important is one's attitude in coping with pain?

10. What is more important than our knowledge and skill in ministering to the hurting?

11. What are some guidelines for those who would be caregivers in helping the hurting.

CHAPTER TWENTY

WHAT DOESN'T HELP THE HURTING

So whatever you wish that others would do to you, do also to them.
Matthew 7:12

Crises and difficult times intrude into our lives. They are unavoidable. They throw us off guard and challenge our ability to cope. These crucial times may be defining moments or key turning points in our lives. Our response to suffering and tragedies determines whether we grow from the experience or whether we regress in our development.

Such difficulties can be so serious that we need the help of others to keep from being overwhelmed and devastated. They can help us in handling the experience of suffering. The privilege of helping others should not be taken lightly. We need to give careful thought about how our words or actions will be received by those we seek to comfort. We do not want to be *"miserable comforters"* as Job described his friends (*Job 16:2*). Well-meaning people can be thoughtless and insensitive in what they say and do.

Philip Yancey tells of his friends, John

I. "I Know Just How You Feel."
II. "You Must Get On with Your Life."
III. "Something in Your Life Is Displeasing to God."
IV. "It Was for the Best. No Doubt This Has Spared You from Worse Problems."
V. "You Do Not Have Enough Faith."
VI. "God Selected You to Be an Example of Faith in Suffering."
VII. "God Took the Person Because He Needed Him or Her in Heaven."
VIII. "You Must Thank God for Making You Suffer. It Is God's Will."
IX. Choosing to Avoid Talking to the Person Suffering or about the Suffering Itself
X. "Please Tell Me the Details of the Person's Death."
XI. "God Must Have Had a Purpose in This. I Believe This Is Why It Happened . . ."
XII. "Think Only Positive Thoughts."
XIII. Quoting "All Things Work Together for Good" (Rom 8:28)
XIV. "It Is Sinful to Be Angry."
XV. "I Know of a Person Who Died of Your Disease."
XVI. Immediately after a Tragic Death: "We're Just Rejoicing in His or Her Victory."

and Claudia Claxton. A year after their wedding, doctors told Claudia she had Hodgkin's disease, a cancer of the lymph glands, and gave her only a 50 percent chance of survival. She had surgery and cobalt and radiation treatments, and visits from many Christians. Unfortunately, her Christian visitors were more confusing than comforting.

A deacon from her church said, "Surely something in your life must displease God."

A lady came with flowers, singing happy songs. When Claudia tried to talk about her illness, the lady changed the subject, seeking to combat the suffering with cheer.

Another visitor, a follower of television faith healers, said healing was Claudia's only escape. "If you have enough faith, just name your promise and claim the victory."

The next visitor said Claudia should praise God for everything that happens. "You must say, 'God, I love you for making me suffer like this.'"

Claudia's pastor said, "Claudia, God chose you because of your strength and integrity to suffer for Christ to be an example to others."

These remarks left Claudia confused (**Yancey,** *Where,* **15-18**). However well-intentioned, these comments did not help Claudia deal with her suffering.

For several years I have asked students in my classes at Ozark Christian College, as well as other groups of Christians, to think about what helped and what didn't help when they faced times of great pain and sorrow in their lives. The material in this chapter and the next came from their comments and from other oral and written testimonies on what helped and what did not help when people were hurting. No doubt exceptions will exist to these suggestions. But it is instructive to listen to what sufferers have to say. This chapter will address some of the things we should avoid saying or doing when we seek to help those who are hurting.

Since a person's suffering is unique to that individual, what helps one may not help another. One thing is clear; we all stand on level ground when it comes to helping the hurting. God uses ordinary Christians to help one another in the healing process. We are to *"help the weak"* (**1Th 5:14**). Love that seeks the other's best interest should guide us as we seek to help the hurting.

Some people are extremely insensitive in their words and actions causing more damage than good. Well-intentioned words of "comfort" may only bring more pain. We need to make every effort to avoid saying things that hurt more than help when our friends are facing difficult times. Here are some real examples of words meant to help that only hurt.

> **We need to make every effort to avoid saying things that hurt more than help**

"I KNOW JUST HOW YOU FEEL."

John Feinberg describes his reaction to this comment:

> Through my experiences, I have learned how inappropriate and unhelpful this comment can be. The problem is really twofold. On the one hand, it isn't true, and the sufferer knows it. Hence, it sounds phony when you say it. Even if you think you know how I feel, and even if the same thing happened to you, you still don't know how I feel and you can't know how I feel. You can't because you are not me with my particular personality and emotions, with my background and experiences, with my family and the relations we share with one another. (***Where*, 40**)

Many sufferers have confided to me that, when someone makes this statement, they do not agree or find it comforting. It is true that one who has faced a similar loss may be able to understand your situation better than others. But that does not mean that they know exactly how you are experiencing the suffering and grief. No one will respond to the death of a loved one in the same way. Each person's relationship with the lost loved one was different and each personality is unique, making every situation different. Each person's suffering is unique. Grief after an accidental death is different from the grief experienced during and after a prolonged illness that results in death. A husband's grieving may be very different from his wife's. The loss is unique to each individual who experiences the loss, and each has to cope with it from his or her personal situation.

When my wife and I were in our early twenties ministering in a church in California, Myrtie Bigelow was a dear servant of God who had lost her mother and nine-year-old daughter in a car accident. Later, her thirty-one-year-old daughter died suddenly leaving her six-

Chapter 20
What Doesn't Help

month-old child for grandparents to raise. Myrtie gave us this wise advice. "Never tell someone, 'I know just how you feel.'" How much better to say, "I don't know how you feel, but I care."

"YOU MUST GET ON WITH YOUR LIFE."

Only persons unacquainted with deep grief would say this. This seems insensitive to those who have lost a loved one because it leaves the suggestion that it is time to forget the loved one. Our "instant potatoes" culture has a shallow view of suffering and grief. Our "stiff upper lip" mentality encourages getting over mourning quickly and getting on with life. But each of us grieves in his or her own way and on one's own timetable. Grieving the loss of a loved one is a coping and adjusting process which continues over many years.

Gerald Sittser, who lost three family members in an accident, says we never recover from a tragic loss.

> We recover from broken limbs, not amputations. Catastrophic loss by definition precludes recovery. It will transform us or destroy us, but it will never leave us the same. There is no going back to the past, which is gone forever, only going ahead to the future, which has yet to be discovered. Whatever that future is, it will, and must include the pain of the past with it. Sorrow never entirely leaves the soul of those who have suffered a severe loss. If anything, it may keep going deeper.
>
> But this depth of sorrow is the sign of a healthy soul, not a sick soul. It does not have to be morbid and fatalistic. It is not something to escape but something to embrace. Jesus said, *"Blessed are those who mourn, for they will be comforted."* Sorrow indicates that people who have suffered loss are living authentically in a world of misery, and it expresses the emotional anguish of people who feel pain for themselves or for others. (*Grace*, 62-64)

A friend of mine said it was three years after his wife died before he felt he could experience happiness again. In some respects one is never completely over feelings of grief.

No one can tell you how long your grief should last.

Some losses require more healing time. No one can tell you how long your grief should last. Norman Wright states,

The unanticipated nature of an accidental death can be a major factor in contributing to a grief reaction that lasts for several years. One study indicated that the majority of mourners who experienced the loss of a spouse or child in an automobile accident were still dealing with the death in thoughts, memories, and feelings four to seven years afterward. (*Life*, 97)

He adds, "Your grief over the death of a child will be more intense and last longer than grief over the loss of any other person significant to you" (102).

> **Controlling persons are not good comforters.**

Allow the person to proceed at his or her own pace. Don't force your own timetable for healing on others. Controlling persons are not good comforters.

Extremes are not healthy. To deny one's grief or to be unwilling to grieve only prolongs the process and makes genuine healing more difficult. On the other hand a fixation on one's grief to the extent that one cannot function in daily life is not normal. When one falls into a clinical depression that involves total withdrawal from all responsibilities in life, counseling or therapy may be helpful. Also a denial of death causing apathy or bitterness may call for special attention.

"SOMETHING IN YOUR LIFE IS DISPLEASING TO GOD."

Many automatically connect suffering with sin. People will say, "If you had been a better Christian, this wouldn't have happened to you," or, "There must be some secret sin in your life."

Job's friends told Job he was suffering because of his sin. God told Job's friends they were wrong. Jesus also rejected this view of suffering (*Lk 13:1-3; Jn 9:1-3*). In the Bible, inspired spokesmen told when God sent suffering as a punishment for sin. One would need to have divine inspiration or a direct statement of Scripture to make this accusation.

A father related that when he and his wife learned that their first-born had problems, they prayed that the problems would go away. Over months of continued praying they successively learned their child was blind, mentally retarded, and had muscular dystrophy and cerebral palsy. Some people distanced themselves from them concluding either they were not spiritual enough or they had angered God by their actions. The father at one time wondered if God was punishing him for his former years of atheism. A minister even suggested that possibility to him (**Clayton, 8**).

Donald Carson shows the inappropriateness of this kind of comment:

> Practically speaking, this means that it is almost always wrong, not to say pastorally insensitive and theologically stupid, to add to the distress of those who are suffering illness, either: (a) some secret sin they have not confessed, or (b) inadequate faith, for otherwise they would certainly have been healed. The first charge wrongly assumes that there is always a link between a specific ailment and a specific sin; the second wrongly assumes that it is always God's will to heal any ailment, instantly, and that he is blocked from doing so only by inadequate or insufficient faith. . . . God may have other reasons for sanctioning illness and sorrow among his people. (*How Long?* 101-102)

Feinberg says, "Scripture is very clear that sometimes the ungodly do prosper (**Ps. 73**), while the righteous suffer (**Job 1:8; 2:3; 1 Pet. 4:12-19**). The truth is that in most instances we don't really know whether someone suffers as a righteous person or as a sinner" (**Where**, 28).

Some suffering is caused by sin, for example, sexually transmitted disease from sexual sin. But not *all* suffering is caused by one's sin. Some suffering is caused by the sins of others (for example, the destruction and death caused by drunk drivers). An innocent person might be the one who suffers in such a situation. Sometimes suffering results from an accident or circumstance where no one is at fault. We encounter suffering because we live in a fallen world.

> **We encounter suffering because we live in a fallen world.**

"IT WAS FOR THE BEST. NO DOUBT THIS HAS SPARED YOU FROM WORSE PROBLEMS."

Death may well be best in some extreme cases where a person has essentially ceased to function as a living person. In most instances, however, only God knows what is best about a person's death. Generally, such a judgment should be left to God. The comforter should stick to caring for the sufferer and giving comfort, rather than speculating about what is best.

The child of a seminary student and his wife died. Later that semester he shared with the class some things he had learned. He reported that he and his wife were told, "You know, it's probably a good thing that your son died. He probably would have grown up to be a problem. Maybe he'd have been a drug addict or would have refused to follow Christ. God knows these things in advance, and he was probably just saving you from those problems." His professor observed, "It is hard to see how that information is a comfort at the time of loss. . . . Their loss is extremely painful, and the pain is not eased, let alone removed, by insensitive speculations about the future. Moreover, the comment is wrong, because it in effect says that it is good that evil has happened" (**ibid., 34**).

"YOU DO NOT HAVE ENOUGH FAITH."

Some believers hold that if your prayer is not answered, something is wrong with your faith. A deaf couple left a church that ministered to the deaf to become a part of a church promising healing. They were excited that, through the church's prayers, they would soon be free from their deafness.

After months of praying for complete healing, the couple remained deaf. Promises changed to blame. Concluding that the couple was not healed because something was wrong with their faith, the congregation asked them to leave. A friend of the couple observes that this case "warns us concerning what happens when we become so sure we know what God will and won't do" (**Mehrens, 2**).

All healing is from God whether it is natural or miraculous. God designed the body to repair itself in many instances. He gave humans intelligence so they could learn healing skills. He allowed us to develop many products that can be used for healing. God at times acts miraculously and heals a person or brings about events that have no natural explanation. But what happens when God does not intervene and heal miraculously? God does not always heal. That does not mean He doesn't like us or that we haven't mustered up enough faith.

The Bible does not teach that sufficient faith will prevent all pain and sickness.

Some have told us, "Sickness is never God's will. God wants you well."

But the NT does not teach that if you have sufficient faith you will never have pain and sickness. God's love for us is not conditioned by our being well or sick. Paul prayed three times for deliverance from his thorn in the flesh, but God said, *"My grace is sufficient for you"* (**2Cor 12:9**). And even Timothy had *"frequent ailments"* for which Paul suggested medicinal help (**1Tm 5:23**).

"GOD SELECTED YOU TO BE AN EXAMPLE OF FAITH IN SUFFERING."

Is this supposed to be comforting? Claudia, whom we met at the beginning of this chapter, did not think so. My wife was told after our son's death that God knew she was strong enough to handle it. That is why He chose her to be an example to others. This was not comforting. Without divine revelation, how could one know this anyway? The problem with this view is that it claims to know that God caused the tragedy. God may use one's faithfulness in suffering as strength to others, but that does not mean He caused the suffering. We need to be careful that we do not blame God for the things that Scripture does not say He does.

> **We need to be careful not to blame God for things that Scripture does not say He does.**

"GOD TOOK THE PERSON BECAUSE HE NEEDED HIM OR HER IN HEAVEN."

God does not "need" any of us in heaven. This comment is especially harmful when made to a small child who has lost a mother or father or brother or sister. What kind image of God does this generate in the child's mind? The child will feel, "I needed the person too." It may generate fear or anger toward a God who just snatches from the earth whoever He pleases.

"YOU MUST THANK GOD FOR MAKING YOU SUFFER. IT IS GOD'S WILL."

This can come across as blaming God for an evil. It can cause a person to react with anger or bitterness. They may think, "What kind of God would want my child to be abused and killed? Do you mean that God wants me to suffer excruciating pain with this cancer?" Does the comment mean God wants horrible things to happen?

It is true that even in the harshest of circumstances there is always that for which we can be thankful. However *1 Thessalonians 5:18—"Give thanks in all circumstances; for this is the will of God in Christ Jesus for you"*—is often misunderstood. We can find things *in* every circumstance for which we can give thanks. But that does not mean we must give thanks *for* evil things.

Paul does say, *"Giving thanks always and for everything to God the Father in the name of our Lord Jesus Christ"* (*Eph 5:20*). When the Bible uses "all" or "every" we must ask if it does so with qualification. John Stott comments on this text:

> We must not press these words literally. For we cannot thank God for absolutely "everything", including blatant evil. The strange notion is gaining popularity in some Christian circles . . . that a husband should praise God for his wife's adultery and a wife for her husband's drunkenness; and that even the most appalling calamities of life should become subjects for thanksgiving and praise. Such a suggestion is at best a dangerous half-truth, and at worst ludicrous, even blasphemous. . . . [We must thank God] for his loving providence by which he can turn even evil to good purposes (e.g. *Rom. 8:28*). But that is praising God for being God; it is not praising him for evil. To do this would be to react insensitively to people's pain (when Scripture tells us to weep with those who weep) and to condone and even encourage evil (when Scripture tells us to hate it and to resist the devil). God abominates evil, and we cannot praise or thank him for what he abominates. (*Ephesians*, 207)

It would be contradictory to thank God for evil "in the name of our Lord Jesus Christ." The context limits the phrase "for everything."

We are not asked to thank God for evil things. But we are to be thankful to God, not just in the pleasant times but in the midst of everything. The above comment assumes that everything that happens is God's will. But that depends on how we define God's will. Sinful and evil acts are not what God wants and wills to happen. Everything that happens is not within God's directive will. God's directive will is what God desires and directs or commands to happen. For example, Jesus is the only way to God.

God in His permissive will allows and permits both good and evil things to happen. He granted to human beings free will, which included the possibility for evil. This fallen world and our fallen human race are not what God desires or approves, but rather what God has allowed.

Later the sufferer may come to see how their suffering fits into God's overall plan. Generally when one is in the pit of intense suffering is not the time to be told "It is God's will." We should avoid other unhelpful statements, such as, "God needs him more than you do," and "He's happy now because he is with God." And "You can always have more children."

I've found it helpful to avoid people who were full of advice. "If I were you, I would do this." Those most helpful don't give uninvited advice or explain things when they are speculating and really don't know.

CHOOSING TO AVOID TALKING TO THE PERSON SUFFERING OR ABOUT THE SUFFERING ITSELF

Some people don't know what to say, feel awkward, or are afraid they will say the wrong thing, so they avoid the sufferer. Or they talk about everything except the reason for the suffering. "Let's talk about the weather . . . or my vacation . . . or our favorite team . . . whatever we can discuss that is happy." Fearing they will make the person sad, they avoid any mention of the lost person. But if you have lost a family member, you don't want that person to be forgotten. The avoidance by friends hurts worse than talking about the person who has died. This kind of silence can communicate a lack of caring. You cannot camouflage disease or death by ignoring it. The sufferer must face the reality of the

If you have lost a family member, you don't want that person to be forgotten.

situation. How much better to say something to this effect, "I'm sorry about your loss. I'm praying for you."

Zig Ziglar, who lost a daughter with leukemia, said,

> Be sensitive but available. Some friends were so afraid of intruding upon our family time that they avoided calling us or asking us to do things as they had before. Other folks felt compelled to start a relationship with us, but in truth, we didn't have energy for new friendships. Send food, do practical things to help, but keep the friendship at the same level as before. If you've been meeting with someone once a week for prayer, keep on doing it. If your acquaintance has been casual, a crisis is not the time to try to deepen it. You want to be surrounded by people who have been close to you. **(143)**

Ziglar's wife made this observation: "Don't avoid talking about the person who has died. I love it when the mother of Catie's best friend recalls things Catie said or did. I realize Catie was important to her, too. It helps when people remember and call or send cards on special dates. Every October 4, Catie's birthday, someone places a pumpkin on her grave site. We don't know who does it, but it means a lot" **(ibid.)**.

Don't abandon the sufferer by avoiding him or her or avoiding talking of the suffering. You don't have to have profound words that will make the pain go away. Most sufferers need someone who really cares to be there to listen to them express their thoughts and feelings.

"PLEASE TELL ME THE DETAILS OF THE PERSON'S DEATH."

The details may be too painful to talk about especially in the early stages of grief. Respect people's privacy. If the person wants to talk about the person's death, listen. But, don't pry thoughtlessly. When we needed to talk, there were friends and family who listened to us express our thoughts and feelings about our son, Mark, his life, and his death. This helped us on our way to healing.

"GOD MUST HAVE HAD A PURPOSE IN THIS. I BELIEVE THIS IS WHY IT HAPPENED . . . ."

Many keep looking for some purpose that God had in a sickness or a tragedy. Generally such opinions are mere speculation and not helpful in times of profound suffering. Grief-stricken sufferers need love and support not theological lectures or philosophical explanations.

Jim and Judy McDoniel's third child was born without arms and with shortened legs. When people attributed this condition to God, Jim responded, "God did not do it." He stated, "God is not to be blamed for armless babies. God is our source of strength and love. I believe we are going in the wrong direction totally when we ask, regarding one of life's tragedies, 'Why is God doing this to me?'" (31)[1]

Some things just happen in this fallen world and we may never know why they happened. Even if we do not know why they happened, we can control our response to the event. We need to see the overall purpose of God in the universe and our lives, but we may never know the reason why a particular tragic circumstance has happened. In most cases, questions about cause are in God's area not ours. It's best to leave it there.

"THINK ONLY POSITIVE THOUGHTS."

This is escapism. It is better to be honest and realistic about one's grief than to try to muster only positive thoughts. If I have a terminal disease, it is neither helpful nor realistic to think and act as if I do not. Everything that happens in this life is not positive. The cheerleaders are not helpful who urge the sufferer to be cheerful or to see the blessing in what has happened. Some good results may come from a loss or illness, but that does not erase the need to grieve in dealing with the harsh realities of the situation. Ultimately our living hope will enable us to endure the trial (*1Pet 1:3-9*).

> **Ultimately our living hope will enable us to endure the trial.**

QUOTING "ALL THINGS WORK TOGETHER FOR GOOD" (*Rom 8:28*)

Quoting this verse may cause sufferers to question their love for God or wonder if they are out of God's will. It can come across to some as an accusation.

[1] See www.allheneedsforheaven.com for information about Jim McDoniel's book, *All He Needs for Heaven.*

This represents a common misunderstanding of this text. The verse does not explain the cause of suffering for the Christian, but rather it shows a result that can come out of suffering. A better translation than that quoted above is "And we know that in all things God works for the good of those who love him, who have been called according to his purpose" (*Rom 8:28, NIV*). This text describes the results God can bring out of suffering but it does not say that God causes the bad situation to bring about good.

Feinberg says, "Clearly, Paul is appealing to the ability of a sovereign God to turn everything that happens to believers, even adversity, into something profitable for them. But in light of *verses 29 and 30*, which explain why *verse 28* is true, it is clear that the good envisioned here pertains to the believer's salvation, not just anything that contributes to worldly convenience or comfort" (*Where,* 35). D.A. Carson says, "If we interpret 'the *good* of those who love him' in selfish, materialistic ways, we shall entirely miss the point of the passage. . . . What the passage promises us, then, is that *in the midst* of such misery [a groaning universe given to death and decay, *Rom. 8:22ff.*] we may be assured that God is at work 'for the good of those who love him'" (*How Long?* 26).

When you have lost a child or a spouse, a future good does not seem better than having your loved one back. It will be hard for the sufferer to see that a future good will make up for the evil. The use of this verse at the time of suffering may appear to say that the loss of the loved one or other situation of suffering is not so bad because God will eventually bring good out of it.

Feinberg advises, "Things happen in our world that really *are* evil! Don't minimize that fact by appealing to the sovereign ability of God to bring good even out of the most horrible situation" (*Where,* 37).

Carson says,

> Doubtless it is true, for instance, that "in all things God works for the good of those who love him" (*Rom. 8:28*), but it is less than obvious that this should be quoted to the couple that has just lost their child in a road accident. If they know the Lord well, then perhaps, with time, they themselves will cite the verse with renewed faith and understanding, but it should not be thrust at them in the wrong way, or at the wrong time, or without tears, lest it seem like a cheap ritual, miserable comfort, heartless proof texting. (*How Long?* 97-98)

"IT IS SINFUL TO BE ANGRY."

Jesus expressed righteous anger (*John 2*). One can be angry and not sin (*Eph 4:26*). Job appeared to be angry at the seeming unfairness of his suffering and wanted to argue his case directly with God. In times of extreme emotional upset godly people may even experience anger toward God, but in their saner, more mature moments they are sorry they were upset with God.

Dan Allender and Tremper Longman III state, "Pondering the character of God does not pacify anger; it deepens it. Our struggle is never that we are too angry, but that we are never angry enough. Our anger is always pitifully small when it is focused against a person or object; it is meant to be turned against all evil and all sin—beginning first with our own failure of love" (**159**). The psalmist advises, *"Be angry, and do not sin; ponder in your own hearts on your beds, and be silent"* (*Ps 4:4*).

"I KNOW A PERSON WHO DIED OF YOUR DISEASE."

My father was in the hospital with a mild stroke. A Christian leader came to visit. He talked for several minutes about a person who had had a stroke. He gave a blow-by-blow account of all the dreary details and the person's eventual death. His visit was not helpful. Even if you do know cases with a similar situation, resist the temptation to tell stories with a bad outcome. When you or a family member is dealing with a serious illness, such stories are neither comforting nor encouraging.

When trying to comfort one suffering a sickness or loss, resist the temptation to recount the story of someone you know who has been in a similar situation. The situations are never the same. It is much better to show genuine interest in the sufferer's unique situation and suffering. Listen to what they want to share of their story.

IMMEDIATELY AFTER A TRAGIC DEATH, "WE'RE JUST REJOICING IN HIS OR HER VICTORY."

This person may imply that if you are sad and grieving that you are not trusting God or do not believe that the lost loved one has eternal life. You may have great confidence in the person's salvation, but there is a time to laugh and a time to cry. Remember it is okay to grieve, but believers do not grieve as the world that has no hope (*1Th 4:13*).

We have all made mistakes in what we have said to the hurting. We need to think before we speak so we can avoid these things that do not help. We must do our best to treat others as we would want to be treated.

Think about It

1. What were some of the inappropriate comments made to Claudia when she was in the hospital?

2. Why should we not tell a sufferer "I know just how you feel"?

3. Why should we not give a timetable for another to get over grieving?

4. Why is it not helpful to avoid the sufferer and to avoid talking about the lost loved one and the suffering? How does avoidance make the person suffering or grieving feel?

5. What is wrong with the comments "You do not have enough faith" and "You are suffering because of your sin" and "It is for the best"?

6. Explain the difference between God's directive will and His permissive will.

7. Why should we be careful telling people why a particular illness or tragedy happened?

8. In what ways is quoting *Romans 8:28* not helpful in the midst of profound grief or suffering?

CHAPTER TWENTY-ONE

WHAT HELPS THE HURTING

Help the weak.
1 Thessalonians 5:14

I. Listen with Genuine Interest and Sympathy.
II. Allow the Sufferer to Express Guilt, Sorrow, or Depression.
III. "I Don't Know What to Say, but I Care."
IV. "We Are Thinking about You and Praying for You."
V. Be Present with the Sufferer.
VI. Allow People to Grieve in Their Own Way.
VII. Do Practical Things to Help.
VIII. Tell Good Memories about the Lost Loved One.
IX. Don't Hesitate to Touch as Appropriate.
X. Be Sensitive to All Who Are Grieving.
XI. "It's Okay to Cry."
XII. "God Weeps with You."
XIII. Continue to Express Understanding and Care Months and Years after the Loss.
XIV. Be Affirmative and Encouraging.
XV. Encourage the Sufferer to Live One Day at a Time.
XVI. Encourage the Sufferer toward Physical Activity.
XVII. Later, Help the Sufferer Focus on the Goodness of God.
XVIII. "Trust God Even When You Do Not Understand."

Every Christian should be prepared to minister to hurting people. We want to help those who are experiencing grief, sickness, or other tragedies. Yancey states, "It would be much easier for us to avoid people in need. Yet ministering to the needy is not an option for the Christian, but a command. . . . As Christ's body on earth we are compelled to move, as he did, toward those who hurt" (*Where*, 239). Helping the hurting is not limited to professionals and specialists. Ordinary people often help the most.

Not everything said by some Christians to sufferers actually helps them, as we noted in the last chapter. We cannot wave a magic wand making pain and suffering go away. We have no completely final and satisfying answer to pain and suffering, yet we can help those hurting by what we say and do.

LISTEN WITH GENUINE INTEREST AND SYMPATHY.

Hurting persons need to talk because they want someone to understand what they are experiencing. Rather than worrying about what you will say to hurting people, concentrate on listening to the words they share with you. Comforters come as listeners not interpreters. Our job is not to explain why the situation happened. Frequently we divert the conversation to side topics because we are uncomfortable in listening to the agony the sufferer is feeling. It tears at our hearts to hear friends pouring out their deep anguish and hurt. If we are not willing to listen, we convey that we really do not care. Comforters share the grief rather than avoid it.

> **If we are not willing to listen, we convey that we really do not care.**

Listen with your heart to see and feel the person's pain. Look at the person while he or she talks. Survivors and sufferers can feel invisible. Let hurting people talk when they want, and about what they want. Allow them to be silent if that is what is desired. Listen attentively, even if a story is repeated again and again.

Don't tell others how they must be feeling; let them tell you what they want to say about how they are feeling. When our 34-year-old son was killed in a truck accident, some people told my wife and me that we must be upset with God. Actually, we weren't. We did not think God caused the accident. It would have been more helpful if they had asked if we were upset with God, rather than assuming that we were. "Listening alone won't make the pain go away completely, but it is a key first step" (**Feinberg, Where, 33**).

Realize that some sufferers would rather express the grief through actions rather than words. My longtime friend, Dr. Wayne Bigelow, told how his father, Balfour, expressed his grief over the death of his seven-year-old daughter, Jane. He was a man of few words. The next spring after Jane's death, his daffodil bed expressed his grief. A surprise to everyone, bright yellow daffodils spelled out JANE.

ALLOW THE SUFFERER
TO EXPRESS GUILT, SORROW,
OR DEPRESSION.

When working through the grief following a severe loss, it is helpful to have someone to whom you can express even your negative feelings as you feel a need. Those who try to make you bury and stifle your feelings are not helpful. "When you don't admit your feelings, they become concealed and withheld. Bottled-up feelings lead to bitterness, vulnerability, and distorted perceptions" (**Wright**, *Life*, **212**). If you do not feel you can express your feelings to anyone, an emotional explosion may occur later. Find someone you trust and who respects you. Usually this person will be someone who has maturely managed his or her own hard times and who does not have a need to tell everybody what you say. While some people deal with their emotions through activities, others need to talk to release their emotions.

At times sufferers may need to pour out their frustrations and feelings. Don't judge or criticize. Don't condemn actions that may have caused the suffering. When a person who has smoked all his life lies in a hospital bed facing death from lung cancer, it is not the time to say, "Well it's because you smoked all those years that you have this disease." Criticism is neither welcome nor helpful when one is grieving and hurting deeply because the sufferer cannot be objective enough to handle it. Even if you think the criticism is justified, at that time it is better left unsaid.

Allow the sufferer to express anger or bitterness, even with God. We find expressions of anger with God in the Psalms and prophets. Job appeared to be angry at the seeming unfairness of his suffering and wanted to argue his case directly with God. Godly people who are extremely upset emotionally may experience frustration with God. Willard Black states, "God can handle our emotional outbursts, our complaints, and questions because He knows that our pain always carries the potential for drawing us closer to Him!" (**237**)

Dealing with a terminal illness or coping with the death of a loved one is a shattering experience. It forces everything in your life to be under reconstruction. We should respond with gentleness and compassion when sufferers express words of frustration.

Norman Wright shows how anger can be dealt with in a positive way.

> You admit it, you accept it, and you release it in a healthy way. You use anger's energy to do something constructive. Mothers Against Drunk Drivers (MADD) was founded because of the constructive use of anger directed toward a major problem in our society—drinking and driving. The MADD organization has made society aware of the problem of drunk drivers on our roads and highways and has helped to establish and reinforce laws to prosecute those who victimize others through their negligence. (*Life*, 69)

Allow the hurting person to express his or her guilt feelings. Many people torment themselves with statements starting with "If only . . ." or "I should have . . ." or "Why didn't I . . ." They may need to confess their guilt to someone. As the initial phase of the grief passes, you may help them separate true guilt from false guilt. In some cases a sense of guilt is based on unrealistic expectations one places upon oneself. True guilt makes us aware of what we have done wrong.

It is helpful to talk with someone who has an objective view of the situation. Norman Wright says,

> If the only one you're talking to about your guilt is yourself, then remember, you are biased. A non-judgmental person can help you look at whatever is creating your guilt feelings, whether they be acts, thoughts, or some perceived omissions. Another person's rationality can help you evaluate your guilt and keep you from overemphasizing the negative. (**ibid.**, 74)

If the guilt is because the person has acted against the will of God, help the person confess his or her sin and seek forgiveness from God. David confessed his sin and sought a clean spirit from God (*Ps 51:1-12*, see also *Ps 32:5; 1Jn 1:9*). When a person refuses to forgive himself or herself, you cannot force it. A loving friend will continue to provide a listening ear. They need to know you love and accept them. This may help them know and accept the love and mercy of God.

When a person refuses to forgive himself or herself, you cannot force it.

"I DON'T KNOW WHAT TO SAY, BUT I CARE."

I have heard many sufferers say that this helped more than anything that was said to them. If you honestly believe that you don't know what to say, do not go ahead and say things that you don't know will help. Nothing you say can eliminate the person's grief or suffering. The person must deal with it personally. Often those who help the most say the least. Trivial platitudes and clichés do not help. Avoid saying, "Time will heal all wounds," "Think of all you still have to be thankful for" and "It's not really so bad." Better to say, "I can't think of what to say. But we are sorry and we are with you in your grief." The assurance that you love and care for them and you hurt with them helps give strength for coping.

> **Often those who help the most say the least.**

Jean Vanier, wisely says, "Wounded people who have been broken by suffering and sickness ask for only one thing: a heart that loves and commits itself to them, a heart full of hope for them" (**Yancey, Where, 168**).

"WE ARE THINKING ABOUT YOU AND PRAYING FOR YOU."

Prayer is powerful. I know personally the encouragement and comfort that comes when you know others regularly pray for you. I'm sure over one hundred people told me they were praying for me daily. We have had the same prayer support during my wife's battle with cancer. We have been strengthened and blessed by many such encouragements.

Yancey commented about his visits to hospitals, "I have been impressed by the huge difference between the measure of comfort that can be offered by believers ('We're praying for you') and unbelievers ('Best of luck—we'll keep our fingers crossed')" (**ibid., 243**). We may be able to list many ways we cannot help. But one way we can all help is to specifically pray for those who are hurting. We should never underestimate the power of prayer. Spurgeon is reported to have said when asked the secret of his ministry, "My people pray for me." That is also a secret to healing.

> **Never underestimate the power of prayer.**

BE PRESENT WITH
THE SUFFERER.

In the words of a grieving person, "People think they have to say something—but it's their presence that counts." Suffering and grief is not a problem to be solved as much as it is a process to be experienced. In some cases you may need to say very little but your presence says loud and clear, "I care." Sufferers may be too weak or not feel like talking. Your presence and companionship can give the strength and support they need. Those to whom you have gone to comfort in a time of great grief probably will not remember what you say, but they will remember that you showed you cared by your presence.

John Mark Hicks says,

> Some of my most precious memories of the events surrounding my wife's funeral involve the presence of people. A friend flew in from Oklahoma to be with me. My sister drove me home to Bowling Green, Kentucky, from Georgia. My father walked with me for several hours. I do not remember anything any of these loved ones said to me, but I remember that they gave their time and presence. . . . Primary comfort for the griever does not come through the words of comforters, but through their presence. (*Anchors*, 26)

When we avoid sufferers, we add to their feeling of being abandoned and alienated. We also confirm their fears that no one cares or will help.

Expressing that you care can bring effective comfort later after the rush of sympathy following the loved one's death. Our friends, Jim and Marj, brought a rose and visited with us on an anniversary of Mark's death. Another friend, Joy, who has lost an adult daughter and daughter-in-law, has over the years expressed her care and concern through letters and cards at special times.

ALLOW PEOPLE TO GRIEVE
IN THEIR OWN WAY.

Since we are all different and our situations are different, it is important that we do not control how others grieve. One person may need to remove the possessions of the deceased soon. Another person may need some time before tackling this difficult task. One may want to look at photos of the departed loved one. Another may find this painful at first. One may want to talk or write about her feelings of grief. Another may prefer not to do so. Another difference can be seen in the need some have to visit the grave frequently. For years a widow walked seven miles round trip every Sunday afternoon to visit the grave of her husband. People will suggest books for you to read to help you with your grief. You may or may not feel like reading material on grief in the early stages. Recognize that what may bring comfort and joy to one may be painful to another.

The kind of death, loss, or crisis will make a difference how a sufferer will grieve. Grieving an unanticipated death differs from grieving a death following a prolonged illness. Men often grieve differently than women. A husband and wife wrote a book *Five Cries of Grief* after the loss of their adult son (**Strommen**). They did not go lock-step through fixed stages of grief. Each grieved in his and her own way. Depending largely upon their age and their interaction with others, children who have lost a parent grieve differently (**Wright,** *Life*, **113-129**). Smaller children experience insecurity and confusion. Older children may experience unrealistic feelings of responsibility or independence. Those who comfort best seek to understand the individual needs of the sufferer and allow each person to grieve in his or her own way.

> **Men often grieve differently than women.**

DO PRACTICAL THINGS TO HELP.

Often the sufferer can't think too well or organize what needs to be done. Sometimes asking "What can I do?" only increases frustration. It places responsibility on the sufferer by giving them an assignment to decide what is appropriate to ask. Instead of general offers to help, it is more helpful when a person sees what needs to be done and goes ahead and does it. One sufferer says, "My reaction when someone offers help in general is not to ask for anything, since I don't want to burden anyone with something they'd rather not do. But if you offer to do something specific, it saves me the time and effort of having to think up something you can do for me. . . . Your offer of something specific . . . tells me that you really do care and are attentive to my specific situation" (**Feinberg,** *Where*, **53**). My wife and I found this very true.

Look for specific, practical ways to help: run errands, mow the yard, wash the dishes, answer the phone, keep a record of visitors and those who brought food, provide needed transportation, babysit, shop for groceries, pick up the mail, care for pets, buy thank you notes and stamps, buy a phone card, clean house (only if the person would feel comfortable for you to do this). Such acts of service express love and care for those who are hurting.

On the day of the funeral for our son, a friend stopped by the house to wash and vacuum our car. He returned to do anything else that was needed. I said, "Would you mind buying pantyhose for my wife?" He did it without hesitation. Barbara was embarrassed when she found out. He did what was needed and we appreciated his help.

In the last chapter I mentioned the baby born without arms to the McDoniels. Jim McDoniel, a minister, spoke of the many ways God's people ministered to their needs. "The ladies took care of our food and house cleaning for weeks. The elders told me to take care of my family, and they would see to the needs of the church." A lady with no grandchildren adopted Chet as her grandchild. "An insurance salesman worked to make Chet one of the first physically handicapped persons in the nation to get life insurance." "Two men welded his powered wheelchair each time it broke. Camp counselors asked to have Chet in their cabins."

McDoniel continued, "Perhaps more than the physical help the church gave, they cried with us. They prayed for us. They loved us and accepted our entire family, including the one without arms." Chet enthusiastically leads worship. He graduated from college, has married and works for a travel company (**31**). The loving practical help of others contributed to his success.

TELL GOOD MEMORIES ABOUT THE LOST LOVED ONE.

Survivors do not want to forget their lost loved ones. Even though grief is painful, they want to talk about the person they have lost. Sharing good memories can bring joy and help people cope with the sadness of loss. This is not reopening the wound but rather helping to heal the hurt.

Sharing good memories can bring joy and help people cope with the sadness of loss.

Encourage the bereaved to tell stories about the lost loved one. Relate the special qualities you appreciated and things you admired in the person. Use the name of the person in your communication. You haven't forgotten this person who is still important to those who remain. Remembering the loved one is an important part in relearning to live in a world without the loved one. The person who is gone cannot return to us, but we want to remember him or her.

A lady from the church where our son, Mark, attended wrote a note to my wife telling her how much she appreciated a communion meditation that Mark had given not long before his death. As a mother to a mother, she said she would be proud if he were her son. This was an encouraging note. A year or so after Mark's death, we were at a fast-food restaurant. A young man came up to us and said, "You don't know me, but I want to tell you that Mark helped me change my life from being a negative person." Comments like these can be very meaningful to those who are grieving the loss of a loved one.

DON'T HESITATE TO TOUCH AS APPROPRIATE.

Illness can disfigure. A terminally ill patient said, "Touch me. I want to be accepted despite the way I may look. Inside, I'm still the same person you always knew."[1] While you pray with the person in the hospital, hold the patient's hand or touch his or her arm. Appropriate touch expresses to the person that you value them.

Zig Ziglar said of friends that comforted them in their grief over their daughter's death,

> I was impressed that each of them asked us if they could hug us, or they volunteered a hug with the utmost respect for our feelings. At no time was there any sense that they were violating our space or invading our privacy. They were sensitive to our needs, and they sensed that we needed the hugs they offered so freely. Sometimes giving a quick hug and just being present speak volumes to the grieving person. (142)

BE SENSITIVE TO ALL WHO ARE GRIEVING.

It is important that we recognize everyone who is hurting and grieving. Try not to overlook anyone: spouse, parents, younger chil-

[1]*The Joplin Globe* (Oct 3, 1996) 11.

dren, brothers, sisters, other close family members, and friends. Nicolas Wolterstorff, who lost a 25-year-old son in a mountain-climbing accident, said, "Now he's gone, and the family has to restructure itself. We don't just each have a gap inside us but together a gap among us. We have to live differently with each other. We have to live around the gap. Pull out one, and everything changes" (99). Think carefully about all those who are grieving. Make a conscious effort to minister to those who are overlooked.

It is easy to recognize those who grieve because of bereavement, serious illness, or tragic accident. We often overlook persons who grieve because of a miscarriage, infertility, divorce, a wayward spouse or child, or from a major economic or personal setback. Norman Wright calls children "the forgotten grievers," who are often ignored by the adults (*Life*, 113). If we really love one another, we will be alert and sensitive to hear cries for help and to recognize even unspoken deep hurts.

> ### Wright calls children "the forgotten grievers."

Siblings are often overlooked as persons suffering the loss of a brother or sister. Our two sons were close friends. Because they were both engineers, they could talk over things that the rest of us could not understand. Since Bryce lived on the west coast, they had long telephone conversations, often late at night, full of engineer talk. Our daughter, Kara, and Mark lived only a mile apart. The two families did a lot of things together and often helped each other. Mark's passing left a void in his brother and sister's lives. Remember *all* the family when you express comfort.

"IT'S OKAY TO CRY."

It is a lie that "Men don't cry." Jesus wept at Lazarus's grave (*Jn 11:35*). The ability to grieve is a God-given avenue helping us deal with the intense pain of personal tragedy and loss. After losing a loved one, going to church or hearing certain songs frequently bring tears. Crying is a natural part of the grieving process. Tears provide a good and natural form of emotional release. Cry when you need to. It is God's escape valve. God has given us tears to provide a healthy expression of sorrow. Tell a person grieving the loss of a loved one that you are okay with his or her crying. The unnatural suppression of grief prevents one from healing from the loss.

Chris DeWelt, who lost a teenage son in a car accident, says, "Were it not for tears and the ability to express them, we would certainly explode (or implode). . . . Tears (and all that goes with them) are indeed the 'oil of the soul.' This is, in fact, a divine gift" (**502**). He affirms, "I'm probably a lot healthier emotionally if I am willing to weep than if I am unwilling to do so" (**503**).

Immediately after a tragic death, the comment "You should just rejoice in his victory" may imply that, if you are sad and grieving, you are not trusting God or do not believe the lost loved one has eternal life. You may have great confidence in the person's salvation, but there is a time to laugh and a time to cry. Believers grieve but not as the world that has no hope (*1Th 4:13*). "*Weep with those who weep*" (*Rom 12:15b*).

> ## There is a time to laugh and a time to cry.

"GOD WEEPS WITH YOU."

God cares. David states,

> *You have kept count of my tossings;*
> *put my tears in your bottle.*
> *Are they not in your book? (Ps 56:8)*

> *When the righteous cry for help,*
> *The LORD hears and delivers them out of all their troubles.*
> *The LORD is near to the brokenhearted*
> *And saves the crushed in spirit.*
> *Many are the afflictions of the righteous,*
> *But the LORD delivers him out of them all. (Ps 34:17-19)*

Our heavenly Father notes our sadness and remembers it. In the words of the songwriter, "His heart is touched with our grief." He weeps with us when we mourn. Our tears become His tears. God sees disease and death as an enemy. He is merciful to us in our grief. He is not an isolated, indifferent CEO pulling strings from heaven. He is our merciful and loving Father who asks us to cast our cares on Him because He cares for us (*1Pet 5:7*). "*In the days of his flesh, Jesus offered up prayers and supplications with loud cries and tears, to him who was able to save him from death, and he was heard because of his reverence*" (*Heb 5:7*). Because Christ endured sufferings when on earth, He is our sympathetic and merciful high priest (*Heb 2:14-18*).

CONTINUE TO EXPRESS
CONCERN AND CARE
MONTHS AND YEARS AFTER
THE LOSS.

Don't just visit in the hospital or attend the funeral, then disappear. Immediately after the crisis or loss much attention and concern is expressed. It helps for friends to continue to be supportive. Anniversaries and holidays can be hard because they highlight the absence of the loved one. If you did not send a sympathy card within a few days, send it later. It can mean a great deal even later. The grief process can last a long time. In some ways recovery is never complete because the sense of loss never goes completely away. Show genuine concern months and even years later. Good friends keep in touch with a brief visit, a phone call, an email, or a note. Cards are helpful and a personal note adds value to the card.

BE AFFIRMATIVE AND
ENCOURAGING.

We must not be gushy and sentimental in an unrealistic way, but we can obey Paul's directive to *"encourage one another"* (*1Th 5:1*). Be honest with those who are suffering. Reinforce their strength. Express love and care for them. Really seek what is best for them. Encourage their reliance upon God.

Help sufferers to start helping others as soon as they are able. It might be later rather than sooner for some. We are all different in how we respond. People coping with grief often withdraw. Encourage past hobbies, give rides to meetings. Help the person get involved in new activities. Encourage by genuinely affirming the good they are doing and expressing your confidence in them.

Help sufferers to start helping others as soon as they are able.

ENCOURAGE THE SUFFERER
TO LIVE ONE DAY AT A TIME.

John Feinberg says he was in a conversation with his father a few weeks after learning his wife's diagnosis of Huntington's Disease. He was saying he did not know how he could handle his wife's illness and also the possibility of their three sons having the disease. His dad told him, "John, God never promised to give you tomorrow's grace for today. He only promised today's grace for today, and that's all you need" (*Where*, 49).

> **God will give us the grace to handle the challenges of each day.**

Feinberg observes, "In that one comment I was reminded both of God's grace and of my need to take each day one at a time. . . . I would begin each day asking God for just the grace needed to sustain me that day" (**ibid., 49-50**). Jesus taught us not to borrow trouble from tomorrow by worrying about it. He says each day has enough trouble for us to handle that day (*Mt 6:34*). God will give us the grace to handle the challenges of each day.

ENCOURAGE THE SUFFERER TOWARD PHYSICAL ACTIVITY.

Some find walking, raking leaves, playing a musical instrument, or some other activity therapeutic. Doing an activity that has visible physical results may be helpful. Later in the grief process one can be directed to engage in productive work or on a needed project which is able to help someone else. When the person is able to do this, definite healing is taking place.

LATER, HELP THE SUFFERER FOCUS ON GOD'S GOODNESS.

While being realistic about the pain and suffering, it is important to think about the ways you are blessed. Timing is important here. The person in the initial stage of coping with grief or a tragedy may not be ready to do this. Coping with suffering can be more bearable if one can focus on God's goodness. Preoccupation with one's troubles can lead to depression. Specifically counting one's blessings helps put the suffering in perspective. Even in the worst of times there is much for which we can be thankful.

Peter instructs us to cast all our anxieties and cares on God because He cares for us (*1Pet 5:7*). Even when it is hard to see anything positive in a situation, we need to be reminded that we have a loving, caring God. Knowing that God does really care for you will give strength to work through the pain, grief, or tragedy.

TRUST GOD EVEN WHEN YOU DO NOT UNDERSTAND.

God never told Job why he was suffering, but God gave Job ample evidence to trust Him. Even though he did not understand, Job kept trusting God. Many things in this life we will never fully understand. I am thankful for a God of infinite wisdom and power who loves us and seeks our best interest. We may never know why some things happen, but we know we have a loving, heavenly Father who is in charge of this universe.

My lung disease was idiopathic pulmonary fibrosis. Idiopathic means the cause is unknown. I was asked how it made me feel that I didn't know the cause of my lung disease. It bothered me at first, but then I realized medical science didn't know and I couldn't know. I decided not to worry about it, but to do what I could to be as healthy as I could be. We asked for God's help and healing at every step of the way. God gives peace to those who trust in Him.

If you demonstrate unshakable trust in God, this will communicate itself to the grieving person.

Trust in God who loves and cares for us is the most important help we can have in dealing with suffering. If you demonstrate unshakable trust in God, this will communicate itself to the grieving person.

Norman Wright reminds us that suffering can lead to growth. He states,

> There is one factor—attitude—that causes a major crisis to become a growth-producing experience instead of a restrictive, crippling, eternal tragedy. Our world is unstable; it rocks our boat. We are unstable; we rock our boat. But if our attitude has been built upon the teachings of the Word of God, then we have hope in the midst of an upset world! *Isaiah 33:6* says, *"And He will be the stability of your times."* (**Life,** 62)

Suffering or loss may limit a person in some significant ways. He may not be able to return to life the way it was. But he can grow through the experience of suffering, finding new opportunities. As time distances you from the initial shock, you can help your friend on the road to a deeper trust in God. The local church can teach Christians to be effective helpers to those who are hurting.

Think about It

1. Why is helping the hurting not optional for Christians?

2. Describe a good listener.

3. How should we handle it when sufferers express negative emotions?

4. Why are these statements helpful? "I don't know what to say, but I care." And "We're thinking about you and praying for you."

5. In times of intense grief why is the presence of a caring friend more important than a theological explanation of suffering?

6. Give examples of practical ways to help hurting people.

7. What people and situations are often overlooked by comforters?

8. Why should grievers not be ashamed of their tears?

9. Why is "one day at a time" good advice?

10. Why does it make sense to trust God even when we do not understand?

WORDS TO KNOW

All-knowing   The quality of God affirming His total knowledge of the past, present, and future. Omniscient

All-powerful   God can do anything He chooses to do that is logically possible and is consistent with His nature. Omnipotent

Animism   The belief that everything in the natural world is inhabited by spiritual forces.

Asceticism   Practicing strict self-discipline and denial of pleasure as an exercise of spiritual discipline.

Asphyxiation   Inability to receive an adequate supply of oxygen.

Atheism   The denial of the existence of a personal God.

Atonement   A sacrifice that brings forgiveness and cleansing from sin.

Auschwitz   A Nazi death camp in Poland.

Bereavement   The loss by death of a loved one which brings a disorienting kind of grief.

Buddhism   Eastern religion emphasizing that desire is the source of suffering. One achieves selflessness through an eightfold path, freeing one from successive reincarnations leading to achieving Nirvana.

Caregiver   One who gives, directs, and/or provides direct care for the needs of someone who is ill, disabled, or otherwise unable to care for themselves.

Creation   God created the physical universe out of nothing and sustains it. He also created human beings after His own image.

Crucifixion	A form of execution in which a person is put on a cross until death occurs. Produces a slow death with maximum pain and disgrace.
Deism	The view that God created the universe but does not supernaturally intervene in the world.
Directive will of God	What God directs or commands to happen.
Dualism	Good and evil are two eternal, opposite realities involved in a never-ending conflict.
Evidential argument from evil	Holds that the existence of horrendous and unwarranted evil provides evidence against the belief in God.
Evil	That which is opposed to the Ultimate Good. It is a corruption of the good.
Evil, Gratuitous	Unwarranted, unjustified, senseless evil.
Evil, Moral	Suffering and harm done by a human agent, such as murder, rape, and hate.
Evil, Natural	Suffering or harm not caused by a human agent, such as hurricanes, droughts, and floods.
Faith	Trust based on sufficient evidence. Also refers to the content of beliefs held by a person.
Fall	The sin of Adam and Eve in the Garden of Eden bringing evil, suffering, and death into the world.
Fallen world	Human beings and the physical universe suffer the effects of sin having been introduced into the world bringing disease, death, thorns and disruption.
Fatalism	Human choice and effort are meaningless because whatever happens does so necessarily.
Finite	That which is limited.
Finitism	View that God's power is limited. Denies that God is all-powerful.
Foreknowledge	In reference to God, He has exhaustive knowledge of the past, present, and future.

Free Will	Ability of moral agents to make genuine choices between alternatives.
Free Will Defense	Justification of God's allowance of evil on the basis that the possibility of evil is logically inherent in giving moral agents free will. Free will is a good that makes possible a greater good.
God's Directive Will	What God commands and directs to come to pass.
God's Permissive Will	What God allows to occur.
Gnosticism	A religious movement of the second and third centuries combining Greek dualism and Christian ideas. It holds that spirit is good and matter is evil. Emphasizes a special higher spiritual knowledge.
Good	Highest ethical quality. For the theist defined by the nature and will of God.
Grief	The mental, emotional, and spiritual pain and sorrow we feel when we lose someone or something we love.
Grief process	The period of time of adjusting to a significant loss in one's life.
"Health and Wealth" preachers	Those who teach that God will always heal and that God will always make you prosperous if you have faith.
Hedonism	The good life is one of happiness and pleasure and the absence of pain.
Hinduism	Dominant religion of India generally holding to many gods, but the underlying view is pantheism. They believe in reincarnation with the goal being for the soul to be delivered from the cycle of reincarnation.
Holocaust	The slaughter of six million Jews by the Nazis during World War II.
Hope	Positive expectation of a future good.
Humanism	The view that human beings are the highest value in the universe. Human values are not God-given but

	are based on human beings and are relative and subject to change.
Image of God	God created human beings with an aspect that is similar to Him. The image of God includes our mind, will, soul, heart, i.e., our inner spiritual being.
Imprecatory psalms	Prayers that God would exercise His wrath on His enemies.
Infinite	Without limits or bounds. God is not limited by time, space, or any other limitation.
Judaizers	Jewish teachers who believed that Christians must also keep the law of Moses, especially the rite of circumcision.
Justification	God's justice is preserved because the penalty for sin is paid, but the believer is declared "Not guilty."
Karma	Belief in Hinduism and Buddhism that one's reincarnation reaps the consequences of what is sowed in a previous life.
Lament	Expression of sorrow or mourning.
Liberalism, Theological	Movement in modern times which reinterprets Christianity in the light of rationalism, naturalism, and humanism.
Logical argument from evil	An argument that holds that the existence of evil refutes the existence of God.
Martyrdom	The faithful witness to Christ even to the point of death.
Messianic prophesies	Passages in the Old Testament making predictions about the person or ministry of Christ.
Miracle	An event in the physical world, worked by the direct power of God, intended as a sign.
Monism	Views all things as being of one kind of reality, e.g., all spirit or all matter.
Mystery	That which surpasses human reason and comprehension but can be revealed to us by God.

Mysticism	Knowledge gained by some experience that transcends human reason and senses.
Naturalism	The physical world is all that exists. Reality is molecules in motion governed by natural laws. Typically denies God, spiritual realities, and life after death.
Natural law	A statement describing observed uniformity in nature.
New Age Movement	A late 20th-century social and religious movement teaching that we are gods and have lived before and will live again. Enlightenment comes through some kind of mystical experience.
Omnipotence	The quality of being all-powerful. See "All-powerful."
Omniscience	The quality of being all-knowing. See "All-knowing."
Open Theism	A theological position holding that God knows the past and the present but does not know what will happen in the future. This is because he cannot know what future decisions will be made by free agents.
Paganism	Belief in many gods who are worshiped through various rituals.
Pain	A sensation of extreme discomfort.
Pantheism	Everything is God and God is everything. The whole of reality is identical with the Absolute. Particular items are only appearances.
Permissive will of God	What God allows to happen in this world in which human beings have free will in a world of natural laws. God permits both good and evil things to happen.
Persecution	Harassment and suffering inflicted because of one's beliefs.
Polytheism	Belief in many gods.
Postmodernism	Recent movement that is suspicious of reason and science, holding that objective truth and universal truths are uncertain. A sentence does not mean what the author intended, but the meaning is constructed by society.

Words to Know

345

Problem of Evil, Emotional	The difficulty of reconciling one's belief in an all-knowing, all-powerful, and all-wise God with the feelings you are experiencing because of the suffering you or loved ones have encountered.
Problem of Evil, Intellectual	The difficulty caused by the existence of evil in a world created and controlled by an all-powerful, all-knowing, and all-good God.
Process theology	Holds that God is the soul of the universe. God evolves and changes as the universe evolves.
Prophet	One who speaks under supernatural inspiration of the Holy Spirit.
Propitiation	Offering that turns away the wrath of God against the sinner.
Providence	The loving care and governance exercised by an all-powerful and all-loving God over the created universe.
Rationalism	Human reason is the highest test of truth.
Reconciliation	Restoration of friendship with God after being alienated by sin.
Reincarnation	After death one is reborn in a new body. Hinduism and Buddhism believe one is successively recycled in new lives according to karma (reaping in the next life what was sown in the last).
Resurrection	Rising to life again after having been dead. Christ rose from the dead. The dead will rise at the final judgment.
September 11, 2001	Muslim terrorists flew airplanes into the Twin Towers of the World Trade Center in New York City and the Pentagon in Washington, D.C., killing over 3,000 people.
Sorrow	The distress and sadness at the loss of someone or something loved.
Sovereignty	The possession of ultimate authority and power. An all-powerful God governs the universe according to His will.

Suffering	The experience of enduring pain, disease, disability, distress, loss, or death.
Theodicy	An answer to the problem of evil and suffering that attempts to justify God's dealings with man by giving reasons why God permits evil.
Theism	Belief in a personal God. An infinite, all-powerful, all-knowing, personal God exists and has created and sustains the universe.
Truth	That which corresponds to or adequately expresses what is real.
Worldview	One's beliefs about the basic questions about the world and life, covering topics such as reality, truth, God, humanity, morality, and history.

WHAT OTHER AUTHORS SAY

A SELECT ANNOTATED LIST OF BOOKS ON SUFFERING

Attig, Thomas. *The Heart of Grief: Death and the Search for Lasting Love.* New York: Oxford University Press, 2000.
Based on many interviews with grieving persons on how they relearned the world and life after their loss.

_____. *How We Grieve: Relearning the World.* New York: Oxford University Press, 1996.
Attig holds that grieving is a process of relearning life as loving our loved one in their absence after having loved them in their presence with us.

Brand, Paul, and Philip Yancey. *Pain: The Gift Nobody Wants.* New York: Harper Collins Publishers, 1993.
The inspiring story of the fifty-year career of Dr. Paul Brand of studying pain and its implications for medical treatment, overall health, and human happiness. Helps one see the positive role that pain plays in the human experience.

Camus, Albert. *The Plague.* Trans. by D. Gilbert. New York: Modern Library, 1948.
A novel by a French existentialist atheist which presents a dilemma of a choice between the belief that there is no God and man must struggle in futility and the belief in a God who is the cause of evil.

Carson, D.A. *How Long, O Lord? Reflections on Suffering and Evil,* 2nd ed. Grand Rapids: Baker, 2006.
Excellent study of the issue of suffering and God from both a biblical and practical perspective

Feinberg, John S. *The Many Faces of Evil: Theological Systems and the*

Problem of Evil, revised and expanded edition. Wheaton, IL: Crossway Books, 2004.
Discusses how various theological systems approach the problem of suffering and evil.

_____. *Where Is God? A Personal Story of Finding God in Grief and Suffering*. Nashville: Broadman and Holman, 2004.
Theologian details his struggle with the religious problem of suffering and evil after learning that his wife has Huntington's disease.

Geisler, Norman L. *The Roots of Evil*. Grand Rapids: Zondervan, 1978.
An apologist analyzes philosophical options proposed to answer the apparent contradiction between the existence of evil and God, e.g., illusionism, dualism, finitism, sadism, impossibilism, atheism, and theism. Biblical theism is defended in its answer to the problem of evil.

Hicks, John Mark. *Yet Will I Trust Him: Understanding God in a Suffering World*. Joplin, MO: College Press, 1999.
Bible teacher explains his struggle with believing in God through the tragedy of the death of his first wife and the sickness of his son.

Kreeft, Peter. *Making Sense Out of Suffering*. Ann Arbor: Servant Books, 1986.
Catholic apologist wrestles with the problem of suffering.

Lewis, C.S. *A Grief Observed*. San Francisco: HarperSanFrancisco, 1961, 1996.
Observations by Lewis as he watches his wife suffer and die. It is brutally honest. Shows how suffering may bring anger and bitterness with God. Lewis's faith wins in the end over these feelings. Here we see Lewis the sufferer.

_____. *The Problem of Pain*. San Francisco: HarperSanFrancisco, 1940, 1996. Classic apologetic statement of the free-will defense in dealing with the problem of suffering and evil. Here we see Lewis the apologist.

McGrath, Alister E. *Suffering and God*. Grand Rapids: Zondervan, 1995.
Brief, readable discussion relating God to suffering. Good illustrations.

McQuilkin, Robertson. *A Promise Kept: The Story of an Unforgettable Love*. Wheaton: Tyndale House, 1998.
A Christian college president resigned early to care for his wife suffering from Alzheimer's disease. A touching story of commitment to honor marriage vows through unselfish service.

Plantinga, Alvin C. *God, Freedom, and Evil*. Grand Rapids: Eerdmans, 1977.

> Important brief statement of the free-will defense by a noted Christian analytic philosopher. Shows that it is not logically inconsistent to acknowledge the reality of evil and the reality of a personal God.

Sittser, Gerald L. *A Grace Disguised: How the Soul Grows through Loss*. Grand Rapids: Zondervan, 1995.

> A moving story of the ministry of God's grace through a terrible family tragedy.

Sittser, Jerry. *When God Doesn't Answer Your Prayer*. Grand Rapids: Zondervan, 2003.

> Deals with the difficulties experienced by believers when God does not grant their requests.

Stott, John R.W. *The Cross of Christ*. Downers Grove, IL: InterVarsity, 1986.

> Readable discussion of the meaning of the cross.

Wright, H. Norman. *It's Okay to Cry: A Parent's Guide to Helping Children through the Losses of Life*. Colorado Springs: Waterbrook Press, 2004.

> Offers practical help for parents. Explains the symptoms of loss and unresolved grief so that parents can recognize them and walk alongside their children on the path to recovery.

_____. *Recovering from the Losses of Life*. Grand Rapids: Fleming H. Revell, 2006.

> Discusses in practical terms the emotional healing process in working though tragedy. Two following books are similar.

_____. *Will My Life Ever Be the Same? Finding God's Strength to Hope Again*. Eugene, OR: Harvest House, 2002.

> Offering principles to help people recover from even the worst circumstances. How to avoid the traits shared by those who continue to struggle and how to find the way out of the despair of trauma and back to a joy-filled life.

Yancey, Philip. *Where Is God When It Hurts?* Rev. ed. Grand Rapids: Zondervan, 1990.

> Excellent, readable book for those who want to make sense out of suffering. It helps the sufferer understand pain and suffering and gives practical guidelines on how to help hurting people.

Ziglar, Zig. *Confessions of a Grieving Christian*. Nashville: Thomas Nelson, 1998.

> Traces his journey in grief following the death of his oldest daughter to pulmonary fibrosis.

WORKS REFERENCED IN THIS VOLUME

This list includes all the works cited in this book. In the text itself, all sources are cited by the author's last name and page number only, except as follows: (1) If the same last name occurs more than once, the author will be cited in the text by first and last names. (2) If the same author has more than one bibliographical entry a **key word** in the title of each of his entries will be printed below in **bold letters**, and the reference in the text will include the author's last name, the key word in the title, and the page number.

Alexander, Pat and David. *Zondervan Handbook to the Bible*, 3rd ed. Grand Rapids: Zondervan, 1999.

Allender, Dan, and Tremper Longman III. *The Cry of the Soul: How Our Emotions Reveal Our Deepest Questions about God.* Colorado Springs: NavPress, 1994.

Aquinas, Thomas. *Summa Theologica.*

Archer, Gleason L. *The Book of Job: God's Answer to the Problem of Undeserved Suffering.* Grand Rapids: Baker, 1982.

Arnold, Bill T., and Bryan E. Beyer. *Encountering the Old Testament: A Christian Survey.* Grand Rapids: Baker Books, 1999.

Attig, Thomas. *The **Heart** of Grief: Death and the Search for Lasting Love.* New York: Oxford University Press, 2000.

_____. *How We Grieve: **Relearning** the World.* New York: Oxford University Press, 1996.

Augustine. *The Confessions of St. Augustine.* Trans. by E.M. Blaiklock. Nashville: Thomas Nelson, 1983.

Baker Encyclopedia of the Bible. 2 Vols. Ed. by Walter A. Elwell. Grand Rapids: Baker, 1988.

Barclay, William. *The Gospel of **Matthew**,* vol. 1. 2nd ed. Philadelphia: Westminster Press, 1958.

_____. ***Jesus** as They Saw Him.* New York: Harper & Row, 1962.

_____. *The Letters of **James** and John.* Philadelphia: Westminster Press, 1976.

_____. *The Letters to the **Corinthians**.* 3rd rev. ed. Louisville, KY: Westminster John Knox, 2002.

Bayly, Joseph. *The View from a Hearse.* Elgin, IL: David C. Cook, 1969.

Bellinger, W.H. Jr. *Psalms: Reading and Studying the Books of Psalms.* Peabody, MA: Hendrickson, 1990.

Black, D.A. "Weakness." In *Dictionary of Paul and His Letters.* Ed. by Gerald F. Hawthorne et al. Downers Grove, IL: InterVarsity, 1993.

Black, Willard. "God's Existence, Presence, and Love in Human Suffering." In *A Humble Defense*, pp. 229-240. Ed. by Mark Scott and Mark Moore. Joplin, MO: College Press, 2004.

Blank, Jeanne Webster. *The Death of an Adult Child: A Book for and about Bereaved Parents*. Amityville, NY: Baywood, 1998.

Blomberg, Craig L. "Healing." In *Dictionary of Jesus and the Gospels*. Ed. by Joel B. Green et al. Downers Grove, IL: InterVarsity, 1992.

Bock, Darrell. *Luke 9:51–24:53*. Grand Rapids: Baker Books, 1996.

Boethius. *The Consolation of Philosophy*. New York: Barnes & Noble, 2005.

Boice, James Montgomery. *Philippians: An Expositional Commentary*. Grand Rapids: Baker Books, 1990.

Boles, Kenny. *Galatians and Ephesians*. College Press NIV Commentary Series. Joplin, MO: College Press, 1993.

_____. "Word Studies," www.occ.edu.

Boyd, Gregory A. *Is God to Blame? Beyond Pat Answers to the Problem of Suffering*. Downers Grove, IL: InterVarsity, 2003.

Brand, Paul, and Philip Yancey. *Pain: The Gift Nobody Wants*. New York: Harper Collins, 1993.

Brooks, Garth. "Unanswered Prayers." Written by Patrick Alger, Larry B. Bastian, and Troyal Garth Brooks. Major Bob Music/Mid-Summer Music/Universal Music/Universal Polygram International, 1991.

Bruce, F.F. *Paul: Apostle of the Heart Set Free*. Grand Rapids: Eerdmans, 1977.

_____. *The Epistles to the Colossians, to Philemon, and to the Ephesians*. Grand Rapids: Eerdmans, 1984.

_____. *Peter, Stephen, James and John: Studies in Early Non-Pauline Christianity*. Grand Rapids: Eerdmans, 1979.

Bullock, C. Hassell. *Encountering the Book of Psalms: A Literary and Theological Introduction*. Grand Rapids: Baker Books, 2001.

Carson, D.A. *Basics for Believers: An Exposition of Philippians*. Grand Rapids: Baker, 1996.

_____. *How Long, O Lord? Reflections on Suffering and Evil*. Grand Rapids: Baker Books, 1990.

Clayton, John. *Does God Exist?* Vol. 29 (May/June 2002).

Clement of Alexandria. *I Clement*.

_____. *Hypotyposes*.

Colson, Charles, and Nancy Pearcey. *Developing a Christian World-view of The Problem of Evil*. Wheaton, IL: Tyndale House, 2001.

_____. *The Problem of Evil*. Wheaton, IL: Tyndale, 1999.

Cottrell, Jack. *The Faith Once for All*. Joplin, MO: College Press, 2002.

Cushing, W.O. "Under His Wings." In *Great Songs of the Church*. Compiled by W.L. Jorgenson. Cincinnati: Standard, 1997.

Davids, Peter H. *The First Epistle of Peter*. Grand Rapids: Eerdmans, 1990.

_____. *James*. Peabody, MA: Hendrickson, 1989.

DeWelt, Chris. "Helpful Words to Those Who Are Hurting." *Christian Standard*, CXL (August 7, 2005).

Dorsett, Lyle W. *Seeking the Secret Place: The Spiritual Formation of C.S. Lewis*. Grand Rapids: Brazos Press, 2004.

Dostoevski, Fyodor. *Brothers Karamazov*. Trans. by Constance Garnett. New York: Barnes & Noble, 1995.

Eareckson, Joni, with Joe Musser. *Joni*. Grand Rapids: Zondervan, 1976.

Edwards, William D., Wesley Galel, and Floyd Hosmer. "On the Physical Death of Jesus Christ." In *The Journal of the American Medical Association*, vol. 256 (March 21, 1986).

Elliot, Elizabeth. *On Asking God Why*. Old Tappan, NJ: Revell, 1989.

Eusebius. *Ecclesiastical History*.

Fee, Gordon D. *Phililppians*. Downers Grove, IL: InterVarsity, 1999.

Feinberg, John S. *The Many Faces of Evil: Theological Systems and the Problem of Evil*. Rev. and exp. ed. Wheaton, IL: Crossway Books, 2004.

_____. *Where Is God? A Personal Story of Finding God in Grief and Suffering*. Nashville: Broadman and Holman, 2004.

_____. "Why I Still Believe in Christ, in Spite of Evil and Suffering." In *Why I Am a Christian*, pp. 237-254. Ed. by Norman L. Geisler and Paul K. Hoffman. Grand Rapids: Baker Books, 2001.

Ferguson, Everett. *Backgrounds of Early Christianity*. 3rd ed. Grand Rapids: Eerdmans, 2003.

Fisher, David. "Joseph Tson: Giving Wings to Others." In *Ambassadors for Christ*. Ed. by John D. Woodbridge. Chicago: Moody Press, 1994.

Flew, Antony. *God and Philosophy*. London: Hutchinson, 1966.

Frankl, Viktor. *Man's Search for Meaning: An Introduction to Logotherapy*. New York: Pocket Books, 1959.

Garland, David. *Mark*. The NIV Application Commentary: Grand Rapids: Zondervan, 1996.

Geisler, Norman L. *Baker's Encyclopedia of Christian Apologetics*. Grand Rapids: Baker Books, 1999.

_____. *The Roots of Evil*. Grand Rapids: Zondervan, 1978.

Geivett, Douglas. *Evil and the Evidence for God: The Challenge of John Hick's Theodicy*. Philadelphia: Temple University Press, 1995.

Gowan, Donald E. *The Triumph of Faith in Habakkuk*. Atlanta: John Knox, 1976.

Green, Michael. *The Day Death Died*. Downers Grove, IL: InterVarsity, 1982.

_____. *The Empty Cross of Jesus*. Downers Grove, IL: InterVarsity, 1984.

_____. *New Life, New Lifestyle*. Downers Grove, IL: InterVarsity, 1973.

_____. *Runaway World*. Downers Grove, IL: InterVarsity, 1968.

Grudem, Wayne. *The First Epistle of Peter*. Grand Rapids: Eerdmans, 1988.

Guinness, Os. *Unspeakable: Facing Up to Evil in an Age of Genocide and Terror*. San Francisco: HarperSanFrancisco, 2005.

Guthrie, Donald. *The Apostles*. Grand Rapids: Zondervan, 1975.

_____. *New Testament Theology*. Downers Grove, IL: InterVarsity, 1981.

Habermas, Gary R., and Michael R. Licona. *The Case for the Resurrection of Jesus*. Grand Rapids: Kregel Publications, 2004.

Hafemann, Scott. "Suffering." In *Dictionary of Paul and His Letters*. Ed. by Gerald Hawthorne et al. Downers Grove, IL: InterVarsity, 1993.

_____. *Suffering & Ministry in the Spirit: Paul's Defense of His Ministry in II Corinthians 2:14–3:3*. Grand Rapids: Eerdmans, 1990.

Hayden, Edwin V. *Beloved Sufferer: How One Man Copes with His Wife's Disabling Illness*. Cincinnati: Standard, 1987.

Hick, John. *Evil and the God of Love*. Rev. ed.. San Francisco: Harper and Row, 1974.

Hicks, John Mark. *Anchors for the Soul: Trusting God in the Storms of Life*. Joplin, MO: College Press, 2001.

_____. *Yet Will I Trust Him: Understanding God in a Suffering World*. Joplin, MO: College Press, 1999.

Hiebert, D. Edmond. *James*. Rev. ed. Winona Lake, IN: BMH Books, 1992.

Howard-Snyder, Daniel, ed. *The Evidential Argument from Evil*. Bloomington, IN: Indiana University Press, 1996.

Hume, David. *Dialogues on Natural Religion*.

The Joplin Globe. October 3, 1996.

Justin Martyr, *Second Apology*.

Kaiser, Walter C. Jr. *A Biblical Approach to Personal Suffering*. Chicago: Moody, 1982.

_____. *Mastering the Old Testament: Micah, Nahum, Habakkuk, Zephaniah, Haggai, Zechariah, Malachi*. Dallas: Word, 1992.

Kent, Homer A. Jr. *Faith That Works: Studies in the Epistle of James*. Grand Rapids: Baker, 1986.

Kidner, Derek. *Psalms 1–72: An Introduction and Commentary on Books I and II of the Psalms*. London: InterVarsity, 1973.

Kistemaker, Simon J. *Exposition of the Epistle of James and the Epistles of John*. Grand Rapids: Baker, 1986.

Knight, George W. III. *The Pastoral Epistles*. Grand Rapids: Eerdmans, 1992.

Kreeft, Peter. *Making Sense Out of Suffering*. Ann Arbor: Servant Books, 1986.

_____. *Three Philosophies of Life: Ecclesiastes: Life as Vanity; Job: Life as Suffering; Song of Songs: Life as Love*. San Francisco: Ignatius Press, 1989.

Kushner, Harold. *When Bad Things Happen to Good People*. New York: Schocken, 1981.

Laetsch, Theo. *Bible Commentary: The Minor Prophets*. St. Louis: Concordia, 1956.

Latourette, Kenneth Scott. *A History of Christianity*. New York: Harper and Row, 1953.

Lewis, C.S. *Christian Reflections*. Ed. by Walter Hooper. Grand Rapids: Eerdmans, 1967.

_____. "Evil and God." In *God in the Dock*, pp. 21-24. Grand Rapids: Eerdmans, 1970.

_____. *The Great Divorce*. New York: Macmillan, 1946.

_____. *A Grief Observed*. San Francisco: HarperSanFrancisco, 1961, 1996.

_____. *Mere **Christianity***. Rev. ed. New York: Macmillan, 1952.

_____. *Miracles*. New York: Macmillan, 1963.

_____. *The **Problem** of Pain*. San Francisco: HarperSanFrancisco, 1949, 1996.

_____. *The World's Last **Night***. New York: Harcourt, Brace Jovanovich, 1960.

Limburg, James. *The Anchor Bible Dictionary*, vol 5. New York: Doubleday, 1992.

Lloyd-Jones, Martyn. *The Life of **Joy** and Peace: An Exposition of Philippians*. Grand Rapids: Baker Books, 1989, 1990.

_____. *Studies in the **Sermon** on the Mount*, vol. 1. Grand Rapids: Eerdmans, 1959.

_____. *Why Does God Allow Suffering?* Wheaton, IL: Crossway Books, 1994.

Lowell, James Russell, "The Present Crisis." In *Yale Book of American Verse*. Ed. by Thomas Lounsbury. New Haven, CT: Yale University Press, 1912.

Luter, A.B. Jr. "Martyrdom." In *Dictionary of the Later New Testament & Its Development*. Ed. by Ralph P. Martin and Peter H. Davids. Downers Grove, IL: InterVarsity, 1997.

Mackie, John. "**Evil** and Omnipotence." In *The Philosophy of Religion*. Ed. by Basil Mitchell. London: Oxford University Press, 1971.

_____. *The **Miracle** of Theism*. Oxford: Clarendon Press, 1982.

Madden, E.H., and P.H. Hare. *Evil and the Concept of God*. Springfield, IL: Charles C. Thomas, 1968.

The Martyrdom of Polycarp.

May, Sharon Hart. "Loss and Grief Work." In *Caring for People God's Way: Personal and Emotional Issues, Addictions, Grief, and Trauma*. Ed. by Tim Clinton, Archibald Hart, and George Ohlschlager. Nashville: Nelson Reference & Electronic, 2005.

McCartney, Dan G. *Why Does It Have to Hurt? The Meaning of Christian Suffering*. Phillipsburg, NJ: Presbyterian and Reformed, 1998.

McDoniel, Jim. "Birth of disabled child teaches me about suffering, God and true hope." *The Christian Chronicle* (January 2007).

McGrath, Alister E. *The **Mystery** of the Cross*. Grand Rapids: Zondervan, 1988.

_____. *Suffering and God*. Grand Rapids: Zondervan, 1995.

_____. *The Unknown God*. Grand Rapids: Eerdmans, 1999.

_____. *What Was God Doing On the Cross?* Grand Rapids: Zondervan, 1992.

McQuilkin, Robertson. *A Promise Kept: The Story of an Unforgettable Love*. Wheaton, IL: Tyndale, 1998.

Mehrens, Ralph. *Contact from Calvary*, vol. XIV (January 23, 1984).

Michaels, J.R. "1 Peter." In *Dictionary of the Later New Testament & Its Development*. Ed. by Ralph P. Martin and Peter H. Davids. Downers Grove, IL: InterVarsity, 1997.

Moo, Douglas J. *James*. Grand Rapids: Eerdmans, 1985.

_____. *The Letter of James*. Grand Rapids: Eerdmans, 2000.

Moreland, J.P., and William Lane Craig. *Philosophical Foundations for a Christian Worldview*. Downers Grove, IL: InterVarsity, 2003.

Morgan, G. Campbell. *The Crises of the Christ*. New York: Fleming H. Revell, 1903.

Morris, Leon. *The Atonement: Its Meaning and Significance*. Downers Grove, IL: InterVarsity, 1983.

_____. *The Gospel according to John*. The New International Commentary on the New Testament. Grand Rapids: Eerdmans, 1971.

Mounce, Robert H. *Matthew*. The International Biblical Commentary. Peabody, MA: Hendrickson, 1991.

Nash, Ronald H. "The Problem of Evil." In *To Everyone an Answer*, pp 203-223. Ed. by Francis J. Beckwith, William Lane Craig, and J. P. Moreland. Downers Grove, IL: InterVarsity, 2004.

Packer, J.I. *A Grace Sanctified: Through Sorrow to Eternal Hope; Including Richard Baxter's Timeless Memoir of His Wife's Life and Death*. Wheaton, IL: Crossway, 2002.

_____. *Knowing God*. Downers Grove, IL: InterVarsity, 1973.

Packer, J.I., and Carolyn Nystrom. *Praying: Finding Our Way through Duty to Delight*. Downers Grove, IL: InterVarsity, 2006.

Payne, J. Barton. "Psalms." In *Zondervan's Pictorial Bible Dictionary*. Ed. by Merrill C. Tenney. Grand Rapids: Zondervan, 1963.

Peterson, Eugene H. *A Long Obedience in the Same Direction: Discipleship in an Instant Society*. 2nd ed. Downers Grove, IL: InterVarsity, 2000.

Piper, John. *The Supremacy of God in Preaching*. Grand Rapids: Baker Books, 1990.

_____. *When You Don't Desire God: How to Fight for Joy*. Wheaton, IL: Crossway, 2004.

Plantinga, Alvin C. "A **Christian Life** Partly Lived." In *Philosophers Who Believe.* Ed. by Kelly James Clard. Downers Grove, IL: InterVarsity, 1993.

_____. *God, Freedom, and Evil.* Grand Rapids: Eerdmans, 1977.

Pojman, Louis P. *Philosophy: The Pursuit of Wisdom.* 3rd ed. Stamford, CT: Wadsworth, 2001.

_____. *Philosophy: The Quest for Truth.* 4th ed. Stamford, CT: Wadsworth, 1999.

Reasoner, M. "Persecution." In *Dictionary of the Later New Testament & Its Developments.* Ed. by Ralph P. Martin and Peter H. Davids. Downers Grove, IL: InterVarsity, 1997.

Richardson, Alan. *An Introduction to the Theology of the New Testament.* New York: Harper and Row, 1958.

Roberts, J.W. *The Letters of John.* Austin, TX: Sweet, 1968.

Rowe, William L., ed. *God and the Problem of Evil.* Malden, MA: Blackwell, 2001.

_____. "The Problem of Evil and Some Varieties of **Atheism**." *American Philosophical Quarterly* 16 (1979). Reprinted in *The Evidential Argument from Evil.* Ed. by Daniel Howard-Snyder. Bloomington and Indianapolis: Indiana University Press, 1996.

Rubenstein, Richard L. "Auschwitz and Covenant Theology." *The Christian Century* 86 (May 21, 1969).

Schmidt, Alvin J. *Under the Influence: How Christianity Transformed Civilization.* Grand Rapids: Zondervan, 2001.

Schreiner, Thomas R. *Paul: Apostle of God's Glory in Christ.* Downers Grove, IL: IVP Academic, 2001.

Schultz, Samuel J. *The Old Testament Speaks.* 3rd ed. San Francisco: Harper & Row, 1980.

Shakespeare, William. *King Lear.*

_____. *Macbeth.*

Silvester, Hugh. *Arguing with God.* Downers Grove, IL: InterVarsity, 1971.

Sittser, Gerald L. *A Grace Disguised: How the Soul Grows through Loss.* Grand Rapids: Zondervan, 1995.

Sittser, Jerry. *When God Doesn't Answer Your Prayers.* Grand Rapids: Zondervan, 2003.

Smith, Harold Ivan. *A Decembered Grief: Living with Loss While Others Are Celebrating.* Kansas City: Beacon Hill, 1999.

Smith, James E. *The Wisdom Literature and Psalms*. Joplin, MO: College Press, 1996.

Sproul, R.C. *Surprised by Suffering*. Wheaton, IL: Tyndale, 1988.

Stalker, James. *The Trial and Death of Jesus Christ: A Classic Devotional History of Our Lord's Passion*. Grand Rapids: Zondervan, 1950 [1894].

Still, Todd D. *Conflict at Thessalonica: A Pauline Church and Its Neighbours*. Sheffield: Sheffield Academic Press, 1999.

John R.W. Stott. *The Cross of Christ*. Downers Grove, IL: InterVarsity, 1986.

_____. *Favorite Psalms: An Inspiring and Insightful Look at the Psalms*. Grand Rapids: Baker Books, 1988.

_____. *The Letters of John*. Rev. ed. Grand Rapids: Eerdmans, 1988.

_____. *The Message of 2 Timothy*. Downers Grove, IL: InterVarsity, 1973.

_____. *The Message of Acts*. Downers Grove, IL: InterVarsity, 1990.

_____. *The Message of Ephesians*. Downers Grove, IL: InterVarsity, 1979.

Strobel, Lee. *The Case for Christ*. Grand Rapids: Zondervan, 1998.

_____. *The Case for Faith*. Grand Rapids: Zondervan, 2000.

Strommen, Merton P., and A. Irene Strommen. *Five Cries of Grief: One Family's Journey to Healing after the Tragic Death of a Son*. San Francisco: HarperCollins, 1993.

Suetonius. *Life of Nero*.

Swinburne, Richard. *Providence and the Problem of Evil*. New York: Oxford, 1998.

Tacitius. *Annals*.

Tada, Joni Eareckson, and Steven Estes. *When God Weeps: Why Our Sufferings Matter to the Almighty*. Grand Rapids: Zondervan, 1997.

Taylor, James E. *Introducing Apologetics: Cultivating Christian Commitment*. Grand Rapids: Baker Books, 2006.

Tertullian. *Address to Martyrs*.

Thielman, Frank. *Philippians*. Grand Rapids: Zondervan, 1995.

Tolstoi, Lyof N. [Tolstoy, Leo]. *My Confession, My Religion*. Midland, MI: Avensblume Press, 1899, 1993.

Tolstoy, Leo. *Divine and Human*. Grand Rapids: Zondervan, 2000.

_____. "**Prayer**." In *Divine and Human*. Grand Rapids: Zondervan, 2000.

Ton, Josef. *Suffering, Martyrdom, and Rewards in Heaven*. Lanham, MD: University Press of America, 1977.

Tournier, Paul. *Creative Suffering*. San Francisco: Harper & Row, 1983.

Travers, Michael E. *Encountering God in the Psalms*. Grand Rapids: Kregel, 2003.

Van Inwagen, Peter, ed. *Christian Faith and the Problem of Evil*. Grand Rapids: Eerdman, 2004.

Vitz, Paul C. *Psychology as Religion: The Cult of Self-Worship*. Grand Rapids: Eerdmans, 1977.

Ware, Bruce A. *God's Lesser Glory: The Diminished God of Open Theism*. Wheaton, IL: Crossway, 2000.

Warren, Thomas B. *Have Atheists Proved There Is No God?* Nashville: Gospel Advocate, 1972.

Webb, W.J. "Suffering." In *Dictionary of the Later New Testament & and Its Development*. Ed. by Ralph P. Martin and Peter H. Davids. Downers Grove, IL: InterVarsity, 1997.

Wenham. John W. *The Goodness of God*. Downers Grove, IL: InterVarsity, 1974.

Wesley, Charles. "And Can It Be That I Should Gain." In *The New Church Hymnal*. Lexicon Music, 1976.

White, Willie W. *What the Bible Says about Suffering*. Joplin, MO: College Press, 1984.

Whitney, Barry L. *Theodicy: An Annotated Bibliography on the Problem of Evil: 1960–1990*. New York: Garland, 1993.

Wiesel, Elie. *Night*. New York: Avon Books, 1960.

Wilder-Smith, A.E. *Is This a **God of Love**?* Costa Mesa, CA: The Word for Today, 1991.

_____. *The **Paradox** of Pain*. Wheaton, IL: Harold Shaw, 1971.

Willard, Dallas. *Renovation of the Heart: Putting on the Character of Christ*. Colorado Springs: NavPress, 2000.

Wilson, Seth. *Learning from Jesus*. Joplin, MO: College Press, 1977.

Wolfelt, Alan D. *Understanding Grief: Helping Yourself Heal*. Bristol, PA: Accelerated Development, 1992.

Wolterstorff, Nicholas. *Lament for a Son*. Grand Rapids: Eerdmans, 1987.

Woodson, Meg. *Making It through the Toughest Days of Grief*. Grand Rapids: Zondervan, 1994.

Wright, H. Norman. *It's Okay to Cry: A Parent's Guide to Helping Children through the Losses of Life.* Colorado Springs: Waterbrook Press, 2004.

_____. *Recovering from the Losses of Life.* Grand Rapids: Fleming H. Revell, 2006.

_____. *Will My Life Ever Be the Same? Finding God's Strength to Hope Again.* Eugene, OR: Harvest House, 2002. Previously published by Servant Books as *Resilience* (1997) and as *Why Did This Happen to Me?* (1999).

Yancey, Philip. *Prayer: Does It Make Any Difference?* Grand Rapids: Zondervan, 2006.

_____. *Reaching for the Invisible God.* Grand Rapids: Zondervan, 2000.

_____. *Where Is God When It Hurts?* Rev. ed. Grand Rapids: Zondervan, 1990.

Youssef, Michael. *If God Is in Control, Why Is My Life Such a Mess? Experiencing God's Sovereignty during Dark and Difficult Days.* Nashville: Thomas Nelson, 1998.

Zacharias, Ravi. *Can Man Live without God?* Dallas: Word, 1994.

_____. *Cries of the Heart: Find the God Who Heals Your Pain.* Nashville: Word, 1997.

_____. *Jesus among Other Gods.* Nashville: Word, 2000.

Ziglar, Zig. *Confessions of a Grieving Christian.* Nashville: Thomas Nelson, 1998.

Zonnebelt-Smeenge, Susan J., and Robert C. De Vries. *The Empty Chair: Handling Grief on Holidays and Special Occasions.* Grand Rapids: Baker Books, 2001.

Scripture Index

Subject Index

373

Person Index